# The
# *Rivers*
## of
# INDIANA

# The
# Rivers
## of
# INDIANA

*Richard S. Simons*

Indiana University Press • Bloomington

Library of Congress Cataloging in Publication Data
Simons, Richard S.
    The rivers of Indiana.

    Bibliography: p.
    1. Rivers—Indiana.    2. Indiana—Description and
travel.    3. Indiana—History.    I. Title.
GB1225.I3S55    1985        551.48'3'09772        84-47745
ISBN 0-253-17476-7
1 2 3 4 5      89 88 87 86 85

Manufactured in Japan

To my Three Favorite Girls:
Rosmarie, my wife;
Charlotte, my daughter;
and Hermine, my mother-in-law.
And to the memory of my parents,
Philip and Tillie Simons.

# Contents

# *Preface*

Who has not sped down a highway, crossed a bridge and for a fleeting moment been intrigued by the sight of a beautiful river flowing beneath it?

Perhaps the view has raised questions: Where does it begin? What is the terrain at its headwaters? How deep? How swift? What lies around the bend? Where does it go? To what mother river does it belong? If it could speak, what stories would it tell? I have wondered, and to satisfy this curiosity, I undertook this work, pinpointing on a United States Geological Survey map the precise source of each river and following its course to the mouth.

This is the story of thirty Hoosier rivers—a number that astonishes many persons—and it attempts to delineate their individual characters, describe their contributions to Indiana's heritage and impart an understanding of their historical, cultural, and economic significance.

The characters vary widely and contrast sharply. There are the gentle, scenic Tippecanoe and the swift, rushing Whitewater; the ugly, idling Calumets and the beautiful, majestic Ohio; the contradictory Patoka and the Lincoln-shadowed Anderson.

Rivers, such as the Mississinewa and the Eel, belonged to the Indians. Some, such as the Maumee and the Little, belonged to the French voyageurs. Others, such as the Kankakee, belonged to the sportsmen. Some, such as the Pigeon, still do.

Before highways, railroads, or the thought of air travel arrived, rivers were the bright wedges of civilization that carried pioneers into an unknown wilderness. They gave settlers power for their mills and factories, provided water supply, and drained off surplus rainfall. They determined the locations of settlements, nourished them, and sometimes helped them grow into important cities.

There is a special romance about each river drawn from its scenery, history, wildlife, industry, agriculture, transportation, archaeology, geology, and, in many instances, its Indian associations. It is this romance that this book attempts to capture.

Its nucleus comes from an *Indianapolis Star Sunday Magazine* series and I am indebted to Publisher Eugene S. Pulliam and his late father, Eugene C. Pulliam, for policies that allowed ample time for research and travel. I also am grateful to the Indiana Historical Society for generous support.

As the trail wound through libraries and along riverbanks, many persons helped enthusiastically and without them this book could not have been written. I am profoundly grateful to Mrs. Floyd Hopper, retired Indiana Division head, Indiana State Library, and to her assistants and successors who frequently went to much trouble to assist me. Librarians at *The Indianapolis Star*, at various libraries throughout the state, and particularly Mrs. David Byrum and her reference staff at Marion Public Library patiently gave time and enthusiastically showed interest. Several county historians, city engineers, county surveyors, and chamber of commerce executives were more than helpful.

I owe special thanks to the Indiana Department of Natural Resources, particularly Jim Parham, Public Information Director, and Nancy Ruthenbeck-Neff, Division of Outdoor Recreation; Indiana Geological Survey, particularly State Geologist John B. Patton and R. Dee Rarick, retired head of Educational Services; Indiana Department of Commerce, particularly Susan A. Lindner, photo librarian; The Nature Conservancy, headed by William Weeks, and the Chicago and Louisville offices of the U.S. Army Corps of Engineers.

Many have walked that extra mile to verify a questionable fact or update an elusive figure. Foremost among them are Thomas McCaffrey and other Indiana and Michigan Electric Company administrators; Rhys D. Rhodes of Paoli; the late Worth N. Yoder Sr., Sturgis, Michigan, city manager, and Bill Scifres, outdoor editor of *The Indianapolis Star*.

I am deeply grateful, also, to Dr. Donald F. Carmony and Dr. Henry H. H. Remak of Indiana University; Dr. Howard H. Peckham, former secretary of the Indiana Historical Society; Ed Breen, for advice on photographs; and the late Richard A. Greene of Muncie for constant interest, advice, and encouragement.

And a special note of gratitude to L. Hewitt Carpenter and Edward Murray, who made multiple trips, and other friends who accompanied me on more than 11,000 miles of travel that went into preparing this narrative, all acting as navigators and keeping me from becoming lost in the vast, wonderful, beautiful Indiana out-of-doors.

*The*
# *Rivers*
## of
# INDIANA

# The Essence of Indiana

# Wabash

To Hoosiers the number one river is the Wabash. And to non-Hoosiers the Wabash is Indiana. Long but not large, tranquil yet dynamic, geologically young but historically old, the paradoxical Wabash has shaped the Indiana of today. It is the spawning ground of Hoosier civilization, the cradle of its liberty, and the highway of its maturity. Its valley is the maker of heroes and presidents, the habitat of writers and singers, the proving ground of adventurers and politicians.

Just as Indiana is situated in the heartland of America, so the Wabash Valley occupies the heartland of Indiana. Flowing northwest, west, and finally south for 475 miles, the river drains 33,000 square miles between its source and its junction with the Ohio River below Mt. Vernon. Along the way it is swelled by the contributions of nearly a dozen major tributaries and it washes past eleven county seats. Four-fifths of Indiana's ninety-two counties lie within its watershed.

In the beginning the Wabash was born of ice and flood. Meltwater from retreating glaciers carved the middle valley and for a time, in the dim geological past, the waters of Lake Erie flowed westward in a mighty torrent across Indiana.

Geologically, the Wabash is not one river, but three. Above Huntington it flows through a narrow and shallow trench that wriggles across the flat, fertile prairies. From Huntington to below Lafayette it occupies the valley carved by the mighty glacial runoff of Pleistocene times, which flowed away to the west. Where it crosses the bed of the great Teays preglacial river, the valley widens into beautiful prairies bordered by distant hills. At other points the valley is steep and narrow as the modern stream fights to erode Silurian-age reefs and other tough bedrock that restricts its course. Spectacular formations, such as Hanging Rock near Lagro, are among the results.

Below Lafayette the river hugs the prairies that extend into Illinois. Small streams, flowing sluggishly through the flatland, create numerous picturesque cascades as they tumble suddenly into the entrenched valley that is now both deep and wide.

Beyond Covington the river follows a partially filled, pre-glacial valley that was never connected to the great glacial stream above it. Swinging sharply southward, the Wabash is a mighty stream flowing through a broad valley floored with rich, level, fertile land.

Below Vincennes it meanders, shifts, and wriggles, cutting new channels, and blocking old ones, constantly threatening to violate bridge locations and state boundaries. In places the land becomes wild and barren.

When the Indians found the Wabash, they named it *Wah-Bah-*

*Left to right*: Potawatomi Indians, near Logansport, painted by George Winter in 1848. ❧U.S. Geologist David Dale Owen lived in this laboratory-home at New Harmony. ❧Grouseland, the home of William Henry Harrison in Vincennes, was built in 1803–04.

*Shik-Ki*, meaning "pure white." The French corrupted the word to *Ouabache*, and the English changed it to Wabash. The French name disappeared, but it was revived in 1962 when the Ouabache State Recreation Area was established above Bluffton.

The Wabash is a river of great events and greater men. Along its banks the Indians built important villages in which they were living when white men came. On its waters the French fur traders, mingling with missionaries and explorers, floated their canoes and pirogues on the great trade route linking the lower Great Lakes and the Mississippi River. In its valley the French constructed a chain of forts from which they vainly sought to turn the advancing British tide. The great wrestling match for the New World was carried on here in earnest. Below Lafayette the Wabash passes reconstructed Ouiatenon, one of the forts the French built in their unsuccessful attempt to hold the Wabash Valley. The annual Feast of the Hunter's Moon pageant now attracts thousands to the site.

Along the Wabash the British and the Americans marched and fought to determine the size and shape of America as the nation's heartland bounced back and forth under their control and Indian influence. On its bank sat the capital that once provided the heartbeat of the West, the seat of government for a domain stretching from Ohio to the Rocky Mountains. No capital, except Washington, D.C., has been responsible for so large an area in the United States.

The Wabash begins its race to the sea two miles beyond the state line of Indiana and five miles south of Fort Recovery, Ohio. Thirty meandering miles, first as a prairie ditch, then as a small creek, bring it to Fort Recovery, where it once ran red with the blood of General Arthur St. Clair's American army, massacred here in November 1791. It was the most complete American rout up to the time of General Custer.

Three years later the dashing and courageous General "Mad Anthony" Wayne, acting on direct orders from President Washington, swept in to avenge St. Clair's defeat. Always dramatic, Wayne chose to build a fort where St. Clair had fallen. Typically, he named it Fort Recovery. The Indians described Wayne as the "general who never sleeps," a title whose accuracy was proven when he broke the Miami farther north. Although Wayne crushed the Indians and opened the way for white settlement in the treaty he negotiated at Greenville, Ohio, in the summer of 1795, peace had not yet come to the Wabash.

It took more blood and battle in 1811 to break the spell of Tecumseh and his one-eyed brother, The Prophet, leaders of the

Tecumseh and his one-eyed brother, The Prophet, leaders of the Shawnees. Governor William Henry Harrison, marching his army up the river from Vincennes, routed the Indians in the pre-dawn Battle of Tippecanoe above Lafayette and became a new national hero. His victory, now marked by an imposing monument, eventually put him in the White House. "Tippecanoe and Tyler, Too" was the campaign cry nearly thirty years later.

Even before Wayne and Harrison fought their battles against the Indians, George Rogers Clark had wrested the land from the British, just as they had taken it from the French. Is there a Hoosier schoolchild who does not know of Clark's fantastic dead-of-winter march in 1779 across frozen, flooded southern Illinois? Leading a ragtag little army of 172 men, weakened by hunger, Clark arrived at the gates of Vincennes while Colonel Henry Hamilton, the British "Hair Buyer," sat comfortably before the fireplace, secure in his assumption that no one would be foolhardy enough to attack him before spring. Clark's men used the weapons of surprise, deceit, and uncanny marksmanship to force the astonished Hamilton to surrender.

With the fall of Vincennes, the British hold over the area, which would become the Northwest Territory, crumbled in a single day, the result of Clark's effort to push his fledgling country's western boundary from Pennsylvania to the Mississippi River. Thus Vincennes be-

came the cradle of Hoosier liberty. It served as the first capital of Indiana Territory, and after the Louisiana Purchase the vast territory from the state of Ohio to the Rocky Mountains was administered from an unbelievably tiny frame structure in Vincennes that has now been reconstructed as a state memorial.

Eventually a grateful United States government, acting with state and local units, erected an impressive $2,500,000 memorial to the indomitable spirit of Clark and his army. Nowhere are the persons who contributed to a city's history so well remembered as they are in Vincennes. Markers and restorations catch the eye from every direction to recall the local associations with Presidents Harrison, Taylor, and Lincoln; patriots Francis Vigo and Father Pierre Gibault; and the legendary figures of Alice of Old Vincennes and Madame Marie Goderre, the Betsy Ross of the Northwest Territory.

Above Vincennes the Wabash flows through a country rich with military exploits of the Revolutionary and Indian wars. At Fort Harrison, above Terre Haute, future President Zachary Taylor gallantly withstood an Indian attack on the fort that future President William Henry Harrison had built on his march to the Battle of Tippecanoe. Farther downstream, at Point Coupee, the only naval battle on the Wabash was fought when Clark's men intercepted supplies coming down from Detroit for the relief of Vincennes.

The fertile river valley, above and below Vincennes, attracted dreamers and visionaries who were seeking a heaven on earth. Although Utopias rarely succeed, the dream persists. In Indiana the Shakers tried it first, establishing West Union in Sullivan County in 1810. Officially known as "The United Society of Believers in Christ's Second Appearing," the Shakers were a peaceful, industrious, idealistic people who lived in communal villages where they were bound by a strict moral code regarding health, observance of the Sabbath, separation from the world, and celibacy. Their search for Utopia bore no fruit, and by 1827 they were gone from the state.

Of the nine other attempts to establish Utopias in the Wabash Valley, the most famous is the New Harmony experiment. The first actors in the two-part drama were the followers of Father George Rapp, stern and inspiring leader of a German religious group that reached the Wabash in 1814, after first establishing themselves in Pennsylvania. The Rappites were builders as well as dreamers. During their ten years at Harmonie they cultivated fields, established factories, erected a multitude of sturdy buildings, and prepared to march at the head of the parade when the millennium arrived.

Worried that their material success might weaken their spiritual dedication, the Rappites decided to return to Pennsylvania. In 1825 they sold their entire holdings in Indiana to Robert Owen, the Welsh-born idealist, who attempted to smother all mankind's problems under a blanket of super-education. To bulwark his dream of communitarian socialism, he imported a "Boatload of Knowledge," filled with scientists and teachers. The bubble burst within three years. The New Harmony State Memorial and the restorations by Jane Blaffer Owen preserve the best of what is left.

The Wabash has always been a winding thread bringing together diverse communities and interests. As settlers filled the valley, they wove a colorful tapestry of inland transportation. The entire saga unfolds at tiny Transportation Park along old U.S. 24 between Wabash and Peru. The water, carrying canoes, and the riverbank pathways, pounded by moccasined feet, were the first two highways through the valley. When the steamboat tried the water, the few brave vessels that ventured upstream were more inclined to stick on the bottom than to float on the surface.

Then man improved the waterway and built America's longest canal, the 464-mile Wabash and Erie, which funneled thousands of settlers into the valley and later transported their farm produce to market. The canal brought the Irish, whose brawn and sweat built it and whose rowdiness once caused the militia to be called out near Lagro to enforce a peace settlement in the "Irish War," whose cause Irishmen in Belfast are still trying to settle. The canalboat had scarcely

*Left to right*: Dogtown Ferry between Posey County, Indiana, and White County, Illinois, in 1944. ❧Passengers on top of a canalboat on the Wabash and Erie Canal. ❧Fording the Wabash River in the 1840s.

begun its trip through the valley when the locomotive in 1856 sounded its doom. Within twenty years the canal was dead.

Next came the interurban, the would-be successor to the passenger train, but it lasted only until paved highways completed the transportation tapestry and drove the speeding cars into oblivion. Their demise did not take place, however, before two cars had crashed head-on at Kingsland, seven miles north of the Wabash at Bluffton, and left forty-one dead in the nation's worst interurban disaster. Despite their failures, each method pushed the valley's development on to a new level, much as succeeding waves strike ever higher on a beach.

The canal was the first strong influence and it brought immigrants who developed a succession of cities evenly spaced along the upper Wabash River. Huntington, Wabash, Peru, Logansport, Delphi, Lafayette, Attica, and Covington grew because the canal came to their doors. Towns like Lagro and Pittsburg were canal towns, too, but they flourished and declined just as the waterway did.

The railroad, however, brought a prosperity that the canal never could offer. No less than seven erstwhile canal towns became railroad division points and shop towns. The Erie Railroad (later Erie-Lackawanna) was Huntington's largest employer, the former Penn-

sylvania (now Conrail) dominated Logansport's economy and the Monon (now Seaboard System) had operating headquarters in Lafayette. Wabash and Attica also were shop towns but Peru won the championship. It served as crew change point for each of its three railroads. Two operated extensive shops. Until 1971, the fabled "Wabash Cannonball" connected six of these cities with St. Louis and Detroit, and, although the blaring diesel horn is gone, the legend lives on as part of American folklore.

Into the Wabash Valley spread diverse religious and ethnic groups: Irish and German Catholics, Mennonites and obscure Swiss sects along its upper reaches; Scotch-Irish and English from the South, followed by Germans and Italians, along its middle course; and French Catholics and German Rappites along its lower waters. Each left its mark on modern Indiana.

In the upper valley novelists put the scenes, sights, and sounds of the river country into print. Foremost among them was Gene Stratton Porter, whose nature novels sprang from the Limberlost country around Geneva. A state memorial there preserves her home and its furnishings.

Geneva sits at the edge of the Swiss country, not far from Berne, which was settled by Swiss immigrants in 1852. Amish farmers till the

land along the upper Wabash, and the Mennonites, from whom they sprang, have at Berne one of the two largest churches of their denomination in the United States. The gutteral sounds of "Schwyzer Dütsch" are still heard among the farmers of a small Swiss sect, which built one of Indiana's most impressive country churches near Vera Cruz.

In summer the valley is awash with seas of corn, soybeans, wheat, and oats and in its lower reaches with melons and peaches. It is the breadbasket of Indiana. But it also is highly industrialized. Its cities produce an endless flow of automotive, industrial, heating, and electrical equipment; rubber, plastic, and paper products; furniture; insulating materials; steel castings; aluminum extrusions; chemicals, pharmaceuticals, and foods.

Although the cities usually established themselves at the water's edge, they took advantage of the terrain in different ways. Wabash, dominated by its hilltop courthouse, quickly spread up the steep hillsides and across the bordering highlands. From across the river it resembles an ancient European city and only a little imagination can convert the courthouse into a mighty fortified castle. History was made at that courthouse on March 31, 1880, when the world's first municipally operated electric street lights, which were mounted on

its tower, were turned on and flooded the city with such brilliance that it reputedly was possible to read a newspaper three blocks away. Wabash was a birthplace of the world-famous Minneapolis-Honeywell Regulator Company, a fact constantly on the minds of Wabashites because of the magnificent Honeywell Memorial Center. The city also produces paper, rubber, metal, and electronics products; building materials and water meter equipment.

Fourteen miles downstream, Peru spreads across a floodplain far from the distant hills. Unlike Wabash, which can watch floodwaters safely from its hilltops, Peru has been badly battered by the river. The 1913 catastrophe left tremendous property damage and high loss of life, but this is less likely to be repeated since completion of the three upper Wabash Valley reservoirs and construction of floodwalls.

Peru again is enjoying the limelight it occupied as the "Circus City." Some of the country's best-known big top shows—Hagenbeck-Wallace, Sells-Floto, John Robinson, and others—were headquartered here until they were sold to John Ringling in 1929 and moved to Sarasota, Florida. But an annual home talent circus festival of professional quality brings in circus lovers from far and near each summer and resurrects the days of sawdust and spangles.

The city also is known for the galaxy of nationally famous persons who called it home: Comedian John (Ole) Olson, Composer Cole Porter, New York Stock Exchange President Emil Schram, and at least four high-ranking generals and admirals of the World War II period.

Farther downstream, Logansport was first an important Indian trading post at the mouth of the Eel River. As it grew, it became a busy transportation hub and was dominated for years by a railroad economy. Below the city, the river spreads over a wide, shallow bed which steamboats attempted unsuccessfully to navigate in floodtime. Country roads at the water's edge offer pleasing views of the river's beauty. Industrial products include cement, automotive parts, electronic equipment, and meats.

Lafayette, largest city in the upper valley, was the canal's western terminus for several years and this gave it an early importance. Before the city spread up from the valley, malaria was a recurring problem and among its victims was Dr. William W. Mayo, who deemed it wise to seek a healthier climate. Had he remained to rear his family there, his sons might have founded their famous clinic at Lafayette instead of Rochester, Minnesota. Modern Lafayette, heavily industrialized, produces heavy machinery, aluminum extrusions, automotive gears, electric meters, foods, and pharmaceuticals.

Purdue University, opened in 1874 in West Lafayette, is famous for its engineering and agricultural schools, but it is a johnny-come-lately in the farming field. As long ago as 1804 Little Turtle, a great leader of the Miami, perceived that his people must learn the white man's way of farming if they were to survive. Consequently, the Quakers of Baltimore dispatched one of their number, Philip Dennis, to conduct one of America's first agricultural schools. Not as far-sighted as their leader, however, the Indians termed this "squaw work," and the school, located near Andrews, had no lasting effect. Indiana has given the Indian chief's name to the Little Turtle State Recreation Area along the Huntington Reservoir on the Wabash.

Swinging sharply southward past Attica and Covington, the Wabash squeezes Vermillion, Indiana's shoestring county, against the Illinois border. This is the beginning of the coal-mining country, which brought boom times to such cities as Clinton, Terre Haute, and Sulli-

van. Clinton, which mushroomed with the demand for coal during World War I, once boasted of having nearly thirty nationalities resident simultaneously. The flavor is still so Italian in one section that it is known as "Italy."

Below Clinton, Terre Haute emerged as the queen city of the lower valley, developing into an early transportation hub and manufacturing center. More than any other city, it helped the Wabash become famous in song and story. One of its sons, Paul Dresser, wrote Indiana's official song, "On the Banks of the Wabash, Far Away." Theodore Dreiser, the famous novelist, was his brother. Eugene V. Debs, five-time Socialist presidential candidate, also came from Terre Haute.

An important manufacturing and mining center by the turn of the century, Terre Haute is noted as the birthplace of the distinctively shaped Coca-Cola bottle. During World War I, it produced acetone, a vital munitions ingredient, for the British government and paid royalties to Dr. Chaim Weizmann, the British scientist who invented the acetone process. Weizmann's royalties from Terre Haute production helped build his personal fortune which he unselfishly used to help found the State of Israel. He became its first president. Chemicals, pharmaceuticals, aluminum, and heavy machinery remain among the city's industrial products, although coal mining has nearly disappeared. Terre Haute is the home of three colleges and universities, Indiana State University, Rose-Hulman Institute of Technology, and St. Mary-of-the-Woods.

On its way to Vincennes the river becomes the boundary between Indiana and Illinois. Except for New Harmony there is no Indiana town on the river below Vincennes.

The river is always restless as it carries away waters that have fallen on two-thirds of the state. Today, as in the beginning, the Wabash is a river of dreamers and doers, victors and vanquished, peace and war, success and failure, farm and factory.

# Rivers of the Indians

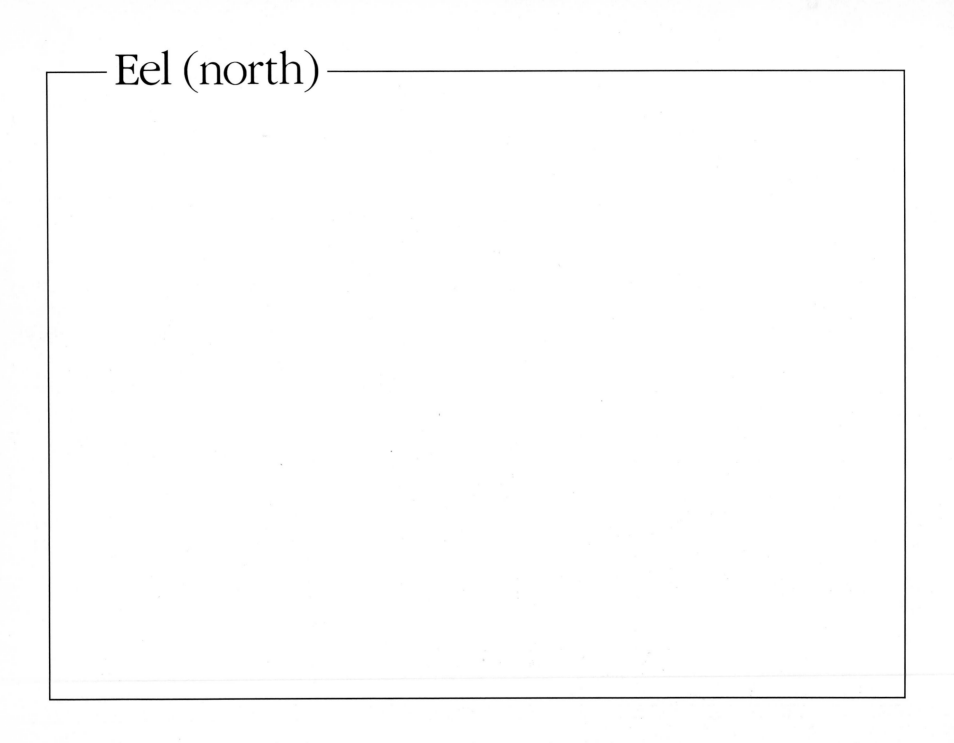

Eel (north)

The Indians called the river *Ke-na-po-co-mo-co*, which in the Miami tongue means "snake fish," and so the first settlers translated the name to Eel, by which it has been known ever since. This quiet, picturesque northern Indiana stream could more properly be called the embattled Eel, for more warfare raged along its banks than on any similar-sized stream in Indiana. It is the state's ABC river—stream of ambush, battle, and conquest. It is also, to a remarkable degree, the story of a single man. His name was *Me-she-kin-no-quah*, which the white man translated into "the Little Turtle." Many historians describe him as the greatest Indian who ever lived, and as the story of Eel River unfolds, it will be easy to see how this claim scarcely can be disputed.

Rising as an insignificant ditch in a flat, barren, swampy area in northern Allen County, two and a half miles southeast of Huntertown, the Eel strikes out westward toward its rendezvous with the Wabash, 110 miles away. Almost immediately it begins to cut a shallow but noticeable valley, threading its way through miles of rich, black farmland. Gradually it becomes a forest stream rippling between tree-bordered banks and in the early days providing water power for numerous grist mills.

Long before the white man drained its swamps and put its water power to work, the Potawatomi, an upper Great Lakes tribe related to the Ojibwa of Longfellow's *Hiawatha*, had swept into Indiana pushing the Miami southward to the Eel. Here the Miami dug in and held fast. They halted the Potawatomi at the north bank and the stream became the uneasy boundary between these powerful nations.

To protect their lands, the Miami for years garrisoned an elevated triangle south of the present Columbia City. Known as "the island," it was surrounded by Eel River, Mud Creek, and a swampy area that cut off invasion from the east. Despite this fortification, reports of conflict between the two tribes were common, and the valley's bloody history therefore predates the white man. It was at "the island" that Little Turtle first earned recognition as a warrior. In later years, as the white man encroached, Little Turtle carried warfare up and down the turbulent valley, earning a fearsome reputation as a brave soldier and a talented strategist.

Even as conflict with the Potawatomi tapered off and the valley briefly became more peaceful, a new foe appeared, presaging events to come. He was a dashing French soldier of fortune with the unwieldy name of Augustin Mottin de la Balme and he was a man with a plan. Little Turtle upset his plan; otherwise, the course of the American Revolution, as well as the War of 1812, might have been changed drastically. Inspired by George Rogers Clark's success at Vincennes, La Balme there conceived a bold plan to wrest Detroit from the British. Beyond Detroit lay Canada; perhaps that fitted into his plan also.

Gathering a little army, mostly Frenchmen, he started up the Wabash in 1780, pausing to destroy the important Miami village of Kekionga, where Fort Wayne now stands. Flushed with this victory and believing that he had forced the Indians into headlong flight, he decided to replenish his supplies by raiding a British trading post on Eel River. He turned in that direction and purportedly camped for the night at a location marked by a memorial tablet on the river road east of Columbia City. But La Balme had reckoned without the military genius of Little Turtle, who silently encircled his army during the night. With a mighty war whoop, the Indians fell upon the sleeping soldiers. Only one captive survived to tell the story. The Eel once again ran red with blood, and the victory catapulted Little Turtle into an even higher position of leadership among his people and of respect among the British, with whom they often were allied.

The upper Eel now was indisputably Little Turtle's land and the great chief returned to his village five miles above the present Columbia City. The Potawatomi respected his ability and did not threaten him.

Peace lasted on the Eel for a decade. This time the threat was far more formidable than La Balme's had been. Alarmed by clashes on the frontier, the federal government ordered General Josiah Harmar, commander-in-chief of the army, to quell the unruly Indians. He was authorized to arm 1,500 men. Arriving at Kekionga, Harmar found the village deserted and he destroyed it. Believing the Indians had fled, he sent Colonel John Hardin with 210 men out to find them and to administer the whipping the General had been instructed to give.

Following a well-marked trail to the northwest, Hardin's men marched gaily along, assuming they were pursuing fleeing Indians. But Little Turtle, who knew his country like a suburbanite knows his

Little Turtle, chief of the
Eel River Miami.

crabgrass, was busy with other ideas. Hastily collecting about 300 men, he headed for a marshy, timber-bordered prairie which stretched up and away on both sides of the river. Here he hid his men. Then he waited.

Confident that no Indians would attack a force as formidable as his, Hardin marched his men boldly into the ambush. At precisely the right moment the Indians opened fire and advanced on the familiar paths through the marsh. Most of the soldiers fled immediately and the few who fought were killed. Little Turtle then followed up his victory with another over Harmar's forces on the Maumee River, a short distance below its source in what is now Fort Wayne.

Back in Philadelphia, the then federal capital, there was no joy. The next year, General James Wilkinson was sent out to raid the Miami towns, and he struck at Kenapacomaqua, an important village on the Eel about seven miles above the present Logansport. He destroyed it, along with food and supplies, in what is known as the Battle of Old Towne. Once again, the Eel was a battleground.

Wilkinson fortunately had escaped an encounter with Little Turtle, who was waiting for bigger fish to fry. Leading an army to the headwaters of the Wabash at what is now Fort Recovery, Ohio, Little Turtle routed a large American force led by General Arthur St. Clair and administered the worst defeat ever dealt by Indians anywhere. Almost two-thirds of St. Clair's army was killed or wounded.

Invincible against four white armies, Little Turtle rode the crest of a victory wave. Yet three years later, when General Anthony Wayne was sent by President Washington to win the elusive victory, Little Turtle advised against further warfare: "Brothers," he addressed the main chiefs of the ten-tribe confederation, "the Americans are now led by a chief who never sleeps. The night and the day are alike to him. During all the time he has been marching on our villages, notwithstanding the watchfulness of our young men, we have never been able to surprise him. Think well on it. There is something that whispers to me it would be prudent to listen to his offers of peace."

His fellow chiefs accused Little Turtle of cowardice and chose Blue Jacket, a Shawnee, as their commander. Spurning Little Turtle's advice, they were soundly defeated at the Battle of Fallen Timbers on the lower Maumee, and their power was crushed permanently. In the peace treaty that followed at Greenville, Ohio, they lost two-thirds of Ohio and part of southeastern Indiana. Little Turtle was vindicated. As he signed the treaty, he said, "I have been the last to sign this treaty; I will be the last to break it." He never did.

General Wayne was so impressed with Little Turtle's dignity and

*Left to right*: In 1951 James H. Deck examined flour produced by his Stockdale mill, built in 1856, near Roann. ❧Eel Valley's Dunkards—members of the Church of the Brethren—still make apple butter in the traditional way.

ability that he urged him to visit President Washington at Philadelphia. When he did, Washington gave Little Turtle a sword and a peace medal and commissioned Gilbert Stuart to paint his portrait.

Little Turtle was subsequently received by John Adams and by Thomas Jefferson, who was empowered by Congress to suppress the liquor trade with the Indians. In urging passage of the law, Little Turtle addressed Congress, declaring, "More of us have died since the Treaty of Greenville than we lost by the years of war among us, and it is all owing to the introduction of this liquor among us." On one of his trips, Little Turtle learned about vaccination, which was being hesitantly introduced from England. Realizing its importance, he not only was vaccinated but he also brought vaccine back to Indiana for his people. Most Americans had not yet accepted its use.

Now that peace had come to his valley Little Turtle realized that his people could survive only if they adopted the best of the white man's ways. They must refuse liquor, fight disease, and give up the diminishing hunt for the bounty of the farm. He persuaded the Quakers of Baltimore to send a teacher of agriculture to the Indians and successfully urged Congress to appropriate $15,000 toward his support. Selecting land along the Wabash near what is now Andrews, the project was begun. It was a wise move but only partly successful.

Heroic in war, wise in peace, Little Turtle died in 1812. Shortly afterward, American armies again swept through the valley as part of the rapidly developing War of 1812. By special instructions they spared Little Turtle's village. With their departure warfare on the Eel ended permanently.

A little more than a generation later the peaceful Dunkards (Church of the Brethren) migrated into the valley and established the mother church at North Manchester. From there the gentle Brethren spread up and down the river, establishing congregations at Mexico, Roann, Logansport, and other points until they now are one of the largest denominations in Wabash and Miami counties.

When the church purchased a floundering little college at North Manchester in 1895, they established the town as their educational as well as their spiritual capital. Today, Manchester College is among the state's largest private schools.

North Manchester also has the architecturally impressive Estelle Peabody Retirement Community and is a potent industrial force, producing wire products, appliance controls, and castings. The Heckman Bindery claims to be America's largest bookbinder.

Growing steadily, North Manchester recently became the largest city in the valley, surpassing Columbia City, seat of Whitley County.

Columbia City was the home of Thomas R. Marshall, the North Manchester native who became vice president under Wilson; Lloyd C. Douglas, author and minister, and General Merritte W. Ireland, former surgeon-general of the U.S. Army. Manufactured products include automotive parts, plastics, and tools.

Although the Eel skirts a moraine throughout its course, the valley deepens appreciably only below North Manchester, where bluffs sometimes reach seventy-five feet. Geologically it is a young valley and bottomlands are few. Its waters drain from less than 800 square miles and are regulated by the flow from several lakes so that flooding is minimized.

Mills were numerous below South Whitley and several dams remain to impound the water and add placidity to the longtime turbulence of the valley. Stockdale Mill below Roann was one of the state's last operating water-powered mills. Covered bridges, at North Manchester and Roann, add a rustic touch.

Since the valley is fairly straight, it was a natural rail route and by 1873 trains were puffing their way regularly between Logansport and Butler on the Eel River Railroad. Six years later it was leased to the Wabash Railroad, which soon converted it from a local farm-to-market line into the middle link of a vast transcontinental system.

Fourteen passenger trains daily steamed the length of the valley, including a luxury train, the Continental Limited, which connected St. Louis and New York City.

But the chugs of the steam locomotive became as turbulent as the Indian wars once had been and a battle—legal variety—soon embroiled the railroad. When the courts terminated it ten years later, tempers had flared, cities had feuded, the Wabash had lost control of the railroad, and the line once again was quiet, firmly held by the people of the valley, but no longer of national importance. By the mid-1970s it was abandoned.

Like the Indians, the local rail magnates had won the battles but lost the war. Turbulence, it seems, was ever the rule of the embattled Eel.

# Mississinewa

It's a warm spring evening and the lazy breezes that drift slowly over the Mississinewa River beckon toward its banks. As you drive down River Road in Marion, your eye sweeps along the pulsing current to the Charles Mill dam. You watch—and you reflect—as the river comes crashing down in a swarm of boiling water and then flows away, unfettered, leaping vigorously toward the sea.

As you look, your mind relaxes and in its eye the dam melts away. Now the Mississinewa is the unspoiled river that Indians canoed and settlers used as their road. It is swift and musical as it glides among the stones and slips noisily over its rocky bed.

As rivers go, the Mississinewa is young, yet it is more than 15,000 years old. Before there was the river, there was the ice. Nearly a mile high it came, pushing down from the north during the great glacial ages. Then as the southern sun checked its advance at last, the glacier began to recede, halting periodically and piling its debris into long, high moraines. Five sets of these in arrowhead patterns were deposited in east-central Indiana, and as meltwater collected at their edges, flowing streams began to form. One of these was the Mississinewa.

The Mississinewa has a story to tell and it tells it in the changing history of its people.

What's that dark mass rounding the distant bend? Can it be?—yes, it is. A flotilla of Indian canoes. Now you recall that the river's name came from a Miami word meaning "falling water." The white man's science has corroborated the Indians' judgment, for the Mississinewa is, indeed, central Indiana's swiftest river, falling 3.3 feet to the mile between western Ohio, where it begins its race to the sea, and its discharge into the Wabash near Peru, 110 miles away.

The Miami considered the Mississinewa THEIR river. It was, except when angry, a gracious and gentle stream flowing through a pleasing country. However, the Indians grew unruly in their Mississinewa paradise, so the federal government sent Lieutenant Colonel John B. Campbell and 600 troops to chastise them. The army arrived at a point seven miles below what now is Marion. They reddened its banks and filled its forests with the smoke of burning villages as they destroyed food supplies and shelter, taking forty-two prisoners, and killing eight warriors. Then they pitched camp for the night on a terrace above the river.

Shortly before daybreak on a horribly frigid mid-December day in 1812 a hideous yell followed by the thunder of hoofs startled the camp into life. Fighting was desperate, often hand-to-hand. Legend has it that an Indian skilled at animal imitations stampeded the army's horses so that many plunged over the cliff, variously reported as twenty to forty feet high, to their deaths. In any event, official records show that 107 horses were lost, an unusually large number.

The American army recorded 12 dead and carried away 48 wounded. Worse, however, were the rigors of winter which rendered 303 men unfit for duty because of severe frostbite. Long marches brought the unhappy army back to its Greenville, Ohio, base in seven days.

The Miami learned a lesson and thereafter were peaceable. The white men learned, too, the high cost of Indian warfare. After the battle, which was the last major Indian encounter in Indiana, the Indians drifted back to their villages—Metocinyah's, near the battlefield; Osage, near the river's mouth, and between the two, the settlement of Chief Shepoconah.

To the Indians, Shepoconah's wife was Maconaquah, the Little Bear Woman. To the whites, she was Frances Slocum, Lost Sister of the Miami, and daughter of a Pennsylvania Quaker family. Her story is one of the most romantic in the pages of American history. Indians carried five-year-old Frances into captivity in 1778 from her parents' home near Wilkes-Barre, Pennsylvania. For years her family held to its hope of finding her and each succeeding generation pledged itself to carry on the pathetic search. More than a half-century after her capture, believing the end was near, she related her fragmentary recollections to George W. Ewing, an Indian trader, who pieced them together and sent word back to Pennsylvania.

The story finally reached her nephew who had accepted the family challenge to continue the search. At his direction her two aged brothers and a sister made the journey to Indiana and after fifty-nine years found Frances living along the Mississinewa, the respected widow of Chief Shepoconah. Her family urged her to return to Pennsylvania, but she would not. "I am an old tree," she said, "and I would die if you would move me." And so she remained among her people and was buried with them when she died ten years later in 1847.

By that time the Miami had been sent to new lands beyond the Mississippi; although Frances and her family and Chief Meshingomesia's band were allowed to remain. For the latter group, the government set aside a reservation fronting for ten miles on the swift, murmuring Mississinewa. A school and a Baptist church were established one mile north of the battleground opposite the village. The reservation, the last in Indiana and the last east of the Mississippi for the Miami, remained intact until 1880 when it was divided among the individual Indian families. Once the white man's culture had assimilated them, there was little to remember the Indians by—mounds to be plowed down, arrowheads, dust of bones, and a fashionable country club bearing the chief's name.

Your reverie bursts apart. But wait. What's happening on the river now? You look and in your mind's eye you see men busy with timber and tools standing knee-deep in the rapid current. The pioneers have arrived. The river has served them as a highway to lands of their own, and they have not overlooked the potential of the river's willful strength. They built dams and harnessed the water to grind their grain, make their flour, and saw their timber. Near the spot where you are sitting, they wisely and skillfully erected the stately Charles Mill in 1856. It stands today almost as it did then. Mills rose up and down the river and on its tributaries in great profusion. Fifteen were built near Jonesboro, where the township, quite naturally, was named Mill. One of the most picturesque was Conner's Mill, which stood until modern times opposite the Mississinewa battleground.

Such towns as Marion, Hartford City, and Fairmount sprang up in the valley, each to grow to prominence in its own way. Fairmount, settled by North Carolina Quakers, became known for the Fairmount Academy and the academy, in turn, influenced many residents into literary and educational fields. Now a quiet town of 3,286, Fairmount at one point had a ratio of 1 person listed in *Who's Who* for every 230 residents. This added up to fourteen times the national average. The list includes three college presidents, a noted marine scientist, college professors and deans, historians, artists, librarians, and authors in the fields of economics, sociology, and religion. Fairmount Township was a home of Bishop Milton Wright, father of the aviation pioneers; Mary Jane Ward, author of *The Snake Pit*, and Leroy Scott, noted author of the muckraking days; Captain David L. Payne, the swashbuckling "Father of Oklahoma"; a General Motors vice-president; and a Chicago loop bank president. The late actor James Dean, and

One of the many advertisements inviting manufacturers to come to Marion during the natural gas boom days.

Jim Davis, creator of Garfield, the favorite cartoon cat, grew up in Fairmount.

Settlers who streamed into the Mississinewa country found a scenic river. In places it is marked by grandeur, in others it is rugged, picturesque, or pastoral. They found its beauty primitive and unspoiled, and in isolated localities it remains so today.

In the uplands of its birth, not far from the source of the Wabash, the Mississinewa is a tiny unpretentious drainage ditch. Hesitant, undecided in direction, it flows through a broad, shallow valley. Arrow-straight in long sections as the result of numerous drainage projects, the infant Mississinewa strikes out toward Indiana. It is a pastoral stream, calm and serene, its valley shallow and its meadows tenanted by grazing livestock.

Agriculture is a multimillion dollar business in the valley. Corn and soybeans are the principal crops and hogs and cattle the principal livestock. In Indiana, Grant, Delaware, and Miami counties are among the nation's principal tomato producers, and Wabash County ranks high in hog, chicken, and egg production. Popcorn and fruit are important specialty crops. Chester Troyer, repeatedly crowned International Corn King, grew his prize grain on fields stretching down to the riverbank.

Darke County, Ohio, where the river begins, stands thirteenth in

the nation in the number of high production farms. It is a national leader in hog, chicken, turkey, and soybean production, standing no lower than the upper 3 percent in each category.

Widening from the strength of a thousand brooks, the river cuts a steeper valley as it approaches Marion, where it first reaches bedrock. The land changes slowly and the Mississinewa becomes a stream of often spectacular beauty, winding past such startling geologic oddities as Split Rock, Bear Cave, and the Seven Pillars, where the onrushing current surges stubbornly against a limestone cliff and carves grotesque formations that are easily the river's most spectacular wonder.

You gaze reflectively at the water cascading over the dam. Suddenly you are back in the gay nineties and the colorful, free-swinging, exciting natural gas era. Hissing comes from wells that flow perpetually, and flambeaux illuminate the countryside and are left to burn night and day. The gas would never give out, they said, so why bother to turn it off? For a very few dollars a year, a householder could have unlimited gas for heating, lighting, and cooking. For factories, the fuel was free.

Although natural gas was discovered at Eaton on the upper Mississinewa in 1876, the well was abandoned as worthless, and the era did not begin in the valley until 1887 when the discovery well came in at Marion. For the next two decades the valley was a great beehive of industry, immigration, and ingenuity.

Marion became the Queen City of the gas belt and within three years 8,769 persons had swelled the village to city size. The population doubled and re-doubled in successive decades. Glass factories, which hastened in to utilize the inexpensive fuel, elbowed aside mills and small woodworking industries. Real estate developers laid out sprawling additions, tempting the factories which would employ the men who would buy the residential lots along the newly platted streets. Merchants rushed in to take advantage of the expanded market.

Marion incorporated as a city and such country towns as Upland, Fairmount, and Hartford City shook themselves awake. Harrisburg, with a population of 145 in two successive census counts, suddenly exploded to 3,600 and celebrated by changing its name to Gas City. Losing population drastically after the boom, it has now rebounded to a count of 6,370. In addition to glass, it snared one of the world's largest tin plate mills. Hartford City claimed one of the nation's largest window glass factories. Sleepy little New Cumberland, Grant County's second oldest settlement, was swallowed by the newly established town of Matthews, which quickly attracted nearly a dozen glass factories, a foundry, railroad shops, and other industries.

*Left to right*: The Mississinewa carved the spectacular Seven Pillars near Peru. ❧The Charles Mill at Marion, built in 1856, has been converted into shops and apartments.

In midseason 1901, it spirited the professional baseball team away from Indianapolis.

As full of life as a Roman candle lighted at both ends, Matthews boomed and died in little more than a decade. Skilled Belgian and French glassblowers swarmed in, overflowing the hotels and rooming houses until tabletop and hallway sleeping space brought premium prices. Money flowed freely along the ninety-foot-wide main street, and the town, its promoters insisted, would become the Pittsburgh of the Middle West. When the gas supply—which everyone but the geologists absolutely knew would last forever—failed, Matthews collapsed. Factories closed. Scores of houses were moved away or razed, businesses closed their doors and the buildings were left to decay. Population shrank from a reported 5,500 to 500 almost overnight, and for many years the silent hulks of crumbling buildings gave Matthews a western ghost town appearance.

Far more durable than the brittle, unrealistic economy is the Matthews covered bridge, the only one remaining across the Mississinewa. A single span 183 feet long, it was built in 1877 and is best known for the wild ride it took during the devastating 1913 flood. Lifted off its abutments, it floated against a thick growth of bankside trees one-quarter mile downstream and lodged firmly. It was returned to its original location on rollers. Sturdy and lovingly maintained, the bridge still carries traffic, and the Matthews Lions Club, with obvious hometown pride, has developed a park at its entrance, erected handsome markers to tell of the strange odyssey, and uses it as the centerpiece for its annual covered bridge festival.

At Marion, promoters worked feverishly during the boom. They built streetcar lines in such profusion that rival companies once sent rails side by side up Third Street hill before coming to their senses and agreeing on a joint track. They built the state's second interurban line to link Gas City with Marion, and it became the kingpin of the sprawling central Indiana network. One company platted a vast development and sold lots three miles from the public square at the unbelievable price of $1,000 each. In its center they erected the York Inn, a rambling four-story structure with towers, turrets, and assorted gingerbread and connected it with downtown by a streetcar line. Russell Harrison, son of the president of the United States, was company president. But like the boomtime embellishments of Matthews, the York Inn faded away and the factories closed. An oil boom followed, but it never gained the proportions of the fabulous natural gas days.

An exciting story, you muse, and a little sad that the color and life and vigor disappeared so completely. Yet, they left their mark. The valley settled down to a more stable existence, and the institu-

After the 1913 flood floated it downstream, contractor George A. Lemon rolled the Matthews covered bridge back to its original location.

tions which grew upon the foundations of the ephemeral gas boom proved more durable.

Taylor University, for example, moved to Upland from Fort Wayne at the peak of the gas era and remained to grow and prosper long after the gas supply gave out and the glass factories had disappeared. Today its 1,467 students study on a 260-acre campus, which has added 17 buildings at a replacement cost of more than $40,000,000 since 1965. It has become one of Indiana's outstanding private universities and a strong cultural factor in the valley.

Marion Normal College, which educated several generations of central Indiana teachers, disappeared after the boom and Marion College succeeded it. Now in its greatest expansion, it has become an important community college for Grant and surrounding counties. The Wesleyan Church, which operates it, also has its world headquarters in Marion. It is Grant County's fastest growing major Protestant denomination, edging past all but the United Methodist Church in membership.

As the gas boom began, the federal government located a soldiers' home in Marion. Continually enlarged, it is now a Veterans' Administration Hospital and covers 189 acres with its 99 buildings.

But now you look across the river. That was the boyhood farm of Willis Van Devanter, for twenty-six years a U.S. Supreme Court justice

in the court's heyday. You recall other "greats" in the local legal world: Caleb B. Smith, Lincoln's secretary of the interior; Judge Kenesaw Mountain Landis, first commissioner of organized baseball; and Major George W. Steele, Oklahoma's first governor. Steele's son, Captain George W. Steele, was a pioneer Atlantic aviator, making the crossing three years earlier than Lindbergh.

Your gaze sweeps downstream where the light green reflections of spring edge the musical water and the river extends a slender, tantalizing finger toward Mississinewa Lake. The roar of motorboats is loud in summer on the 3,200-acre flood-control impoundment, which proves that the river still demands that men spend money and energy to deal with its eccentricities.

Here the present and the past have flowed together. Army engineers scrubbed clean and drowned much of the 14,386-acre flood-control basin in which lies Indiana's fourth largest lake. Orchard and shade trees joined in the funeral pyre of bulldozed frame dwellings as 4,500,000 cubic yards of earth and concrete were thrown across the valley near Peoria to form a dam 8,000 feet long and 140 feet high. The picturesque village of Somerset, elbowed close to the river by the hills, has been rebuilt on higher ground, and the hilly countryside that attracted innumerable artists and beckoned to James Whitcomb Riley to sing its raptures now lies under hundreds of acres of water. Bankside resorts like Pearson's Mill, Riverside Park, and Liston Glens have disappeared. The ground that Frances Slocum trod is now buried under millions of gallons of water, and motorboats race over the doorsill of her cabin. The Frances Slocum Trail, a scenic county road tying together the region's principal points of interest has been partially relocated.

The river is clean today. Not as pure as it once was but cleaner than it has been. There is good bass fishing and enough walleye and northern pike to lure the avid angler. Below the dam, it is the same Mississinewa that has tumbled restlessly and unceasingly over its rock-strewn bed for thousands of years. The water slides over rippling shallows, glides among the rocks, and nestles in a valley backed by steep wooded hills.

Near Peru the stately, white-pillared home of composer Cole Porter suddenly bursts into view, reflecting the aristocratic life in which he was reared. This is the heart of the Miami Indian country, a fact recalled by names once painted on the barns. A short distance downstream, the Mississinewa slopes between the rolling hills for the last time as it passes the farm of Emil Schram, former president of the New York Stock Exchange.

The valley flattens as it merges with the bottomlands of the nearby Wabash. Elephants, giraffes, lions, and tigers once paced here at the winter quarters of America's best-known circuses: Hagenbeck-Wallace, Sells-Floto, and John Robinson. Ringling Brothers owned them at the end. Resting from the rigors of the high trapeze and the wild animal acts, they made Peru the Circus City. Those were great days, filled with color and excitement.

The bubble bursts. The animal trainers and the barkers disappear. You are back on the riverbank. But your imagination must have one final exercise. You have seen the Mississinewa's story unfold before your eyes: First, the Indians in their sleek, birchbark canoes. Then, the pioneers who drove them from the soil. Next, the glassblowers for whom the farms were converted into cities and towns. The first press operators at General Motors and tube makers at RCA's world's largest television picture tube plant, all helped build the present industrial complex in Marion, which includes automotive parts, paper, glass, wire, and plastics producers. The poets, the composers, and the scholars. For a brief, fleeting moment they are all there. Then you blink your eyes and they disappear into the mists of history.

# Salamonie

Meet the Salamonie, the river whose future was planned, promised, and guaranteed by the Army Corps of Engineers. Until 1966 the Salamonie hadn't been much to boast about. The second smallest river that was a tributary of the upper Wabash, it was an insignificant stream with a dual personality. To be sure, the lower river was wandering and charming, flowing powerfully between bluffs that shot straight into the air as much as seventy-five feet, but the upper river was shallow and weed-grown, imprisoned in man-made ditches—narrow, straight, barren, and ugly. The water flowed slowly and, sometimes in summer, scarcely flowed at all.

Then the engineers arrived. In five years they threw across the valley a massive dam, 132 feet high and more than a mile long, converting the river into a seasonal lake, seventeen miles long, and creating one of the most scenic areas north of Brown County. Nature, working for thousands of years, had failed to wreak such cataclysmic changes.

There was no Salamonie before the great glacial sheets of geologic times spread out of the north. As the continental ice mass alternately advanced and retreated, it ground down mountains and filled the valleys with the pulverized debris, eventually building a series of parallel ridges, arrow-shaped, across northeastern Indiana. At the base of one of these ridges, as the southern sun melted the great ice mass, the Salamonie was born.

But the glaciers had done more than create the Salamonie. They also created two larger parallel streams—the Mississinewa and the upper Wabash—and left the Salamonie flowing between them, squeezing it into a drainage basin of little more than 500 square miles. Wedged between its larger neighbors, it began small and was destined to remain that way.

Like many Indiana streams, Salamonie's name originated with the Indians. In the Miami tongue it was *On-za-la-mo-ni*, which meant "bloodroot," a plant from which they made yellow dye. The Indians have stamped their name indelibly on the map with an angular tract above Montpelier that was set aside for Chief Godfrey and is still known as the Godfrey Reserve.

To find the beginning of the Salamonie, one must travel to southeastern Jay County, a mile south and one and three-quarters miles east of the aptly named village of Salamonia, and about eighty-eight miles from the river's mouth. Willows nearly obliterate its source, and tall, sturdy prairie grasses choke the tiny channel that issues from a field drain lying behind the site of an abandoned farmhouse.

For nearly half its length—through Portland and past Pennville

*Left to right*: Quiet waters below Belleville Mill, near Warren, attracted fishermen. ◄§While neighbors watched, a gas well blew in about 1895 in Jay County.

in Jay County—a succession of straight, shallow ditches carries the sluggish Salamonie through flat farmlands. There is no recognizable valley and man is hard pressed to provide adequate drainage for the adjacent fields. Near Montpelier, however, the stream assumes the appearance of a small river, bounding over boulders and bedrock and receiving scores of tiny brooks whose contributions swell the huge reservoir downstream. No longer sluggish, it becomes a pretty stream whose placid meanderings carry it past wooded banks and over ever-murmuring riffles.

For many years pump jacks bobbed importantly in bordering fields as they lifted oil from the Trenton limestone, 1,000 feet below. But in more recent years a few scattered wells were all that remained of the Salamonie's love affair with the far-flung Indiana oil field of eighty years ago. Now an attempt is being made to revive production but there is no promise of a return to the boom days. Stretching from the Ohio border nearly to Marion, forty-five miles westward, the Trenton field was the hottest thing going in its day. And since the Salamonie neatly bisected the field from Pennville to Warren, oil wells and the Salamonie became inseparable partners.

Appropriately, the great oil boom began near the riverbank in 1890. On the D. A. Bryson farm north of Montpelier the drill struck the underground reservoir and oil gushed out at the rate of sixty barrels a day, immediately creating a fever pitch of excitement that was to spread far beyond the placid stream's valley. Three months later a cathartic of nitroglycerin pushed the flow to a hundred barrels daily. Excitement rose accordingly. Oilmen streamed in from everywhere by the hundreds, perhaps thousands. They raised derricks, bit into the earth with their drills, hauled in machinery, and established supply depots, all the while responding gleefully to the ever-increasing oil production.

Most of the men chose the quiet village of Montpelier as headquarters. In one great surge of feverish activity, the town more than quadrupled its population, and its residents smiled happily as 14,000 barrels of oil each day passed through its pumping station, largest in the field. Two 25,000-barrel storage tanks loomed importantly on its skyline. All this unaccustomed commotion prompted the local newspaper editor to write enthusiastically that Montpelier was "destined to become the metropolis of northeastern Indiana." But he was a slaphappy optimist, intoxicated by the oily excitement of the day.

When the bubble burst, half the people moved away, and Montpelier reverted to its accustomed role of farm-trading center and small producer of such diverse items as gloves, shipping containers, and rubber products. Its reversion ended its threat to Portland, then and now the ruling city of the valley. Seat of Jay County and largest settlement on the river, it is a rich farming center and manufacturer of clothing, forgings, and automotive equipment.

Below Montpelier the Salamonie flows its quiet way toward Warren, once the busy corner of the great oil field but now better known as a trading center and location of the United Methodist Memorial Home for the Aged. The bloom had begun to fade from the oil fever when Mr. and Mrs. William Chopson donated $37,500 and 200 acres of land to the Methodist Church. The Warren Commercial Club enlarged the donation with fifty-eight additional acres, and in 1910 the home's first building opened the doors of its thirty-seven rooms. Steadily expanding, the home moved at its fastest pace during the 1950s when it added two $1,000,000 wings and a $500,000 hospital. Additional expansion in the late 1970s added a $6,000,000 residential unit. Nearly 400 persons now reside on the neatly landscaped grounds near the Salamonie.

At Warren the quiet river becomes frivolous, leaping over one of the two milldams remaining from the days when water was the most important power source. Now flowing scenically between gradually rising banks, the Salamonie spills over a dam again at Belleville, the site of one of Indiana's last waterpowered mills. Above the dam a country road rides the riverbank and the mirror-like water charms travelers on wheel and foot as it glides past quiet woods and distant hills.

Below Belleville, the Salamonie suddenly assumes its new personality, winding between steep hills and looping around a never-never land known as Heiney's Bend. Here at last is the real Salamonie, the grown-up river, delight of anglers, darling of nature lovers, and magnet for scenery oglers. Entering a series of convulsive loops, the river takes a detour said to be seven-and-a-half fish-swum miles before returning to within 1,000 feet of itself. The bluffs here are high and steep and the river twists and turns like a snake enjoying the sunshine, meanwhile dropping thirteen feet as it loops around the bend.

Inside the light-bulb-shaped loop there is a heavy quiet and a feeling of isolation. The Indiana Department of Natural Resources operates a boating and fishing area here that connects with others downstream in the 11,506-acre Salamonie Reservoir area. The upper limit of the reservoir, it has become an angler's delight. Conservation officials opened the project attempting to kill every fish they could find in the Salamonie and its tributaries. Then they planted nearly 90,000 bass and bluegill, along with 20,000 channel catfish. At the same time 1,020 acres were developed into the Lost Bridge State Rec-

Many years after oil was discovered, scattered wells using primitive equipment continued to produce.

reation Area on the south shore of the reservoir between Mt. Etna and the dam, and 619 acres into the Salamonie River State Forest in Wabash County near Lagro.

In summer—when the lake fills to its seasonal pool of 2,855 acres—swimmers, boaters, anglers, and kindred water worshippers turn out by the thousands. There are five recreation areas, complete with boat-launching ramps, picnic grounds, camping facilities, and a beach for their recreation.

Bluffs along the reservoir reach seventy-five feet in places and the scenic beauty is memorable. A sunset on the water is a treasure that can never be erased from memory. While the reservoir obviously is long and narrow like the valley, two embayments give it width. One covers the site of Monument City, the other the site of New Holland. From May 1 to September 15 the water remains at seasonal pool level. Then it is lowered gradually by twenty-five feet, the level which it retains until April 1, when the dam gates clang shut and the water is stored to prevent flooding along the Wabash.

Having experienced the glaciers and conquered their thrusts, the Salamonie is not likely to be unduly disturbed by what man has done to its waters. Confined and perhaps tamed, the river still flows on its course to the Wabash.

# Tippecanoe

Along the north edge of Whitley County, where rolling green hills and steep wooded ridges conspire to conceal some of Indiana's most beautiful lakes, a tiny stream, a few feet wide and less than a city block long, flows sluggishly from the grassy shallows of Little Crooked Lake. Entering the mile-long waters of Crooked Lake, it continues into nearby Big Lake. From the far end, the tiny stream issues again as a westward-flowing ditch. Thus, in the quiet beauty of the Indiana lake country, begins the Tippecanoe River.

Once beyond Big Lake and on its own, the Tippecanoe, here sometimes known as Stangland Ditch, flows quietly through undulating fields filled in summer with rippling oceans of wheat and oats and great green expanses of ripening corn. Its course is a succession of long, straight tangents dredged to drain the surrounding farmland. As it gathers the water of numerous small lakes, it etches its way into the earth, creating a gentle valley, while it skirts thickly forested hills and cuts its way through field and swamp into Smalley Lake.

Beyond Smalley Lake, the infant Tippecanoe suddenly dives into a green thicket of willows, laurels, and beeches huddled so closely together as to blot out the sunlight. The water slides over murmuring shallows and the current grows noticeably strong. Fish seek the quiet pools and turtles clamber up and down the banks. Here, as through its entire course, the Tippecanoe is nature's stream, bearing a minimum of silt, unsullied by industrial wastes and bordered by lush green fields and clean, cool forests. It is a gentle river, gracious and inviting; its charms are never-ending, and those who see its glories surely can never forget the river's beauties.

The Tippecanoe has long been known for its beauty. As far back as 1888, when Assistant State Geologist Will H. Thompson, younger brother of famed author Maurice Thompson, made an official survey of the valley, he wrote:

> I have called it a "beautiful" stream, but neither that word nor any other is strong enough to properly characterize its exceeding loveliness.
> There are many fine streams in the state of Indiana, but not one that can be compared with this river. Its rare beauty, its splendid fishing, the good shooting to be found along its banks, the numberless cold springs that bubble out of the high bluffs, the small green islands that are met at almost every turn of the stream, the clear water flow-

ing over the assorted sand and boulders of the northern drift, or the masses of heavy green grass attached to the bottom and waving in the moving water like a tiny forest in a "broad and equal blowing wind," lend a charm against which few hearts are proof.

From source to mouth the Tippecanoe is a bountiful pantry to wild ducks floating on the water, warblers busily grubbing lunch from the bankside willows, redheaded woodpeckers winging overhead in their characteristically majestic flight, and bobwhites whistling cheerily across the fields. It is a river of kingfishers, alert and poised, waiting for the proper moment to dive, of groundhogs scurrying along the banks, and of turtles sunning themselves on its rocks. Cities, for the most part, have been content to build a few miles from the water and to leave nature to its unspoiled self.

A child of the lakes, the Tippecanoe is totally controlled by them, flowing through two of the state's largest—Tippecanoe and Webster—as well as nearly a dozen smaller ones on its 166-mile course. In its 1,900-square-mile basin, the river drains eighty-eight natural lakes and each acts as a settling basin to reduce the flow of silt and regulate the water level. Damaging floods in the valley are rare. The Tippecanoe is described as the clearest stream in the state, and aquatic grasses, which line the bed, are unique.

Although the Tippecanoe is a quiet river of nature, as well as a

*Left to right*: The Shawnees led by the Prophet fought General William Henry Harrison and the army at the Battle of Tippecanoe, November 7, 1811. The Billy Sunday Tabernacle at Winona Assembly was dedicated in 1920.

gay companion to water sports lovers and fishermen, it also is a working river, harnessed early by man to turn mill wheels and later to produce electrical power. Its farthest upstream duty was at Wilmot, where a milldam created the twelve-acre Wilmot Pond in the 1840s. State Road 5 now passes over the dam at the foot of the willow-lined lake, which lies in a setting as beautiful as any to be found along the Tippecanoe.

Below Wilmot the river winds along the steep face of a moraine and into Lake Webster, a 524-acre playland formed when a milldam raised the water level to combine several lakes. It is one of Indiana's rare lakes to be churned by steamboat paddles; the *Dixie* has been a fixture since 1929. Webster is better known, however, to thousands of Methodists as the home of Epworth Forest and Camp Adventure, where nature's strength ministers to man's spiritual needs.

As the Tippecanoe is a river of nature, so also is it a river of God, for organized religion, ranging from the mainline United Methodists to the embattled, ultra-conservative Faith Assembly, has taken a strong hold through its upper valley. One of the more famous American ministers, the Reverend Lloyd Douglas, best-selling author of *The Robe, Magnificent Obsession*, and other novels, grew up along the upper river. Numerous religious groups have developed retreats in the Tippecanoe's lake country. The best known is Winona Lake at

Warsaw. Now a separate municipality, it is a fascinating blend of lakeside resort and religious revival meeting reminiscent of the day when chautauquas were a driving cultural force.

The Winona Assembly, which dates to 1895 and was the forerunner of the town, resulted from the vision of such influential men as H. J. Heinz, the food processor; John M. Studebaker of the automotive family; and Dr. J. Wilbur Chapman, an eminent evangelist. William Jennings Bryan and the great evangelist Billy Sunday figured prominently in Winona Lake's growth. To provide convenient transportation, the Assembly founded the Winona Interurban Railway, but since its officers were strong Sabbatarians, they refused to allow the cars to operate on Sundays. A unique problem within the industry, it ended when empty-handed bondholders threatened to sue.

Winona Lake today attracts 60,000 summer visitors annually and revolves around the 5,000-seat Billy Sunday Tabernacle. It also is world headquarters of both the Free Methodist and Grace Brethren churches. The latter operates Grace College and Seminary there.

Warsaw, seat of Kosciusko County, is the valley's largest city and in summer is the bustling hub of a vast recreation industry scattered among the county's scores of lakes. Numerous factories which turn out orthopedic equipment make the city a national leader in that field. Other industries produce automotive and airplane parts, foundry

products, glass, furniture, clothing, and publications. Three lakes adjoin the city and provide attractive beaches and parks.

Warsaw is the center of a rich agricultural region which produces millions of eggs for midwestern and eastern markets. The long, low hen-houses, of wood or metal, are a trademark of Kosciusko, which ranks fourteenth in the United States in chicken sales. At one time, the industry kept a fleet of nearly forty refrigerator cars rolling on the Winona Interurban and connecting steam railroads.

In Kosciusko County the Tippecanoe becomes broad and grassy before flowing through 1,037-acre Lake Tippecanoe, the state's deepest and one of Indiana's best-known resort lakes. Here it receives waters from the seven-lake Barbee chain. Below the lake outlet the river's mood changes. Sometimes it is a quiet, winding, wooded stream with beauty at every bend. Elsewhere it is dark and brooding, its waters a succession of quiet pools. Grassy, wooded islands become frequent, particularly in its middle course, and high banks, alternating from side to side, offer breathtaking views. Commercially operated float trips bring the river's beauty to countless fishermen. Summer cottages cluster closely on its banks.

The Potawatomi, the early residents of the valley, gave the stream its name, which derives from their word *Ki-tap-i-kon-nong*, or "place

of the buffalo fish." They built numerous villages along its banks, including Chip-pe-wa-nung, where former U.S. 31 now crosses the river, three miles north of Rochester. The Potawatomi made nine different treaties with the United States at this site; Winamac, a chief of the tribe, signed two treaties negotiated by Governor William Henry Harrison in 1802 and 1803. Nearly 900 Potawatomi camped here in 1838 as they began the tragic removal westward in what came to be known as "The Trail of Death." The tribe has left behind it, firmly attached to the land, such names as Winamac, Manitou, Maxinkuckee, and Monoquet.

Manitou, the resort lake at Rochester, owes its existence to the Indians. In the Treaty of Paradise Springs, signed at Wabash in 1826, the federal government agreed to build a mill on the Tippecanoe and support a miller for the benefit of the Potawatomi. The mill, however, was built on a tributary and the dam combined several small lakes into the present 631-acre Lake Manitou. Rochester's industries today produce clothing, foods, castings, and automotive equipment.

Below Rochester the river flows through a gap in the moraine into the sandy plain of preglacial Lake Kankakee and for nearly sixty miles meanders through the flat, dry bed of the ancient lake. Northeast of Rochester the state has established the Menominee State Fish-

*Left to right*: At Warsaw a streetcar line which became an interurban railroad still hauls freight. ⮜An aerial view of Indiana Beach resort on Lake Shafer, with NIPSCO's Norway Dam in the background.

ing Area, which is named for the Potawatomi chief who fought so courageously against removal from Indiana in 1838.

In this area the Tippecanoe receives the drainage of Lake Maxinkuckee, which is famous not only for its natural beauty and resort attractions, but for the Culver Military Academy, which occupies 1,500 acres on its shore. When Henry Harrison Culver, a stove manufacturer from St. Louis, sat down along the lake shore in 1894 and began to dream his dreams, it is doubtful if he envisioned that the school he planned would become one of the country's leading preparatory schools and its fame would spread well beyond the valley of the Tippecanoe.

Thousands of Hoosiers visit the stream each year at the Tippecanoe River State Park north of Winamac, the Pulaski County seat known for production of control devices and mechanical equipment for the physically handicapped. The 2,761-acre playland stretches along the forest stream for six miles and offers hiking trails, campgrounds, and picnic areas.

Far below Winamac, only a few miles above the river's junction with the Wabash, man in a mighty effort, has wrested the Tippecanoe from nature. Above and below Monticello, behind two tremendous dams, man has shackled the river, diverting to the serious matter of making electricity water that has flowed free and unhampered from Indiana's quiet lakes. The dams, Norway and Oakdale, create the 1,157-acre Lake Shafer above Monticello and the 1,272-acre Lake Freeman below the city. Since their construction in the mid-1920s the lakes have attracted hundreds of thousands who have converted Monticello into a major resort. The city survives despite near annihilation of its downtown by a tornado in 1974.

Below Oakdale Dam the Tippecanoe again flows free, twisting and winding between craggy bluffs. Then, in quiet isolation, much as at its headwaters, the river joins the Wabash. Its mission in Indiana at last is accomplished.

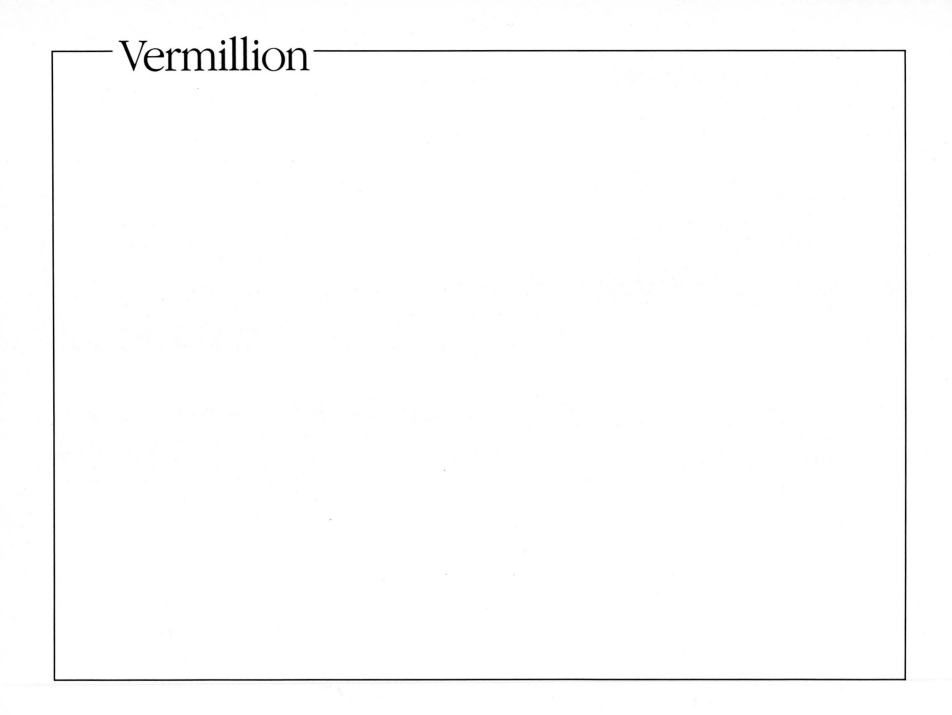

Vermillion

Forty-three miles above Terre Haute, a small, tranquil river called the Vermillion slips quietly into the Wabash. Flushed with the contributions of the Grand Prairie to the west, it spends its final miles flowing across the rich flood plain of the Wabash, where in summer vast seas of green corn surround its mouth and muffle the outside sounds. Remote from highways, the end of its long journey is hidden from the eyes of passing motorists.

It has not always been peace, quiet, and obscurity along the river to which the Indians gave the name *Osanamon*, which means "vermilion paint." In frontier times the Vermillion country was home to tribes of Kickapoo and Piankashaw and some of their principal villages stood at the river's mouth. In warfare between whites and Indians, the river became a turning point, a dividing line from which armies retreated and peace messengers abandoned their missions. For some reason the Vermillion seemed to be a jinx, perhaps because of the savage ferocity of the Kickapoo.

The Vermillion first wooed American attention in 1786, when General George Rogers Clark, hero of Vincennes, marched a 1,000-man army up the Wabash in an effort to break the Indians' power and quiet the restless frontier. By the time Clark reached the mouth of the Vermillion, his men were tired of the whole idea. Half of them mutinied and Clark was able to advance no farther. He left the Indians beyond the Vermillion undisturbed.

Frontier affairs simmered fitfully for the next four years until Major John F. Hamtramck, commandant at Vincennes, sent a peace emissary up the Wabash. All went well until he arrived at the Vermillion. If he crossed, he was warned, he would be killed; so he retreated hastily to Vincennes. Hamtramck then marched a 400-man army up the Wabash to the mouth of the Vermillion, where he found the principal Indian village deserted and destroyed it. Despite this hollow victory, his men refused to advance any farther.

Twenty-one years passed before anyone dared again to advance against the Vermillion. The new hero was General William Henry Harrison, marching up the Wabash toward the Battle of Tippecanoe. Determined to proceed beyond the Vermillion, Harrison constructed a blockhouse and supply base near the river's mouth and added a boat landing so he could receive supplies coming up the Wabash.

With this anchor securely in place, he continued to the famous battle that years later helped elect him president. From this time on, the Vermillion played its new role as a quiet prairie stream.

A distance of 106 river miles away, on a lonesome ridge where endless cornfields lean against the prairie sky, a small stream issues from a field drain and pauses momentarily in a roadside pool. Then it trickles south, growing stronger, emerging hesitantly as a small, narrow prairie creek. As an adolescent river, gurgling over shallows, the most distant fork of the Vermillion begins its irregular course toward the Wabash.

The appearance of the Vermillion varies greatly in its different stretches. In places it is marked by grandeur; in others it is rugged, picturesque, or pastoral. Not only is the Vermillion's appearance contrasting, but it springs from a bistate ancestry and is of two minds about how its name shall be spelled. In Indiana, the river bears little resemblance to the youthful prairie stream, and as if to emphasize the contrast, Hoosiers have added an extra "l" to the spelling so that the Vermilion of Illinois becomes the Vermillion of Indiana. As a further curiosity, it rises from a gentle moraine in Livingston County, Illinois, scarcely 2,500 feet from the source of another river which flows in the opposite direction, and strangely, also is named Vermilion.

The Hoosier Vermillion is made up of a family of rivers which converge on Danville, Illinois, four miles west of the Indiana line. Here the main river gathers its three upper branches and becomes one, flowing a combined total of 239 miles and draining 1,435 square miles of one of the nation's most productive bread baskets.

Despite its rich soil, settlement came late to the Vermilion basin. Being prairie, it lacked the necessary timber for construction and settlers found the tough sod difficult to break. Being flat, it lacked adequate drainage and the headwaters village named Flatville was an obvious accurate description. Being a collection of small streams, the Vermilion could not serve as a water highway and no commerce accompanied the cheerful babble of its waters.

For many miles of the Vermilion's upper life it is serene as it follows the gentle contours of the rich, black prairies. But suddenly it begins to cut a deep swath, sloping between towering hills as its race to the Wabash quickens. The high, bold line of the hills covers a black

*Left to right*: William Henry Harrison, on his way to the Battle of Tippecanoe, crossed the Vermillion on November 3, 1811. ✺ A covered bridge near Eugene, Indiana.

treasure of coal and the placid meadows of the upper reaches give way to a rugged panorama of wild beauty.

Heavy timber crowds the river and obscures a sprawling power plant which hints at the urbanization that has developed downstream. Highways, hesitant to cross the deeply entrenched valley, dead-end on its hills. Now the Vermilion is within six miles of Danville, Illinois, and enters one of the outstanding natural areas along its course.

Kickapoo State park, lying on both sides of the Vermilion, was a wasteland of spoil banks and brackish ponds when Illinois acquired it from the United Electric Coal Corporation for $10 an acre. Subsequent expansion increased the size from 1,290 acres to nearly 1,600. In pioneer times, prolific salt springs drew settlement to the basin and an elaborate riverbank memorial draws attention to this ancient industry. A huge 100-gallon iron kettle, one of twenty-four used to produce a bushel of salt from each filling, forms the centerpiece. In a single year, 3,000 bushels of this vital frontier commodity found their way into markets as distant as northern Indiana, southern Wisconsin, and eastern Missouri.

The beauties of nature have been developed to their fullest along the Vermilion. Near the Indiana line, Forest Glen Preserve, a

Vermilion County (Ill.) nature park operated on state park standards, covers nearly 1,800 bankside acres, and on Middle Fork above Danville, Kennekuk Cove County Park occupies five miles of river frontage.

Forest Glen, older of the two, consists mostly of wooded ravines teeming with birds, reptiles, wild animals, and plant life. Climb the seventy-two-foot observation tower and you'll see it all at one glance. School classes from both Illinois and Indiana regularly take field trips to this true department store of the outdoors that includes more than 150 catalogued species of birds and such unusual plants as wild orchids, Indian pipe, and green dragon. A large multipurpose lodge with a small theater, an interpretive center, two nature preserves, trails, and an administration building help make Forest Glen outstanding.

Nature education took a different course at the University of Illinois Vermilion River Observatory located just beyond the Indiana boundary. Long before satellite dishes became common, astronomers came to track celestial objects with a huge 120-foot-diameter steerable radio telescope. Previously they had covered a five-acre natural ravine with a wire reflecting mesh to collect signals from outer space. Although only five miles from Danville, the site was

The University of Illinois located an early radio telescope in the Vermillion Valley not far from the Indiana border.

chosen because of its freedom from man-made interference, a testimonial to the isolated remoteness of the river.

In many ways the Vermilion dominates Danville and its 38,985 residents. It slices through the city in a deep gorge across which once stalked the towering concrete piers of the abandoned Illinois Terminal traction line. The North Fork is impounded to form Lake Vermilion and provide the city's water supply. It also delights swimmers, boaters, anglers, and picnickers along its eight-mile shoreline.

Below Danville, where the Middle Fork joins forces with its sisters to form the main stream, the river fights valiantly against the crowding of stubborn hillsides and the alternation of hill and valley makes for varied and exquisite scenery. On distant hills, abandoned coal mines leave their roughly chiseled scars.

The river twists and turns as it fights its way through a nameless fold in the hills to reach the Wabash flood plain. Both its appearance and its spelling change here. No longer a placid highway flowing between comfortable green fields, the Vermillion indulges in rugged and expansive moments where the sides pile up their height as much as 100 feet, looking almost mountainous compared to the scenes that came before. A covered timber bridge at the pioneer town of Eugene, Indiana, adds a picturesque charm.

The rich silt the Vermillion carries into the Wabash washes from three counties in Indiana—Vermillion, Warren, and Benton—and five in Illinois which produce an incredible cornucopia that reads like a Who's Who of agricultural achievement. Champaign, Livingston, and Iroquois counties, Illinois, outproduce all but two of the nation's 3,070 counties in corn and soybeans and Vermilion County, Illinois, ranks in the upper one-half of 1 percent. In sweet corn production, Vermilion also ranks in the upper one-half of 1 percent, Iroquois ranks in the upper 1 percent, and Ford County, Illinois, and Warren County, Indiana, stand in the upper 3 percent.

The Illinois counties also have other claims to fame. The number of high income farms in Iroquois and Livingston counties rank them in the nation's upper 1 percent. Champaign County is in the upper 2 percent. Iroquois County stands ninth in the nation in farm machinery value, Livingston is 17th, Champaign is 18th, and Vermilion is 34th. Livingston ranks 35th in the nation in chicken production, Iroquois 78th. Vermilion is the nation's 45th largest vegetable producer. Iroquois, Livingston, and Champaign counties rank among the nation's upper 1 percent in cropland harvested and Vermilion is among the nation's top 2 percent. There can be no doubt that the Vermilion basin is one of America's greatest bread baskets.

# Rivers of the Voyageurs

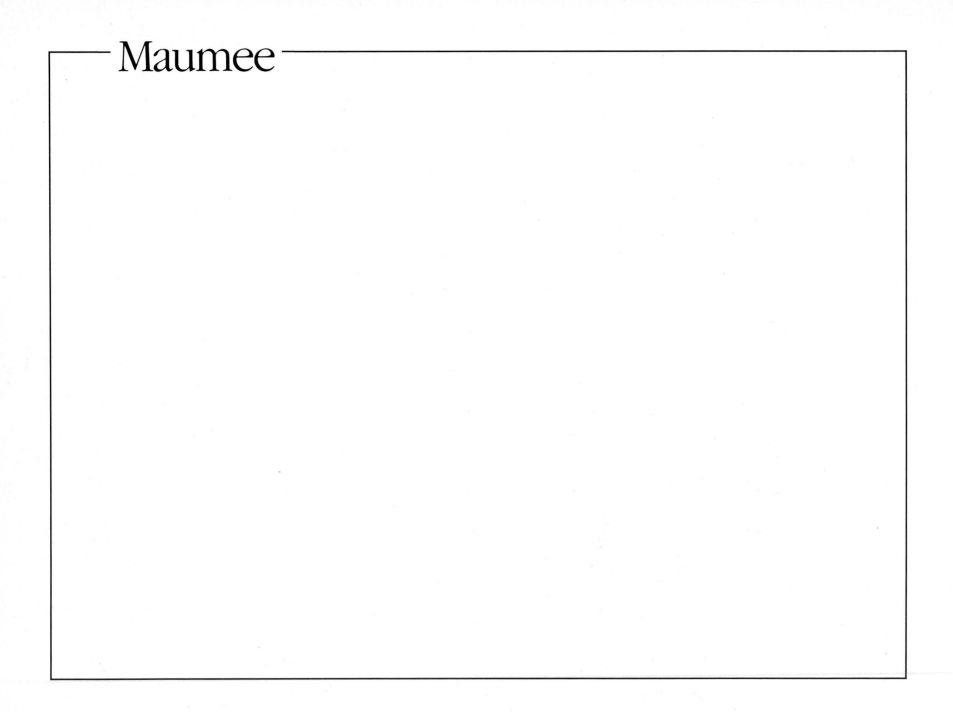

Maumee

The Maumee is a river of distinction. It rises full-grown in the heart of Indiana's second largest city and ends as a carrier of ocean cargo in Ohio's fourth largest city. It is Lake Erie's largest inland tributary, a scenic treat, a 160-mile-long battlefield, and a magnet to industry. It has been a raceway and tramping ground for armies, a molder of empire, and a trade route now beginning its fourth century. Its past is filled with high adventure; its future with bright promise. As past and present have flowed together, it has deeply influenced the life around it.

The Maumee is a nearly unique river. Most streams originate in the flat prairies as obscure farm drainage ditches or high in the mountains as unnamed rivulets. But not the Maumee. It is a major stream by Indiana standards in the first mile it flows, and its beginnings are urban, not rural.

Glamorous and romantic for 300 years, it has long witnessed the human passage over the shortest water route between the important colonial centers of Quebec and New Orleans. It has been the heart and pulse of successive empires—Indian, French, British, American. There can be no doubt; this is a river and a valley worth knowing.

Somewhere in the misty regions of prehistory the story begins, for shaping the Maumee was the work of tens of thousands of years. In the beginning, the land was rough, hilly, and unproductive, like today's Brown County. Then came the ice. More than a mile high it came, smashing down hills, filling in valleys and lakes, blocking rivers with the debris. In this brutal war of nature, rocks, soil, forests, and hills were ground up, as if by a huge mortar and pestle, and fused into the great glacial mass until it resembled a dirty mountain of frozen earth.

When the warming sun checked the great glacier's progress at last, the silent task of melting billions of tons of ice began. Lakes formed in depressions which the ice had gouged out of the earth and rivers gushed from the edge of the retreating glacier. As the ice shrank, the rivers grew longer, like an animal's tail growing before your eyes. As the glacier receded, it stopped occasionally to rest, depositing great loads of ground-up boulders, gravel, sand, and soil in pairs of morainic ridges shaped like arrowheads. These set the course of the Maumee's tributaries.

During one period Lake Erie covered northwestern Ohio and extended as far as the present Fort Wayne. When ice blocked the drainage outlet through the St. Lawrence Valley, the meltwater sought a new path which it found over the low summit on which Fort Wayne now stands. Soon a mighty river flowed across this continental divide and down what later became the Wabash Valley. Eventually the ice retreated, unblocking the St. Lawrence, like the stopper being removed from a bathtub, and the waters which had flowed down the Maumee now moved in the opposite direction, the river becoming a tributary to Lake Erie instead of its outlet.

Rivers soon flowed along the base of each principal moraine, heading toward the lengthening stream that was to become the Maumee. Down from the cool, clear lakes of southern Michigan came the St. Joseph. Up from western Ohio's flat prairies sluggishly wriggled the St. Marys. Where they met at Fort Wayne, they formed the Maumee.

When the first white men arrived, Glacial Lake Maumee, a 100-mile extension of Lake Erie, which had been spawned as the icy harrow remolded the land and redistributed the waters, had shrunk to the oozy, slimy, mosquito-laden Black Swamp. Through its center flowed a liquid backbone—the Maumee.

Improbably crooked in its upper reaches, it sets out for Lake Erie carving such deep loops and convolutions that early explorers reckoned its 100 crow-flown miles to exceed 160 by water. Almost like a lost child, it wanders aimlessly over the glacial fill of the old lake basin, carelessly and without hurry, frequently reversing its direction and abruptly folding back on itself like a ribbon.

Below Defiance, Ohio, where it receives the offerings of the Tiffin and Auglaize rivers, the Maumee assumes a strong new character. Here the valley broadens and the river becomes majestic and powerful, reminiscent on a smaller scale of such grand and mighty streams as the lower Hudson, the scenic Columbia, or the broad Ohio. It becomes a charming river, filled with new beauty at every bend, dotted with picturesque islands and sometimes churned by formidable rapids. Ohio now includes it in its scenic river system.

As early as 1669 La Salle may have seen the Maumee. Jesuit priests followed, pushing across the Great Lakes and up the river from Canada, bent on converting the Indians to Christianity. The In-

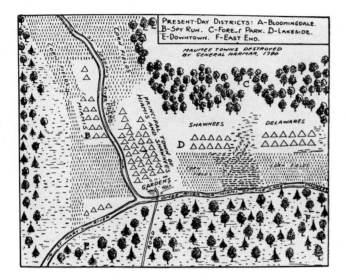

Map of Kekionga (now Fort Wayne) in October 1790 was drawn by an officer in General Harmar's army.

dians came, too, heading for warfare with the tribes farther west. And finally the fur traders arrived, sniffing a huge bonanza from the pelts to be found throughout the valley.

The French, finding the country unpossessed, set out to claim it for their king. Early in the eighteenth century they erected forts designed to protect the fur trade from the Great Lakes to the lower Mississippi. By this time, despite various designations by different tribes, the river had received the name by which posterity would know it. First, they called it "Miami" or "Miami of the Lake" after the Indians who dwelt along its banks. But this led to confusion with the southwestern Ohio river by the same name. In time, the French conveniently corrupted it to the present Maumee.

The Maumee's source was the head of the gentle nine-mile portage to the Wabash Valley. Determined to control the fur trade route, the French built Post Miamis on the St. Marys River a few hundred yards above the source of the Maumee and near Kekionga, the principal Miami village. The original name was Fort Saint Philippe des Miamis. It was the first in a long line of forts which the French, British, and Americans successively erected at Fort Wayne. The French sought trade with the Indians and trapping rights, mixing matrimony with business and living with equality among the Indians. Their missionaries sought no material advantages.

By mid-eighteenth century a small but growing cloud had appeared on the horizon. The British had arrived, intent on colonizing and eventually driving the Indians from their ancestral hunting grounds. But first the French had to go. Despite the chain of protective French forts, the British tide was poised to sweep through the land, drowning Frenchmen wherever it could find them. The great wrestling match for the New World now began in earnest.

With the arena ready for the drama to be played, the peaceful Maumee—river of life to the Indians, river of transport to the French—assumed a strange new role. It became a raceway for armies. Indians, French, British, and Americans—up and down the valley they swept, burning, plundering, looting, taking captives, breaking the backs of empires, shifting title to huge areas overnight. For sixty-five years, wars reddened the river's banks and filled its forests with the smoke of burning towns.

Chief Nicholas of the Hurons started it. His attack was like a spark in the forest, the forerunner of the conflagration to come. In 1747 he attacked Post Miamis, partially burned it, and captured the small garrison. But a mutual need for trade restored peaceful relations and the French returned to the Three Rivers. With Post Miamis

in a bad state of repair, the French eventually moved to a new site on the St. Joseph River a short distance above its mouth. Here they built their second fort, which they occupied until the British took control in 1760 as a result of the French and Indian War.

The British arrived just in time for Pontiac's Conspiracy, and a fresh new conflagration swept the valley. The plot was the same; only the cast was changed. Pontiac, an Ottawa, was a true son of the Maumee. Born in a riverbank village near the present Defiance, Ohio, he organized numerous tribes in a massive effort to drive the whites out of the area for all time. He nearly succeeded. British outposts fell like dominoes. The Indians used every wile at their command, succeeding at Post Miamis by using an Indian girl to entice the fort commander into an ambush. The leaderless garrison surrendered shortly afterward. Eventually the British broke the conspiracy and returned to their forts. An uneasy quiet settled over the troubled valley.

Yet there was to be no peace. One of the causes of the Revolution had been the British government's Quebec Act of 1774 that forbade settlement by the colonists in the area west of the mountains, although many hardy pioneers had done so. The Revolution soon raged in the East and George Rogers Clark's heroic capture of Vincennes transferred the Maumee country and the entire Northwest Territory to the Americans.

The Indians remained, and despite the succession of white owners they defended the land against all invaders. They pounced upon a flamboyant French adventurer, Colonel Augustin Mottin de la Balme, as he marched from Vincennes toward Detroit in 1780, virtually butchering his army. Ten years later George Washington sent an American army under General Josiah Harmar to break the Indian power and make the country safe for Americans. But the Indians, under their famous Chief Little Turtle, routed the army as it forded the Maumee in what is now Fort Wayne. The following year, General Arthur St. Clair sought to vanquish the Miami confederacy, but it hacked his army to pieces long before it reached the Maumee. Washington then summoned General "Mad Anthony" Wayne to do the job.

Wayne drilled his army for two years and set out for the Maumee only when he judged his men completely combat ready. The year was 1794. Striking the river midway on its course at the confluence with the Auglaize, he threw up a sturdy fort, and "defying the English, Indians and all the devils" to take it, he named it Fort Defiance. Leaving the fort secure, he turned eastward, and again, as so often in the past, footsteps of marching armies echoed along the Maumee.

The Indians watched from the bordering forests as Wayne's well-disciplined army marched down river. Then near Maumee, Ohio, a short distance above modern Toledo, they mounted an attack in a

*Left to right*: The Maumee rises full-grown in the heart of Fort Wayne from the junction of St. Marys (left) and St. Joseph (upper right) rivers. ໖Cannon at Defiance, Ohio, marks the location of fort General Anthony Wayne built there.

tangled forest of trees felled by a windstorm. The first barrage drove the Americans back, but they quickly regrouped and routed the enemy. The Battle of Fallen Timbers decisively broke the Indians' resistance and the fires of war flickered out.

Wayne was not content to rest. He marched to the source of the Maumee where he built a strong fort to command the portage. Colonel John F. Hamtramck, commandant, with a flash of astute reasoning, named it for Wayne. Its dedication on October 22, 1794, is considered the birth of the present city. Although the garrison's presence quelled the Indians' tendency to engage in treachery and carnage unauthorized by the United States of America, peace again was fleeting.

By 1812 Americans and British were doing a rerun of the Revolution and warfare again flared along the Maumee. For five days, Indians, prodded by the British, besieged Fort Wayne. They retreated only as General William Henry Harrison and an army of 2,700 men approached from Piqua, Ohio. The Americans turned down river, tracing Wayne's steps in reverse. They paused to erect a new fort at Defiance and another, Fort Meigs, at Perrysburg, Ohio, near the site of Wayne's victory at Fallen Timbers. Bloody fighting flared at Fort Meigs before the British withdrew. It was their last penetration of the Maumee Valley.

At last the fighting ceased and a permanent peace spread over the valley. The old fighters faded away—Anthony Wayne, Little Turtle, Pontiac. All the heroes of the wars were gone. In their place came a new breed of men intent on tilling the soil, building cities, providing transport, establishing factories. They were an interesting assortment. Such men as Johnny Appleseed, that legendary character who wandered barefoot over the Midwest planting apple orchards; Lewis Cass, Michigan's governor and a future presidential candidate, who came as a visitor to dedicate the Wabash and Erie Canal at Fort Wayne and accidentally fell in; Hugh McCulloch, Lincoln's secretary of the treasury, who led the government through the financial wilderness following the Civil War; and that forgotten Fort Wayne native, Whistler's father, whose wife became famous through her artist son's character study. No longer a battleground, the Maumee became a renowned pioneer highway.

By 1819, when the last garrison was withdrawn from Fort Wayne, the surrounding village had begun to take on the character of a regional commercial and manufacturing center. It flirted briefly with riverboats, but when the Wabash and Erie Canal arrived, the future was assured. The canal grew to become the continent's longest artificial waterway and Fort Wayne was one of its principal ports. Finally, stretching 464 sinuous miles from Toledo to Evansville, it reached Fort Wayne in 1843, but laborers sweated, dug, and cursed

another ten years before they reached the Ohio River. By 1875 it was gone, supplanted by the railroads.

The floodtide of immigration that rode the canal from the East doubled Fort Wayne's population each of the two decades following the waterway's arrival. It offered a new route to the state's undeveloped lands and created new competitive markets because of the sharply reduced transportation costs.

The canal changed the river's appearance as well as the valley's population. Engineers threw a supply dam two city blocks long across the river near Defiance, Ohio, and another of nearly a half mile at Grand Rapids, Ohio. They raised the water level along twenty-seven miles of river and added a majesty that the stream had never before known. Both dams remain intact and a canal section has been restored in a scenic state park below Defiance. Another park near Maumee, Ohio, preserves the gigantic water stairs which walked the boats sixty-three feet down the valley wall through six huge locks.

Many Germans who accompanied the Irish to build the canal remained in Fort Wayne and gave the city such a German flavor that it has supported no fewer than fourteen German-language newspapers, including five dailies. As late as 1927 German residents pored eagerly over the daily *Freie Presse-Staatszeitung*. Today Fort Wayne is largely a German city with intense cultural interests. Its residents guard their heritage jealously and never tire of parading local talent in civic theater, music, ballet, and art presentations. They have put millions into the Performing Arts Center and a botanical garden, which supplement excellent museums devoted to local history, art, natural history, and Lincoln lore. Historic Fort Wayne, a resurrected fort near the sites of the early French, British, and American fortifications, turns the calendar back to the frontier days of 1816. The Fort Wayne Philharmonic is acknowledged as one of the nation's leading semiprofessional orchestras and the city's beautiful library is the envy of librarians everywhere. For many years the library not only circulated publications but wrote and printed its own on selected subjects, usually designed to keep the city's heritage ever in mind. Local residents study at seven accredited colleges, taking courses ranging from theology to business to science. For relaxation, they may visit the zoo in Franke Park or attend a performance in its open-air theater, and when blossom time arrives, the beckoning scent of thousands of flowers brings multitudes to Foster Park and Lakeside, which contains what may be the state's largest municipal rose garden. Forever loving celebrations, Fort Wayne pours its energies into the annual Three Rivers Festival, which spotlights the city's unusual blend of past and present, the recently established annual German-fest, and the Johnny Appleseed Festival.

Also sports-minded, the city over the years has supported professional hockey, basketball, and baseball teams and was host to the nation's first professional league baseball game in 1871. It also took an early excursion into the field of night baseball.

Numerous large industries, concentrated in the transportation and electrical fields, turn out such varied products as wire, electric motors, truck trailers, automotive parts, and gasoline pumps. New high-rise bank and government buildings are attempting to revitalize downtown.

In March 1982, the three rivers went on an unprecedented rampage which drove 10,000 from their homes and challenged the city's spirit and resolve. In a drama that gained nationwide attention, laborers and businessmen, housewives and students worked shoulder to shoulder to shore up sagging dikes and reduce the river's appetite for destruction. Even President Ronald Reagan flew in to heave a few sandbags alongside the locals. Consequently no one was startled when the U.S. Conference of Mayors in 1983 made Fort Wayne the first medium-sized city in history to win its Liveability Award. Following the National Municipal League's "All-American City" designation,

the double recognition gave Fort Wayne a reason to swell with rightful pride.

Downriver the Maumee flows past the cities of Defiance and Napoleon, Ohio, and finally reaches Lake Erie at Toledo. More than 100 foreign ships call annually here and together with the sailings of about 1,500 lake vessels impose the fascinating flavor of an international port on a city bordered by corn and soybean fields. Toledo is a major Midwestern rail center, and the fourth-ranking inland port. It is a prime mover of soft coal, boasts of being the glass capital of the world, and the largest oil refiner between Chicago and the East Coast. The famous jeep and a flood of automotive parts come from its factories.

But the past has not wholly disappeared from Anthony Wayne's valley. The armies have departed, and gone are the bawling "canawleers," shouting at the mules, untangling towlines, drinking, and swapping yarns in the taverns. But in a sense their spirit remains in the rebuilt fort, the restored canal sections, and the countless historical statues and markers that dot the valley and border its waters.

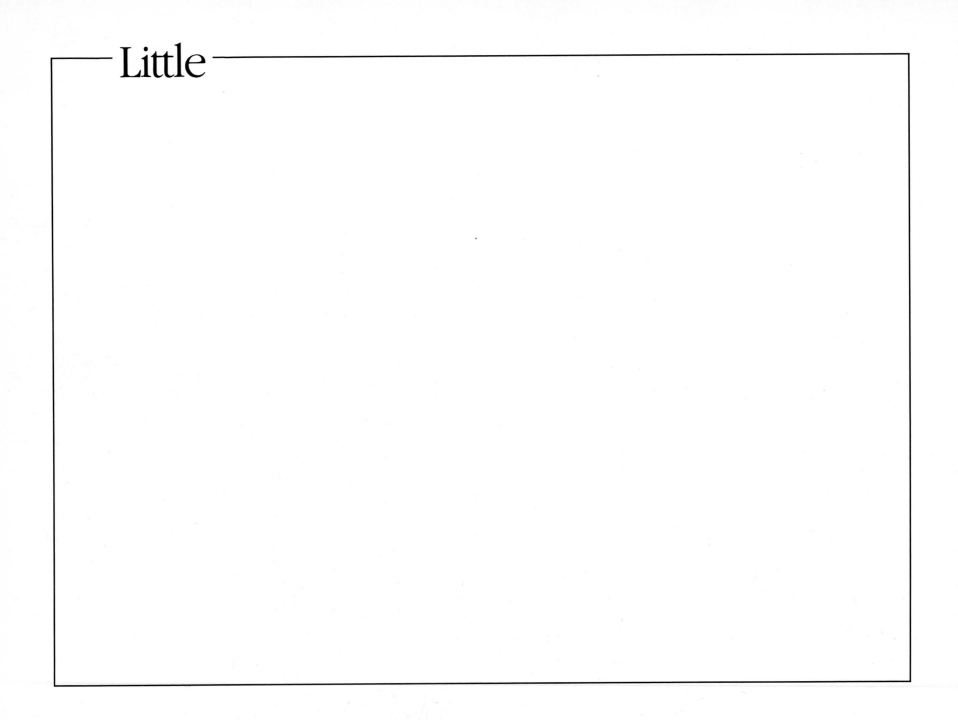

Little

Give yourself thirty minutes and you can drive busy, dual-lane U.S. 24 from Fort Wayne to Huntington with scarcely a conscious effort. But turn the calendar back 300 years and you will find your car replaced by a frail canoe, the hum of your tires by the slap of a paddle, and the driver by fearless Frenchmen caught up in the procession of empire.

For the Frenchmen it had been a long, arduous, and tiring trip up from Quebec. Although they were accustomed to the hardships of the forests, the tough, wiry *coureurs de bois* had fought an exhausting battle as their tiny vessels carried them westward through the Great Lakes and into the little known lands beyond. All the way the voyage had been uphill. First it was up the St. Lawrence, battling the swift current generated by the outpouring of the Great Lakes. Then it was the lakes, themselves; across Lake Ontario, up the treacherous Niagara River, around the mighty falls, and up the length of Lake Erie.

Then they had come to the mouth of the Maumee River at the far corner of the lake Again it was upstream through this broad waterway—all the way against the current until they arrived at the low summit where Fort Wayne now stands. The Indians pointed out the path which led westward across the woodland and prairie. Now it was overland—dragging or carrying the slender canoes and heavy pirogues across the continental divide that stood midway in the nine-mile portage.

Suddenly before them stretched a vast swamp and somewhere in its tangled interior that wondrous thing took place—the birth of a waterway all the way down to the Mississippi. It was a short river flowing from the swamp, a sluggish river, and a narrow river. *La Petite Rivière*, the French called it, and the Americans who were to come later translated the name literally to Little River, sometimes erroneously called the Little Wabash. Scarcely twenty-five crow-flown miles from source to mouth, it was, nevertheless, the beginning of a water highway as important in its day as any majestic pioneer highway in America.

It was a joyous river and the French voyageurs would break into happy song as they began the downhill ride. Now it was downstream, every foot of the way. No more fighting powerful currents. No more risking sudden squalls on the lakes. No more backbreaking toil on the oars and paddles. No more uphill water. This was the easy route to the great hunting and trapping country beyond, the water highway to New Orleans, the gateway to empire for the seventeenth-century French.

Water pumped from the May Stone quarry forms the headwaters of the Little River at the western edge of Fort Wayne.

Today's river is a captured stream, almost uniquely man-made, and it has survived great change. Frontier commerce no longer rides its often muddy waters, and much of the willow fringe along its banks has disappeared. Most of the year, it is only a poor trickle of water.

Yet it is still the valley leading to a country the French found unpeopled and unpossessed by Europeans. It is the valley through which British armies marched when they captured Vincennes, and a valley through which several modes of land transportation evolved as man sought the most efficient way to link the Great Lakes region with the Mississippi Valley. The Little River is more a valley than a river, but it is worth knowing because it ran through another world, back through the centuries, the chain binding empires together. No other Hoosier stream so small has influenced so strongly the making of Indiana and the course of empires.

The story of Little River begins somewhere in the misty regions of prehistory. The great glacial sheet thousands of feet thick that overspread North America dammed the St. Lawrence Valley, forcing the waters to find a new outlet to the south. As the warming sun drove the mighty ice sheet back, the meltwaters uncovered the low divide at the head of Little River. Ice, rocks, sand, and gravel, propelled by the thundering torrent, gouged a deep valley two miles wide. Even-

tually the St. Lawrence Valley became unblocked, and the water reversed itself and ceased to flow over the Fort Wayne summit. Little River became what its name implies, and the feeble current which remained found itself held back by a limestone ledge near Huntington which it could not grind away.

Realizing the importance of rivers to explorers and fur traders, the Miami took control of the head of Little River and established one of their most important villages at the portage. The mouth of the river, known as the Forks of the Wabash, later became the treaty ground and site of an important trading post.

The French, meanwhile, looking ever farther westward from Quebec, became curious about the portage. As early as 1682, La Salle, the region's first explorer, wrote Governor Frontenac of New France about it, and in time the French established an important outpost at the portage, followed by others near Lafayette and at Vincennes. From this time on, the valley witnessed the unceasing human march over the shortest water route between Quebec and New Orleans. The shrewd Miami, however, were waiting, and they exacted a toll for use of the portage, providing guides, carts, and packhorses for the canoes, furs, and merchandise the French transported.

Near the close of the seventeenth century when Iberville led a

colony of settlers from the harsh climate of Canada to the sunnier lands of Louisiana, he used the Little River. Other settlers followed. Missionaries, colonists, and travelers used it, but it was the fur traders who made it famous. In a single year they shipped 20,000 beaver skins up Little River for Europe's burgeoning fur trade.

After the British had won the tug of war for the New World, the valley echoed to the tramp of marching feet rather than the shouts and songs of fur traders. When the infamous British soldier, Henry Hamilton, the "Hair Buyer General," marched from Detroit to capture Vincennes, he used Little River, remarking that beaver dams had raised the water level at the portage.

One of General Wayne's scouts in 1795 reported that Little River could be navigated in floodtime all the way to the portage by boats carrying 10,000 pounds and that all year the water stood from three to ten feet deep. The country, he wrote, was flat and low, and the river current strong only in the lower six miles. He found willows blocking the channel three miles below the portage but said that they could be cleared easily.

Although Little River to the French was a busy artery of commerce only for the canoe and the pirogue, no less a person than George Washington saw that nature clearly had fitted the marsh headwaters for a connecting waterway between the Great Lakes and the Mississippi and he was among the first to recommend a canal along this route. Eventually the Irish came to dig the canal, and by 1835 boats were crossing the summit and traveling the length of the valley. By 1843 the canal connected Toledo, Ohio, and Lafayette, and it was extended later to the Ohio River at Evansville, 464 miles from its beginning. Just as Little River had been the gateway to the west for the French, so it became a great commercial artery to the early Hoosiers, giving them a profitable outlet for their products, reducing the cost of incoming goods and creating a migration route for early settlers.

Just as the gee and haw of the canalers had replaced the songs of the French voyageurs, so did another sound enter the valley. This was the snort of that annihilator of space, the iron horse, which doomed the slow and clumsy canalboat. By 1858 the railroad paralleled the canal from Toledo to Attica and then struck westward for St. Louis. Eventually the interurban, then the highway, pushed through the valley to complete the full evolution of land travel.

Huntington, just above the river's mouth, was first a canal town, then a crew change point and shop location for the now-abandoned Erie Railroad, which once was the city's largest employer. It is the home of Huntington College, and it is known for its singular shop-lined twin bridges across Little River.

*Left to right*: A web of ditches drained the upper valley's swamp in the 1880s. ◄§The river became famous for its shop-lined twin bridges at Huntington. ◄§Huntington converted an abandoned quarry into a garden.

But while the locomotive was hauling produce and passengers along the river, owners of thousands of water-logged acres saw the valley as something more than a convenient transport route. They could see the river straightened, the rock ledge blasted open, the swamps drained, and 35,000 fertile acres made ready for the plow. Accordingly, Huntington and Roanoke citizens organized the Little River Ditching Association in 1874, but opposing landowners took the project to court and effectively killed it. Five more attempts followed before a court-approved contract was signed in 1886. Newly designed steam dredges replaced the pick and shovel and the work was completed in three years. It was said to be the largest such project ever undertaken in the United States.

The swamp is now a flat, fertile valley and Little River flows through it arrow-straight with its tributaries rerouted, bayous cut off, and the once soggy grasslands and scrubby forest gone. Altogether fifty miles of streams lace the twenty-five-mile-long valley where water once stood from one foot to six feet deep all year. Trains no longer crawl through axle-deep water in wet seasons, and what once was the river's soggy sourceland now forms the floor of an immense limestone quarry more than 300 feet deep.

# St. Joseph (of the Maumee)

Out of the lakes and ponds of southern Michigan flow a handful of cool, clear streams. Dropping down from the high ground around Hillsdale, they successively unite, joining rill to rivulet to form streams up to a cow's belly, until they become known as the St. Joseph River. No one seems to know where the St. Joseph really begins. Lakes, ponds, and marshes near the villages of Osseo and Pittsford feed its headwaters. One of its most distant sources flows from a thicket northwest of Osseo. The water is clear and cold, gurgling over a rocky bed in a stream no more than eighteen inches wide and four inches deep. This source is scarcely indicative of the lower river, which is large enough to quench the thirst of Fort Wayne, and once carried a steamboat on its surface and supplied water for the central section of the Wabash and Erie Canal.

From the thicket, the stream disappears into a woods of willow, birch, and aspen, then emerges to trickle through a neat, grassy meadow and provide outlet for numerous small lakes. Growing stronger with these contributions, it courses southeastward, hesitating south of Pittsford to fill a picturesque hill-rimmed millpond and plunge over a dam hidden by a highway bridge. The weathered ruins of an ancient mill stood guard for years at the end of the dam. The river once powered several such industries.

It is a singular fact that this source of the St. Joseph rises within two miles of a larger and more powerful St. Joseph River, which flows away in the opposite direction through Elkhart and South Bend toward its rendezvous with Lake Michigan. No one in Hillsdale, not even the historically minded, seems to be concerned that two unconnected rivers rising within two miles of each other should bear the same name. Near Prattville, where the Potawatomi once camped as they migrated toward what is now Indiana from their Michigan homes, the river turns abruptly southwest and continues in this direction to its mouth at Fort Wayne.

To the Indians who originally inhabited the land, the St. Joseph was *Ko-chis-ah-se-pe*, which in the Miami tongue meant "Bean River." But the French, who first explored its waters, trod its paths, and gathered furs along its banks, renamed it the St. Joseph, sometimes the Little St. Joseph or St. Joseph of the Maumee to distinguish it from the larger river of the same name that flowed into Lake Michigan. Not only did the French control the upper river by virtue of their trapping and trading activities, but by operating a fort near the river's mouth, they effectively made the St. Joseph their own.

Shaping the St. Joseph was the work of tens of thousands of years, and somewhere in those misty regions of prehistory the story begins. The river is a child of the glaciers that once spread over the Midwest. A mile high they came, smashing down mountains and filling valleys, rivers, and lakes with debris. This brutal war of nature fused rocks, soil, hills, and forests into the hulking ice mass until it resembled a great, dirty mountain of frozen earth. The glaciers remained in northeastern Indiana longer than in other areas of the state.

When the southern sun checked the glaciers' progress at last, the silent task of melting billions of tons of ice began. Meltwaters carved new valleys and began spreading thousands of acres of ground-up boulders, sand, and gravel over the land. In the process, the glacier deposited several closely parallel moraines and between two such ridges the St. Joseph flows. Consequently, the drainage basin is small, and the seventy-five-mile stream is a short river, a narrow river, a shallow river. Cedar Creek, its largest tributary, and other smaller streams enter mostly from the west and reach the St. Joseph only by mustering enough strength to burst through the moraine on the river's right bank. Since natural lakes control the headwaters, flooding is minimal.

Cedar Creek is one of three Hoosier streams designated a natural and scenic river by state law and entitled to protection from those who would commercialize its beauty. Auburn, near the creek's headwaters, was an important early automobile producer and some of the best of its products can be seen in the Auburn-Cord-Duesenberg Museum which occupies the former Auburn plant. Present day industrial products include automotive and foundry products, furnace controls and closures.

The glaciers that destined the St. Joseph to remain a small river temporarily made it one of the mightiest streams in America. As ice blocked the lower Great Lakes, the water was forced to drain westward up the Maumee Valley to Fort Wayne and then down the Wabash. For a short distance near its mouth, the St. Joseph carried this torrent on its way from the Maumee to the Wabash Valley. But when the glaciers retreated north of the St. Lawrence, the lakes carved their present path to the sea and the westbound river first diminished and then reversed itself.

The Miami were the first to discover the lower St. Joseph's strategic value as the land link in the shortest water route from the Great Lakes to the Mississippi and established their principal town, Kekionga (now Fort Wayne), at the junction of the St. Joseph and St. Marys rivers. The French capitalized upon the Indians' discovery of its strategic value, and in 1750 erected Fort Miamis on the riverbank. It succeeded an earlier fort a short distance away on the St. Marys River that the Indians had burned in 1747. The French garrisoned the fort until 1760 when they handed it over to the British as a result of the French and Indian War. Three years later the Indians captured it during Pontiac's Conspiracy, but the British regained it, keeping control until the end of the American Revolution.

From its source to its mouth, Montpelier, Ohio, population 4,431, is the only city to break the willow fringe along the river's banks. The St. Joseph is a gracious and gentle stream, coursing through pleasant, fertile valleys where cornfield and pastureland invade hardwood forests. Yet at times the St. Joseph hides itself in dense woods, a lost stream separated from civilization by a rising corridor of banks crowned with elms and maples. One of its few remaining milldams stretches across the river at the head of a scenic loop at Spencerville and at the lower end a covered timber bridge from the 1870s still carries travelers.

An earlier commercial use of its water, however, was by engineers of the Wabash and Erie Canal, whose big ditch through Indiana and Ohio was America's longest artificial waterway. Water supply was a problem at Fort Wayne, since this was the summit section and streams were small. So laborers dug a feeder canal and built a dam about seven miles upstream from Fort Wayne. Although robbed of part of its rightful waters, the St. Joseph helped keep the canal operating for nearly half a century.

In 1896 the area around the west end of the dam became Robison Park, one of the state's most extensive amusement areas, and a double-track streetcar line carried thousands along the onetime canal bank to fun and frolic. For more than a generation fun lovers rode out to swim, picnic, or board the steamer Clementina for a trip up the scenic river.

Not far from the park site, Concordia College covers a rolling campus near the river. Completed in 1958 by the internationally known architect Eero Saarinen, the campus intentionally resembles a north European village, and its innovative architecture reflects the heritage of both the Finnish-born architect and Concordia's Lutheran roots.

Anyone making the trip to the park by streetcar could see the hilltop cemetery where one of America's great folk heroes lies. His name was John Chapman, but millions know him as Johnny Appleseed, the man who brought the bloom of apple orchards into the Midwest.

A native of Massachusetts, Johnny arrived in Fort Wayne about

The Concordia College campus, created by Eero Saarinen, borders the river at Fort Wayne.

1830 and spent the last fifteen years of his life there. A legend in his own time, he was a picturesque figure as he made his way through the forests, clearing little plots of land and planting apple orchards. Dressed in ill-fitting, homemade clothes and carrying a Bible, Johnny served as a missionary of the Swedenborgian, or New Jerusalem, church along with his work as a horticulturist. The post office department honored his contribution to the frontier with a commemorative stamp in 1966.

Although the romantic days of the French, Johnny Appleseed, and Robison Park are gone, the tireless river has found a new and vital role quenching Fort Wayne's thirst. A dam at Cedarville, which is only a few miles northeast of Fort Wayne, blocks the river and backs up a scenic eight-mile-long, 460-acre lake through a valley with such gentle contours that highways run nearly at water level. Gray skeletons of drowned tree stumps jut from the upper lake, but the open stretches below attract fishermen and water sportsmen.

Neither the Indians nor the French were able to master the river during the centuries they controlled it, but the engineers subdued it in a single move when they built the dam on dry land and rerouted the river behind it.

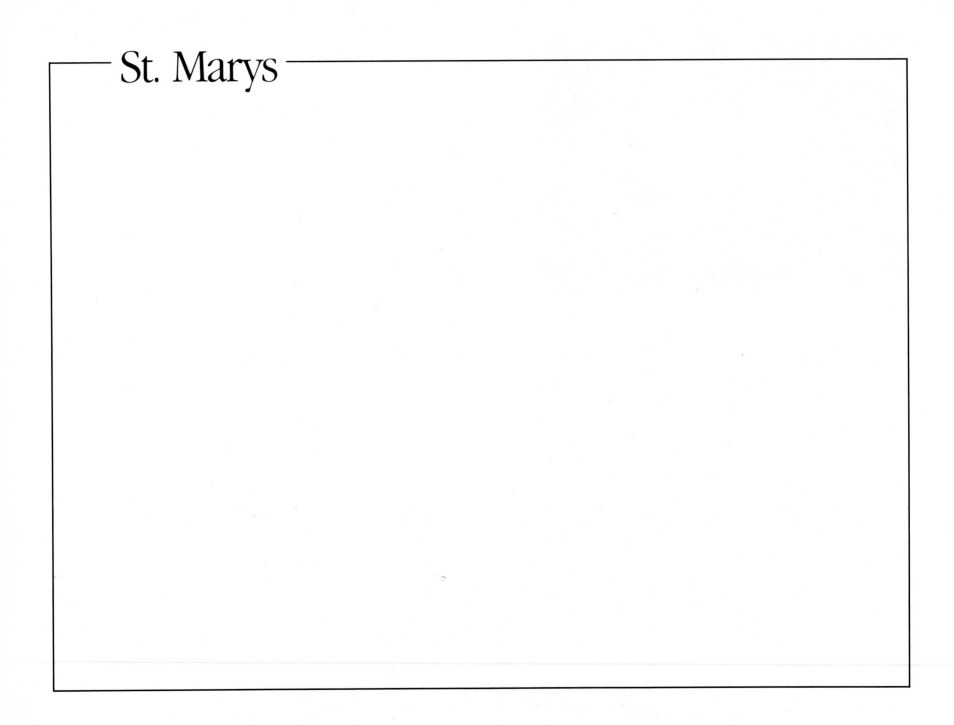

St. Marys

*Left to right*: Just west of New Bremen, Ohio, the river begins its uncertain way toward the Maumee River. ❧St. Marys, Ohio, has preserved a remnant of the Miami and Erie Canal in this downtown park.

The St. Marys is the river that failed twice before it finally found its proper place in the world. As a military highway, it was a washout. As a transportation route, it was a failure. But as a bountiful center of agricultural production, the fertile St. Marys country has gained national recognition on several counts.

Stretching about ninety miles in a series of sinuous curves and placid meanderings, the river's sluggish appearance belies the significant and exciting role it has played in the winning of the West. And at the same time modern drainage hides the reasons why her role was less important than it might have been. Muddy, sometimes sullen, frequently narrowing into insignificance and just as suddenly broadening into a respectable stream, it has known the sound of marching feet heading for the destruction of war and the ring of shovels and axes used in constructing canals to improve transportation.

Long before 1700, Frenchmen penetrating west from Quebec discovered the river's mouth, which is where Fort Wayne now stands, and the pathway that led up the riverbank and across the low continental divide that separates the Great Lakes basin from the Mississippi Valley. This was to become the most vital portage into the west as explorers, missionaries, traders, and armies busied themselves taming Indians, taking furs, and exploring the raw, unknown frontier. The portage extended a scant nine miles and formed the only land barrier on the shortest water route connecting the two French capitals of New Orleans and Quebec.

To the French, the dream of empire lay beyond the portage and they knew full well that to control the portage was to control the country. About the end of the seventeenth century, they established a trading post, Post Miamis, at the head of the portage and by 1712 had fortified it so that it became Fort Miamis. Its site is located on Superior Street, a few blocks west of downtown Fort Wayne.

The river, winding sluggishly from the southeast, never achieved importance as a water highway. It rose in the flat prairies of Auglaize County in western Ohio, wriggled through sticky swamplands and finally flowed along the edge of a ten-mile-wide trough between two glacial moraines. Its banks were too wet to support marching armies, its flow too undependable to carry transport.

Its valley was a different story. Prehistoric glaciers which had crept out of the north, had covered the land to a depth of thousands of feet. Then the warming sun checked the ice sheet's advance and finally sent it in full retreat, leaving a series of parallel, arrow-shaped ridges which set the course of our modern rivers. The St. Marys, rising southwest of the picturesque German Catholic village of New Bremen, Ohio, flowed north until it struck the base of one such ridge and was deflected westward. Then for sixty miles it followed the

north edge of a flat plain from ten to twelve miles wide until it met the St. Joseph River at Fort Wayne to form the Maumee.

Although the French knew the lower river, the slimy swamps kept them out of its upper reaches and this area gained little attention until President Washington dispatched successive armies into the heart of the western Indian country to make it safe for settlement. Gen. Josiah Harmar was the first, and he led his men up from Fort Washington at Cincinnati to the St. Marys headwaters in 1790. Here he struck along the river, penetrating the swamps where he could, detouring around them when he couldn't. Arriving at the site of Fort Wayne, he attacked the Indians but withdrew after suffering heavy losses and returned to his base with little accomplished. After Gen. Arthur St. Clair's devastating defeat the following year at what is now Fort Recovery, Ohio, Washington turned the task over to Gen. "Mad Anthony" Wayne, who marched northward along the west edge of Ohio, pausing at the St. Marys River to build Fort Adams before moving on to crush the Indians at the Battle of Fallen Timbers near Toledo, Ohio. Following his triumph he marched up the Maumee Valley, established Fort Wayne, and then turned his army up the St. Marys.

Wayne hoped to sail his army upstream but the river failed him. A company of scouts sent out to determine the navigation possibili-

ties reported water travel impossible on the shallow, swampy St. Marys and that it would support nothing larger than canoes and those only at high water. Wayne then marched his men on high land paralleling the river, making long detours around the swamps, and reaching the water on the third day after marching thirty-six miles.

During the four decades following its failure as a military highway, the St. Marys slipped into near obscurity, draining farmland, powering a few mills, and carrying occasional flatboats during high water. Then canal fever burst on the pioneer scene like a gold rush. The St. Marys, as few rivers anywhere, found itself boxed in by a canal at each end—the Miami and Erie paralleling its headwaters and the Wabash and Erie bridging it at Fort Wayne. For a time they performed the transportation service the river never was able to carry out.

The Wabash and Erie was the long one. For 464 miles it stretched across Ohio and Indiana, connecting Toledo and Evansville, the continent's longest canal. It crossed the St. Marys at Fort Wayne on a covered wooden aqueduct which later became famous as the city's favorite swimming hole.

At the opposite end of the river, the Miami and Erie Canal, connecting Toledo and Cincinnati, paralleled the St. Marys for nearly twenty miles. To feed it, Irish laborers with pick and shovel created

twenty-seven-square-mile Grand Lake (Lake St. Marys), which today attracts thousands of water worshipers to its fifty-two-mile shoreline.

Now at last the river's failure as a transport route seemed to be turning into success. The canals offered cheap carriage for the farmers' crops and livestock and reduced the cost of bringing in the goods they needed. But almost at their birth the canals heard the ominous wail of the locomotive whistle. Within twenty years, the railroads had shouldered them aside as the principal freight and passenger carriers, and in another twenty years the noisy canalers, shouting at the mules, untangling towlines, and swapping yarns in waterfront hotels, remained only in memory.

Just as it failed as a military highway, the St. Marys Valley lost out as a transport route. Yet clear evidence of both canals remains. Fort Wayne has restored "The Landing," a one-block business area once lined by canal warehouses. A visit to "The Landing," which is opposite the new City-County Building, is like suddenly raising a window blind on scenes of another day. Shops, restaurants, night spots—they all are there to return the visitor to days when the canal landing was the busiest place in town.

At St. Marys, Ohio, site of Wayne's original Fort St. Mary's, and the Indian trading post called Girty's Town, a canal feeder carries water from Grand Lake (Lake St. Marys) to the Miami and Erie Canal, which provides power and water supply northward toward Spencerville, Ohio. An attractive floral park, edged by the Venice-like canal, forms a pleasant recreation spot in the heart of St. Marys.

When the canals died, the valley lost its hopes of becoming a transportation route. The third time, however, its dreams of success were realized because the St. Marys country soon found its rightful role as a rich agricultural region. Three of the five counties through which the river passes rank as national leaders in production of chickens, turkeys, pigs, horses, and tomatoes. Both Mercer County, Ohio, near the headwaters and Allen County at the river's end rank near the nation's top 2 percent in number of high income farms. Mercer also produces so many chickens and turkeys that fewer than 45 of the country's 3,070 counties surpass it. It stands as the nation's seventieth tomato producer. Allen County ranks near the nation's upper 1 percent in chicken production.

With all this agricultural abundance along the St. Marys, it was logical that the Central Soya Company should establish itself in Decatur along the river's banks and that it should grow to become one of the 500 largest industrial corporations in the United States. At its Decatur plant in Indiana and smaller centers elsewhere it can pro-

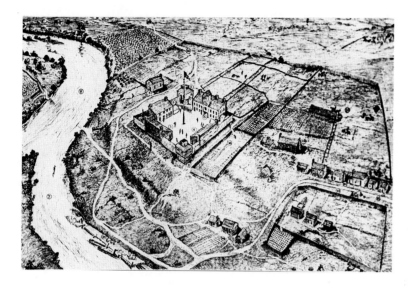

cess 100,000,000 bushels of soybeans annually. In 1984, its sales exceeded 1.72 billion dollars.

Central Soya goes back to the depression's depths when Dale W. McMillen purchased an idle sugar beet refinery at Decatur. In 1934 he ventured into the relatively new soybean processing field and began building a battery of towering concrete silos which now surround the original tiny plant. The products end up in such varied items as livestock feed, flour for the baking industry, and oil for food processors. Soybeans, with their unlimited versatility, make magazines easier to read, enable paints to go on walls faster and stay on longer, and help make cars run more smoothly.

The St. Marys remains a lonely, remote river between rows of trees. Few cities break the green fringe along its banks; few industries sully its waters. But in the fertile, green fields along its borders, it has discovered its lasting claim to fame.

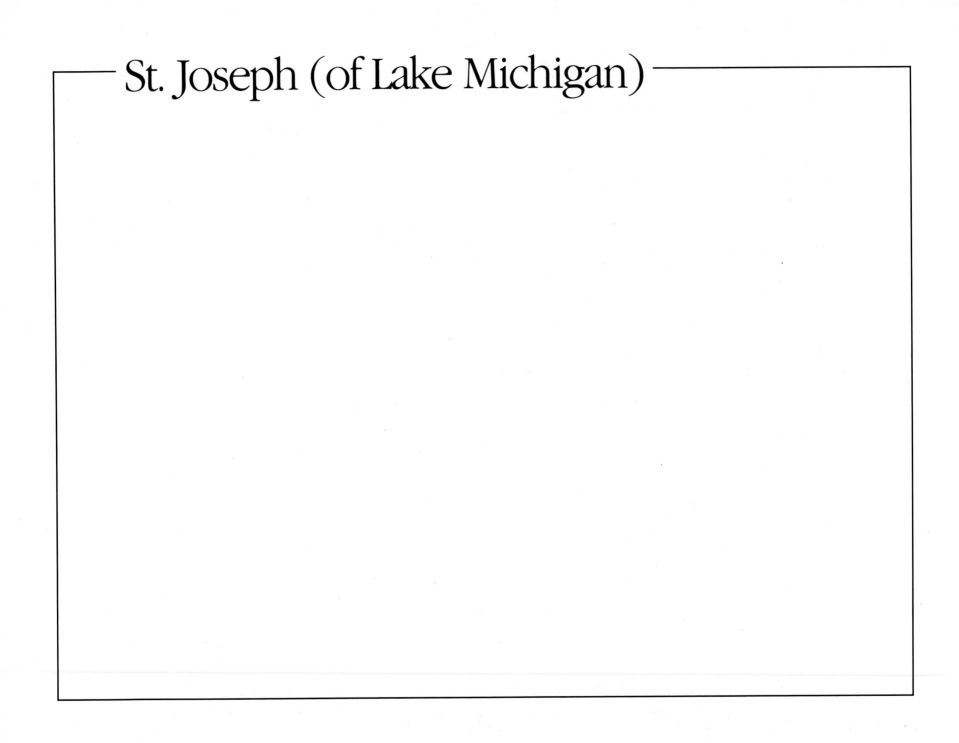

St. Joseph (of Lake Michigan)

At the edge of Hillsdale, Michigan, a stream so tiny that it can be bridged by a single leap issues from a picturesque lake to which a local Indian bequeathed his name: Baw Beese. Leisurely, without hurry, winding ten miles to gain a mile toward the sea, it sets out for Lake Michigan, 210 miles distant. A placid highway flowing between comfortable rows of trees, it crosses half of Michigan, dips into Indiana for forty-two miles, and drains a 4,700-square-mile basin. The Indians canoed it. Early settlers made it their road. Great Lakes cargo boats navigate its lower portion.

To the Miami Indians, the river was the *Sa-ki-wa-si-pi-wi*, which meant "coming out place" and referred to the portage at South Bend which led to the Kankakee, the Illinois, and the Mississippi rivers. However, the Potawatomi, through whose country it flowed, called it *Sag-wa-si-bi*, which to them meant "mystery river." Their derivation sprang from the legend of a mysterious Indian who was discovered along its banks and in time the term applied to the man also was applied to the river.

But René Robert Cavelier, Sieur de La Salle, the first European to navigate the river, called it the River of the Miamis. Frenchmen who followed, and who were the river's first European masters, renamed it St. Joseph for the patron saint of Canada.

On this river, the first French explorers and fur traders entered Indiana 300 years ago. The pioneers who followed them built their homes and factories, raised their grain and livestock, and developed one of America's most prolific fruit cultures along its banks.

Although it is the child of placid lakes, maturing as it flows through restful fields and woods, the river becomes, before it reaches Lake Michigan, Indiana's hardest working stream, a veritable slave in the service of industry. But it would be a mistake to think of the St. Joseph, past or present, as only a workaday river. Its most striking single fact is the way in which it combines scenic beauty with historical association and sheer usefulness to mankind. The St. Joseph is more than a river. It is also a valley, and both the river and the valley are worth knowing.

Three hundred years ago, Frenchmen with furs, empire, and Indians' souls on their minds found the St. Joseph a convenient water highway into the unexplored interior, an irresistible invitation to adventure. As a result, the river long witnessed the human march from the Great Lakes into the unknown. A century later, the British pushed them out, and then, like a tug of war, Indians, Spanish, and Americans successively claimed the valley, the British holding it twice.

Once the dust of battle had settled, the Americans discovered that the St. Joseph made a road and a living place for men, gave them power to use, created trade, and to some degree determined the de-

*Left to right*: The Twin Branch dam, one of seventeen dams on the river, was constructed in 1904 between Elkhart and Mishawaka. ⋖§Studebaker Corporation once flourished in South Bend.

velopment of the region. It exerted a deep influence on the life around it.

To know the St. Joseph, it is best to start at the mouth, where the story begins as far as the explorers were concerned. Although Father Jacques Marquette, an early explorer of the Mississippi, may have traveled the St. Joseph in the early 1670s, it is certain that another French explorer, La Salle, worked his way upstream in 1679 as far as the great southernmost curve that gave its name to the city of South Bend. His expedition then made the short portage to the Kankakee River, where it launched the voyage toward the Mississippi.

Two years later, La Salle returned to the south bend, conferring with the Indians under a huge tree that became known as the Council Oak. With the rich fur trade in mind, he already had erected Fort Miami on a bluff overlooking the river's mouth, the site also of a Jesuit mission.

The French soon were busy the length of the valley. Father Claude Aveneau built a mission at what is now Niles, Michigan, and Fort St. Joseph was erected to protect it. A hundred miles away, the famed Father Louis Hennepin, deep in the unmapped interior, preached to the Indians at a point on the river still known as the Ford of the Gray Robe.

Then in quick succession, as history is measured, the lower val-

ley bounced like a yo-yo from one conqueror to another. The British captured it from the French, the Indians took it from the British, the British regained it and lost St. Joseph, the key fort, to a tiny French-American expedition that marched from the Illinois country near St. Louis. Then in best comic opera fashion, the invaders let their guard down on their way home and were routed by the British who pursued them to a point near Michigan City.

A few weeks later the most unlikely conquerors of all appeared, moving in like the French had done while the British left the fort unguarded. These were the Spanish, led by Don Pierro, commandant at St. Louis, where the expedition originated. Seizing Fort St. Joseph, the Spaniards raised their flags and declared that all land east of the Mississippi belonged to their king by right of conquest. Either frightened or overconfident, the Spanish hurried home the next day. The British returned and the conquest was over.

The Revolutionary War placed the valley permanently in American hands, and once it was over, the Americans began to look at their river. They found that it rose on the divide separating Lake Erie's waters from Lake Michigan's and that it followed a wooded, winding course marked by many graceful and scenic bends. It was a gracious and gentle stream. Four hundred lakes, ranging up to six square miles in size, fed the river. The valley varied from 500 to 2,000 feet in

*Left to right*: Studebaker shop and home in Ashland, Ohio, 1835. ✑§The Memorial Library at the University of Notre Dame was dedicated in 1963. ✑§La Salle met with the Indians under this tree (at South Bend) in 1681.

width, and the banks in places towered sixty feet above the water. Regulated by the lakes, growing with the springs that flowed down to it, widening from the strength of a thousand brooks, it experienced few low flows or rapid rises. Floods were infrequent. Westerly winds, laden with the moisture of Lake Michigan, could make a garden of its lower reaches, and 570 feet of fall could power mills and factories.

Settlers rushed into the valley and introduced flatboats and keelboats as soon as they realized that their rich, new lands which yielded so abundantly also were roadless lands. Steamboats briefly paraded to and fro on the river, which by 1830 had come to be regarded as a wide, deep, majestic bearer of burdens. A shipment of furs is known to have left South Bend by keelboat for New York. Passenger steamers churned the water.

River transportation may have played a part in the iron manufacturing industry that flourished briefly at Mishawaka and South Bend after ore was discovered nearby. But the St. Joseph was a busy artery of commerce only briefly. Progress brought the railroads, and in time they supplanted the steamboats. Traffic was so lucrative that by 1890 two parallel rail lines connected South Bend and Lake Michigan, one on each side of the valley. The Army Corps of Engineers, however, did its best to keep the boats moving by dredging a twenty-one-foot

channel at the river's mouth, where nearly 500,000 tons of shipping is handled annually. The Corps also studied navigation feasibility as far as Elkhart.

Since the beginning of history, people who live along a river have felt the urge to control its flow or at least to discipline its vagaries, and the people of the St. Joseph were no exception. The pioneers looked longingly at the wealth of untapped power and moved to harness it. One hundred fifty-five years after La Salle explored it, a dam had been built on the St. Joseph at Mishawaka. Ten feet high it stood and races on each side carried the waters to their place of work.

The adjoining city of South Bend watched enviously until James Oliver harnessed the river and put it to work powering his plow works. About this time, Henry and Clement Studebaker began manufacturing wagons that they sold largely to immigrants heading west. Together, the two firms brought fame to South Bend and an easier life to the farmer, particularly after Oliver invented the chilled plow.

Where the St. Joseph had once worn an air of proper, orderly well-being, its flow was increasingly interrupted by dams and guided by races. Where it had flowed placidly, it now crashed down in swarms of boiling water, powering plow works and a windmill factory, paper plant, and a woolen mill.

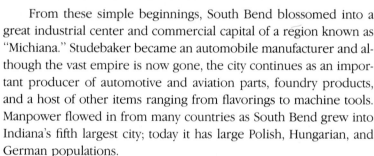

From these simple beginnings, South Bend blossomed into a great industrial center and commercial capital of a region known as "Michiana." Studebaker became an automobile manufacturer and although the vast empire is now gone, the city continues as an important producer of automotive and aviation parts, foundry products, and a host of other items ranging from flavorings to machine tools. Manpower flowed in from many countries as South Bend grew into Indiana's fifth largest city; today it has large Polish, Hungarian, and German populations.

South Bend's twin city of Mishawaka and nearby Elkhart both took power from the river and developed into important manufacturing centers. Elkhart is considered the band instrument capital of the world and also is noted for the manufacture of mobile homes and medicines. Many pretentious homes line the river at Elkhart and skiers and boaters frolic in the water. Campers and picnickers take possession of the river's banks in summer.

As industry grew, so did the demand for power, and the St. Joseph was made to change its function, even its shape, and above all the manner in which man looked at it—from a flowing highway to a powerhouse. Following World War I, at least five power stations were built or expanded in quick succession and the process of transform-

ing the St. Joseph grew so swiftly that many miles of it became unrecognizable. From the one-foot City of Hillsdale Dam at its source to the twenty-two-foot hydroelectric barrier at Berrien Springs, seventeen dams interrupt the river's flow to power industry, produce electricity, or impound water for mill or factory. The Federal Power Commission says that three potential hydroelectric sites remain to be developed, so that the St. Joseph is no longer considered a river in the classic sense but, in a day when progress is measured in kilowatts, as a source of electric power.

Long before the power of electricity had transformed the valley, the power of education appeared. The University of Notre Dame and St. Mary's College at South Bend and Hillsdale College at the river's source were founded in the 1840s. Others followed. The Seventh Day Adventist Church established Andrews University at Berrien Springs, Michigan, in 1901, and the United Missionary Church located Bethel College at Mishawaka in 1947. Indiana University established a regional campus, now called Indiana University at South Bend, in 1940; and Holy Cross Junior College was opened there in 1966.

Notre Dame, with its 9,000 students, grew from a tiny frontier school to a 1,250-acre, lake-dotted campus marked by an amazing style contrast between ornate Victorian-era and startling contemporary buildings. Its thirteen-story library, which seats 2,900, includes a spectacular nine-story mosaic covering its front wall. One of Indiana's "Big Three" universities, it is best known for football fans who swarm in from across the nation to see some of the country's crucial gridiron battles.

Cities along the St. Joseph display an interesting variety of characteristics that range from sturdy, workaday habits to a flair for the occult. Colon, Michigan, population 1,190, likes to think of itself as the "Magic Capital of the World." Quiet, lake-bordered, river-edged, its role seems totally out of place in the simple, rustic world of the upper St. Joseph. The "magic" name centers about the Abbott's Magic Manufacturing Company, which produces paraphernalia for illusions ranging from the inexpensive "Devil Coin Box" to the "Vanishing Elephant" trick selling for as much as $6,000 (without the elephant), and visiting magicians from all over the world nearly double Colon's population when they meet each August.

At the other end of the river, a cult known as the House of David established itself in Benton Harbor, Michigan, in 1903. Its members, who spread their fame with a bearded, semi-pro baseball team, lived in communal style, and neither smoked, drank, nor ate meat. Internal problems led to establishment of a rival group, the City of David, so that Benton Harbor, like Colon, had more than its share of mysticism.

Niles, located eleven miles below South Bend, likes to call itself the "Four Flags City" because of the French, British, Spanish, and American occupations. In addition to its early Catholic mission, Niles was the site of an important frontier Baptist mission more than 160 years ago. Niles, like St. Joseph and Benton Harbor, is located in Berrien County, Michigan, where blue-green orchards unsurpassed in the country, make a festival of spring. Easily the nation's fruit bowl, Berrien ranks fifth among the nation's 3,070 counties in cherry trees, eighth in apple orchard acreage, eleventh in both peaches and pears, eighteenth in grapes, and nineteenth in plums. It also ranks third in cucumbers harvested, eighth in strawberries and twenty-first in tomatoes. Its multi-million dollar vegetable crop places it fiftieth in the nation and its eight-figure fruit-nut-berry crop ranks thirty-fifth.

Plentiful Lake Michigan moisture which helps make Berrien County a garden spot also benefits its neighboring county of Cass. It ranks in the nation's upper 2 percent of cherry, cucumber, and breeding hog production and in the upper 3 percent of apple and tomato producers. Calhoun County, another neighbor, contributes heavily to the nation's onion supply, but this is balanced by the sweet aroma of mint, which also grows abundantly in the valley.

Impressive statistics, these. What better evidence of the richness of the St. Joseph Valley and the industry of her people?

# Highways of Settlement

# Ohio

Name the river that has most powerfully influenced Indiana, and the inevitable answer is the beautiful, majestic Ohio, which paradoxically lies almost entirely outside the state. For 357 miles—more than double Indiana's crow-flown width—its series of sparkling straightaways, majestic curves, and placid meanderings form the state's southern boundary. Its hills are among Indiana's highest, its gorges among the deepest, and its dozens of graceful bends carve picturesque peninsulas which afford sweeping views of Kentucky's border. Its topography, agriculture, architecture, customs, and pace differ from the Indiana to the north and there lingers about it not only the straightforward simplicity of the Middle West, but much of the grace of the South, to which the roots of its people go. Although the Ohio is a gracious and gentle stream, it has been a powerful arbiter of life and in godlike fashion it has both given and taken away. It is a valley where the present and the past have flowed together.

Careers of those who grew up along its banks illustrate its widely varying influences. There were authors Edward Eggleston (Vevay) and David Graham Phillips (Madison), playwright William Vaughn Moody (New Albany), actress Irene Dunne (Madison), newsmen Elmer Davis and Edwin C. Hill (both of Aurora), baseball great Billy Herman (New Albany), acting president of Hawaii Henry E. Cooper (New Albany), presidential cabinet members Edwin Denby and George W. McCrary (both of Evansville), and two notable engineers, James Buchanan Eads (Lawrenceburg), who threw the great bridge across the Mississippi River at St. Louis, and Elwood Mead (Patriot), who built Hoover Dam.

For nearly 200 years the Ohio was considered a wholly Kentucky river, its low-watermark on the Indiana bank being the state boundary. But in 1980 the U.S. Supreme court settled a long-drawn-out boundary squabble by declaring the line to be the river's bank as it stood in 1792, rather than the low-watermark of the constantly shifting stream. Channel changes and water levels raised by dams consequently gave Indiana at least 100 feet of river width and in some places a good deal more. Bankside industries and marinas now fall unquestionably within Indiana's jurisdiction.

Ever since the days when Indians canoed it and the first settlers made it their road, the Ohio has exerted a deep influence on Hoosier life. It has provided not only a route for conquering armies and an avenue for settlement, but a highway for trade, a protective moat against rambunctious Confederate armies, and a water supply for an increasingly controversial bankside industrialization. It interferes in politics, dabbles in real estate, and rearranges geography. Until the days of the railroad, it was the primary route to the West, meeting the settler's early needs; yet it remains equally essential to the teeming millions of today. It is not only a river, but also a valley and one worth knowing.

To the French, first white men to see it, the Ohio was *La Belle Rivière*—the beautiful river. They only echoed the Iroquois word for "beautiful," and those who view it today and feel its sense of romance as it tosses between its steep, tree-crowned banks cannot question this early description.

By definition, the Ohio begins in downtown Pittsburgh, Pennsylvania, where the Allegheny and the Monongahela meet to create the fountainhead that starts the great, surging Ohio on its powerful way toward the sea. Its most distant waters come from Pennsylvania's northern counties and West Virginia's mountains. When they meet, they assure the Ohio a stature afforded few infant rivers.

But it was not always so. The Ohio's history is long and cannot be measured in mere centuries. Shaping the Ohio was the work of at least half a thousand million years as the waters busied themselves with their evolutionary struggles. It is said by the men who read the rocks that somewhere in the dim mists of prehistory the Ohio was a series of disconnected streams flowing in diverse directions. One principal divide stood at Madison, near the present highway bridge. The great ice mass of the glaciers blocked and rerouted the streams, rearranged the land, and sent the waters flowing along the path that is now the Ohio. Once consolidated, the river, joined by scores of tributaries, began its 981-mile course toward Cairo, Illinois, and the Mississippi.

From the beginning, men found the Ohio convenient to their westward penetrations, the chain binding the beckoning West to the settled East. During the late 1700s, it carried George Rogers Clark, the hero of Vincennes, to conquest and Colonel Archibald Lochry's army to annihilation by Indians near what is now Aurora. Behind them, bent on subduing the Indians, followed Generals Harmar, St. Clair, and "Mad Anthony" Wayne. To Harmar and St. Clair, the Ohio was the road to humiliation and defeat; to Wayne, it meant resounding victory. Once Wayne had stabilized the frontier, the Ohio became a majestic water highway, bringing thousands of restless pioneers in pursuit of fertile land and the promise of a new life.

During the great migration of the early 1800s, most settlers either floated down the Ohio from the East or crossed it from Kentucky and beyond. One traveler wrote of seeing more than a hundred boats moored above Pittsburgh awaiting the river's rise. In 1807, 2,000 flatboats and keelboats floated down the Ohio to New Orleans, and in 1820, 84 percent of Indiana's population resided in southern Indiana.

The river attracted diverse groups. Among the earliest were French Swiss who established Vevay in 1802, intent on continuing their native occupation of grape culture. Opposite Louisville, Kentucky, early settlers were men who acquired land in Clark's Grant, awarded to the hero of Vincennes and his soldiers for their gallant services. Farther downstream, German Swiss founded Tell City which came to be peopled primarily by Germans.

From the springboard of Cincinnati's "Rhineland," Germans migrated downriver to settle New Albany, Tell City, and Evansville, which was once a port of entry to the United States. More than twenty German language newspapers appeared in these three cities and they no doubt were read, also, by the large German populations of Madison and Aurora.

Since the river was the road to the nation's interior, many pioneers strayed no farther than its banks. New Albany shortly became Indiana's largest city, and in 1850 two of the three largest, each with approximately 8,000 residents, were located along the Ohio. To New Albany, Madison, and Evansville, the river gave life, maturity, and importance.

In that day, the river dominated everything. Settlements were laid out to accommodate the river; the river was the town's lifeline. County seats, instead of being centrally located as logic would dictate, were established bankside in ten of the thirteen riverfront counties, and one inland seat later lost out to a river city. Names of the settlements that dot the riverbanks hint at the richness of the local tradition and the root of its culture: Aurora, Rising Sun, Patriot, Vevay, Fredonia, Tell City, Rome, Troy, and Grandview in Indiana; Rabbit Hash and Brandenburg in Kentucky.

As the country matured, the Indiana river towns fell into three groups. There were the upper Ohio settlements, marked by palatial homes of the river captains, merchants, and manufacturers. Then came a cluster of little towns straitjacketed today in timelessness and tucked away in a fold of the past, Rip Van Winkle style. Finally came vibrant communities fueled by manufacturing and mining and clustered about the tri-state metropolis of Evansville.

From the time men first dreamed of making the river a highway of trade, they sought vessels more effective than the clumsy keelboats and flatboats. And when steamboats churned the water they knew they had the answer. Traffic leaped as the means arrived to return after delivering a cargo downstream.

Despite the shallow draft of the vessels, boats wrestled daily with the perils of the Ohio. None knew better than the colorful pilots the dangers inherent in the river's swift rage at floodtime and its treacherous shallows, changing channels, and lurking snags at low water. Hidden sandbars, shifting currents, points, bends, and eddies were daily assignments in their process of education.

But there was a lure to the river that few men could resist and as ornate boats paraded to and fro in ever-increasing numbers, the Ohio became a busy artery of commerce. As early as 1824, the federal government appropriated money to improve the channel. Boatyards sprang up at Madison, Jeffersonville, and New Albany, the latter producing both the *Robert E. Lee* of song and racing fame and the snagboat that Henry Shreve invented to clear the western waters for safe navigation. Jeffersonville was home of the famous Howard Ship Yards, now Jeffboats, Inc., which turns out vast numbers of inland water vessels. Barges also are constructed at Tell City.

Occasionally, during the romantic days when men would boast loudly of the palatial steamboats they raced on the river's currents, their vessels would run afoul of each other or become snagged on the unexpectedly shallow bottom. Passengers' fates ranged from discomfort to death. The *United States* and the *America*, two of the finest palaces afloat, collided near Patriot in 1868 and sent an estimated 70 persons to their deaths in the fire and sinking that followed. Less serious was the wreck above Cannelton in 1825 which interrupted the triumphal tour of the Marquis de Lafayette. The famous hero of the American Revolution managed to escape and spend the night huddled in a shallow cave at a spot known ever since as Lafayette Spring.

The boatmen had a more persistent problem, however; the Falls of the Ohio opposite Louisville, Kentucky. In reality, it was a rapids of about two and one-fourth miles which fell approximately twenty-six feet. Whatever its name, it was steep enough to halt navigation most of the year. This barrier forced even the low-draft boats of the day to unload their cargoes above the falls and to reload below. It created a prosperity that built Portland (now part of the larger city) and Louisville on the Kentucky side and Jeffersonville, Clarksville, and New Albany, in downstream order, on the Indiana side.

Men do not submit to such barriers easily, and as early as 1804 plans were afoot to circumvent the falls with a canal. Indiana tried it first, digging and blasting briefly until the solid limestone forced its builders to surrender dejectedly. Kentuckians were more persistent, and their Louisville and Portland Canal, completed in 1830, carried more than 800 boats the first year. During the 25 years preceding the Civil War, traffic averaged 1,300 steamboats annually. Louisville's growth as a result outstripped its three Indiana rivals. Legend has it that a contractor named Hoosier worked on the canal and that his employes, drawn mostly from Indiana, became known as "Hoosier's men," thus giving Indiana its nickname.

The river gave its towns a prominence they would not have enjoyed otherwise, and men who gained affluence because of it have left their marks in palatial mansions that echo a way of life. Most notable are the J. F. D. Lanier State Memorial and the privately owned Shrewsbury House at Madison, whose stately columns and free-standing spiral staircases place them among the finest Greek Revival-style houses remaining in the Midwest. Other notable structures include Hillforest and Veraestau at Aurora, the courthouse at Rising Sun, a cluster of homes at Vevay, Culbertson Mansion State Memorial at New Albany, and others at Newburgh and Evansville.

Although younger than some of its neighbors, Madison quickly became the queen city of the upper valley. By 1850, 8,000 persons had swelled this wilderness town to city size, the alluvial product of those two tireless streams, time and the river. It missed being the state's largest community by only 170 persons. It was the river that built Madison and dominated her life. Because it was a major port, it also became a focus of inland transportation and both the first highway to penetrate the interior—the Michigan Road—and the first railroad—Madison and Indianapolis—originated here.

Pioneers scarcely could have chosen a more unlikely place to strike inland. Madison, squeezed close to the river by 400-foot bluffs, lay like a dachshund, a tenth of a city wide and a city and a half long. Yet the future appeared so certain that few discouraged the battle to thrust highway and rails up through the perpendicular hills.

While the Michigan Road was being pushed toward Michigan City, Madison swarmed with shipping and boomed with manufacturing. It produced steamboats, railroad cars, steam engines, foundry products, brushes, soap, cooperage, and beer. Its slaughterhouses, fed by thousands of hogs herded down the Michigan Road, were so busy that thoughts of overtaking Cincinnati as America's "porkopolis" danced in Madison heads. When Jenny Lind, the famous "Swedish Nightingale" squeezed a Madison concert into her big city tour, townspeople hastily whitewashed a packinghouse, converted it briefly into a concert hall and presented the rare event in grandiose style.

When the snort of the Iron Horse accompanied the blast of the steamboat whistle, Madison figured it had found a surefire road to permanent prosperity. Many a town had a river and a selected few had a railroad, but rare was the city that had both. The obvious way out of town was UP and hordes of laborers attacked the perpendicular limestone bluffs with scrapers and black blasting powder. They refused to rest until they had carved a path of one and one-third miles to the top on a grade that averages 5.9 percent, steepest standard gauge in existence today in the United States. Cogwheels were required until 1868 when Reuben Wells, the railroad's master mechanic, designed a powerful locomotive that eliminated the need forever. The City of Madison Port Authority now operates the railroad and is attempting to assure its future by establishing a river-rail terminal.

With so much going for it, Madison presumed that it always

*Left to right*: The Uniontown, Kentucky, dam is fourteen miles southwest of Mt. Vernon.  ✑Fluorspar figurine carved by the Middle Mississippi people was found at Angel Mounds in Vanderburgh County.

would remain the upper river's premier port. But it reckoned without the Civil War, which denuded the Ohio-Mississippi system of its traffic, except for returning war casualties. When the firing ceased, the railroad replaced the steamboat, and Madison became the city that caught the boat but missed the train. During their westward expansion, the railroads wouldn't even think of penetrating Madison's perpendicular topography and so they passed it by.

Faced with economic strangulation, Madison's population peaked it 1870 and declined through a long stream of years until 1940, a sleeping beauty dreaming of her romantic past. Reflecting the days when opulent living was an ingrained habit, she remained an astonishingly handsome city with ancient houses everywhere to delight an artist's soul.

With commercial pressure absent, much of the city's old elegance lingered, along with an easy beauty and a charm that wouldn't quit. Many luxurious homes, where graceful living, warm hospitality, and expression of culture were a matter of course, survived into the present.

In recent years, Madison has enjoyed what it likes to think of as a modest industrial renaissance; yet it remains a museum-piece town, neat, trim, and gracious, where the beautiful hills smile down from all sides, changing in color as the season shifts. When a nationally

known museum's curator first saw Madison, he exclaimed, "Put a fence around the entire town and don't let anyone touch anything in it."

Madison has heeded his advice, and in few other cities are old buildings so loved and preserved. Virtually the entire lower city—133 blocks—was declared a national historic district in 1973. Four years later the National Trust for Historic Preservation placed Madison in the spotlight again. This time it chose the city from among sixty-nine applicants for a Main Street study to develop renovation methods for often unused upper floors of business buildings.

The catalyst responsible for all this architectural activity was John T. Windle, who, with his wife, Ann, discovered Madison, fell in love with it, and transplanted themselves from Chicago to enjoy it. Madison, they quickly realized, was ripe and mellow with the fullness of time and they felt the placidity and charm of its well-being.

In 1960 Windle inspired the organization of Historic Madison, Inc. The latent interest in architecture expanded into a jealous guardianship of the gems scattered throughout the city, and any landlord who harbored thoughts of razing architectural masterpieces realized that he might incite a full-scale riot. Historic Madison eventually acquired properties to make an antique lover drool in ecstacy. They include the Second Presbyterian Church, an outstanding Greek Revival temple, and Federal-style homes, including one known for the fanlight over the door.

In addition to Federal styles and Classic Revivals that pleasantly dot the city, there are generous dashes of Georgian, Gothic, and Italianate. Neat gray row houses and buildings sporting pressed iron facades, produced in Madison foundries, are relics of a vanished phase of American life that adds to the charm. An Italian campanile tower crowns a city fire station.

As part of its mellow charm, Madison remains one of the few cities of its size to rely on volunteer fire companies. Her citizens are fond of remembering its heritage when social prestige swung on membership in the "proper" company. Such individualistic early names as Fair Play, Western, and Washington companies still exist. The mixture of architectural charm, breathtaking scenery, and the lively annual regatta on the Ohio impresses thousands of visitors each year.

Hanover adjoins Madison. Known for Hanover College, an early higher learning institution founded by Presbyterians in 1827, its drives curve among classic Georgian buildings with spectacular views of the winding Ohio, far below.

Between Madison and Hanover, Clifty Creek, tumbling over a seventy-foot rock ledge, forms the centerpiece for beautiful Clifty Falls State Park. The 1,309-acre spread offers overnight accommodations, swimming, hiking, and enough rugged scenery to please any lover of the outdoors.

Upstream, the river edges past Vevay, one of its oldest towns, and like Madison known for its pretentious mansions. But the French Swiss who founded it are gone. So is the wine-making industry they hoped to establish, although the annual Wine Festival maintains a contemporary link. But all is not lost for the thirsty. Joseph E. Seagram & Sons and Schenley Distillers, Inc., produce bourbons, gins, and other whiskeys at their sprawling plants at Lawrenceburg.

While many cities busied themselves with loading cargo and supplying boats, Jeffersonville and New Albany built vessels to sail the inland waters. During the years when steamboating reached its fullest expression, New Albany operated at least nine boatyards. As this industry vanished, it became a pioneer plate-glass producer and a veneer, plywood, food processing, and electronic equipment manufacturer. But New Albany's past is not a remote thing and visible evidences remain in the mellow antiquity of some commercial buildings and the lingering elegance of some of her mansions. Indiana University's Southeast Regional campus is located here. Sherman Minton, a United States senator and Supreme Court justice, came from here, and Walter Q. Gresham came from nearby Lanesville.

Gresham had the distinction of serving in two presidential cabinets, heading three different departments and being appointed successively as a Republican and a Democrat.

Much change is evident. The abandoned New York Central Railroad bridge stands isolated high in the sky, its three miles of approaches abruptly removed. The twenty-two-room E. J. Howard mansion in Jeffersonville now houses the Howard Steamboat Museum, which honors the Howard Ship Yard boats and others built along the river. The Census Bureau now operates in the Army Quartermaster Depot complex. The former state prison is now the Colgate-Palmolive Company, famous for its huge clock that can be read more easily from the Kentucky side. Upstream, Charlestown has settled into a less hectic existence than during its wartime munitions center days.

Squeezed between Jeffersonville and New Albany stands rapidly growing Clarksville, oldest American settlement in Indiana. It occupies the river side of 149,000 acres granted to George Rogers Clark and his men in return for their Revolutionary War services.

Although Clarksville is the cradle of American settlement, Corydon, twenty-two miles west, is the cradle of state government. About thirteen miles inland, it is one of the few interior seats of river counties. The picturesque hip-roofed capitol served both territorial and state governments until Indianapolis became the state capital.

The first state constitution was written here; on stifling June days in 1816 the lawmakers abandoned the capitol and moved to the cool, welcome shade of a huge tree which became known as the Constitution Elm.

The capitol building today is the central point of a state memorial that includes the Governor William Hendricks home. The elm's stump is a local shrine. The streets are sun-flecked and green with old trees; colorful window boxes gaze down from buildings and add to the atmosphere of pleasant and gentle living. Markers, dripping with history, dot the town. They also tell of Morgan's mercurial raiders, who invaded Corydon in 1863 and fought the only Civil War battle on Hoosier soil. It left 12 dead and 35 wounded. The Confederates captured 345 men and rode into Corydon, where they operated more like circus performers than disciplined soldiers.

Corydon is headquarters of the 7.7-mile Louisville, New Albany and Corydon Railroad, historically the state's second shortest independent road. In keeping with the region's self-reliant traditions, the builders forded Little Indian Creek and trains still cross without benefit of bridge. Like many other short-line railroads, during the '70s, the Corydon ventured into the freight-car-leasing business and more than 750 units carried the obscure road's name across the length and breadth of America. When the recession arrived and de-

mand fell, dozens of idle cars came home to Corydon to await better days. A stub switch, relic of an earlier day, survives in the railroad yards.

In the Corydon area, the Ohio carves its most tortuous path, heading variously to every point of the compass. At Leavenworth, the view from the bluff is unsurpassed as the river makes a surprising change of direction and is swung around to an abrupt about face. But go back to the great Ohio River flood of 1937, and the same beautiful view lay under tens of feet of angry water, sweeping Leavenworth before it as a broom sweeps crumbs from the floor.

When the flood had receded and Leavenworth had dried out, there wasn't much left to return to. The willful strength of the river had nearly obliterated it; so a new town was built 400 feet higher, perched safely on top of the bluff. It was complete with streets, dwellings, stores, and church. A few hardy souls, accustomed to combatting the river's floodtime possessiveness, braved their way back into what little was left of the old town. Yet as a former county seat and thriving river port, Leavenworth no longer existed. Elsewhere, the flood left a legacy of sturdy walls that sprang up to protect Lawrenceburg, the three Falls cities, Cannelton, Tell City, and Evansville.

Indiana's only Civil War naval encounter occurred upstream from Leavenworth. A Confederate detachment under Capt. Thomas H.

Hines had crossed the Ohio and penetrated northward into Orange County before being discovered. Once identified, they hastily retreated and sought refuge on Blue River Island opposite the mouth of Blue River. They fought briefly against bankside Union forces, but when the gunboat *Izetta* appeared from Leavenworth and fired a single shot from its six-pound cannon, the Confederates quickly surrendered.

Below Leavenworth, something bordering on fantasy is happening today. Whole pockets of Hoosierdom have been set apart and cut off from the present as if controlled by a time machine. Once the steamboat era had passed, they became the towns that time forgot—Fredonia, Cape Sandy, Alton, Magnet, Derby, and Rome. Two were early county seats. All were ports. One shipped about 25,000 pounds of pork annually from its packinghouse. Now scattered buildings in the grand style look totally out of place among the vacant lots and simple dwellings that surround them.

Beyond the next bend lie Cannelton and its sister, Tell City. Cannelton has several distinctions. The first company chartered to mine Indiana coal dug into the steep hills behind the town. The Indiana Cotton Mills, its huge Romanesque building now idle and awaiting rescue, was the state's largest industry after it was completed in 1849. General Lafayette's boat was wrecked nearby in 1825. A midair explosion killed 63 in a Northwest Airlines plane a few miles upstream in 1960.

Tell City did not grow from the river's seedbed as did the other towns. It appeared full-blown in 1858 when Swiss colonists from Cincinnati laid out an attractive town of wide streets and gave them such classic names as Schiller, Mozart, Pestalozzi, and Gutenberg. Germans followed the Swiss, but the apple pierced by an arrow, for the legendary William Tell, remained the community trademark, appearing in such diverse places as the newspaper's masthead, the bank, and the once-thriving William Tell Hotel. The city is known as the home of the sprawling Tell City Chair Company, which keeps America rocking, and for its pretzels, plywood, electric motors, and barges.

Not far below Tell City, the tiny Anderson River enters the Ohio near the old port town of Troy. This is the Lincoln country. The family, migrating from Kentucky, crossed the Ohio here and young Abe later operated a ferry across the Anderson's mouth. Not far downstream, at Rockport, Lincoln began his famous voyage to New Orleans. Legend has it that he first saw slavery then and vowed to hit it hard if he ever was given the opportunity.

Industrialization sets in once more. A large electric generating station of the Indiana and Michigan Electric Company was placed on line in 1984 at Rockport, and the sprawling Aluminum Company of America (ALCOA) smelter covers a vast acreage near Yankeetown. Several million tons of coal annually find their way to river barges from the mines of Warrick County, Indiana's No. 1 producer.

Newburgh, one of the oldest cities in the "pocket" area and eastern gateway to Evansville, clings like a halyard to the river's steep hills. Some of its buildings, now mellowed by time, looked down on the first of three Confederate raids onto Indiana soil.

Evansville, the commercial, cultural, and financial hub of a three-state area, is the lower river's principal city. It is German through and through. Frontiersman Hugh McGary chose it as a townsite in 1812 and its growth surged during the 1850s, '60s and '80s. It became an important rail center, terminus of that wondrous hand-dug ditch, the 464-mile Wabash and Erie Canal down from Lake Erie, and an interurban hub that featured a private ferry for the trip to Henderson, Kentucky.

Miners dug coal beneath its streets and manufacturing came early but it cast a changing shadow: first, saw mills and furniture, then automobiles, and finally so many refrigerators that Evansvillians liked to think of their city as the ice cube capital of the world. Manufacturing now has diversified into air conditioning, machinery, household appliances, plastics, foods, furniture components, closures, and nutritional products.

Nearly half a thousand years before McGary established the modern city, Mound Builders, those prehistoric ancestors of contemporary Indians, found the river equally attractive. They built a vast complex near what is now the eastern edge of the city, throwing up mysterious mounds and leaving fascinating remains of their village life. The Indiana Historical Society and Eli Lilly rescued it in 1938, and it is now preserved and interpreted as the Angel Mounds State Memorial.

Ever mindful of its heritage, Evansville has preserved the best of its fascinating architecture in no less than four historic districts. Its Museum of Arts and Sciences warrants a visit and its Zoo houses a startling number of exotic animals. It also has a nature sanctuary of "original" trees. The University of Evansville and University of Southern Indiana provide higher education.

Through Evansville's many changes, the river remains constant. It continues to lap at the city's feet, bringing commerce, recreation, and sometimes destruction. People, business, industries marched across the stage, but the river remained, as immutable as the Rock of Gibraltar.

Ever since history began, Ohio River dwellers have felt the urge to control the river's flow or at least to impose some sort of disci-

pline on its vagaries. By 1929, man's ingenuity had tamed the river through a system of forty-six locks and dams which maintained a nine-foot channel and guaranteed a year-round flow sufficient to move coal, grain, steel, fuel, and other bulk commodities. It sometimes was described as the "world's greatest engineering feat." Prior to completion, boats often were hung up on sandbars or snagged by submerged debris. Many an unlucky vessel lies in the graveyard that is the river's bottom. River traffic increased so dramatically that terms like "The American Ruhr" and "The Industrial Heartland" were applied to the rapidly industrializing valley, and tonnage on this wide, deep, majestic bearer of burdens grew to astronomical proportions. In 1981, tow boats pushed barges carrying 150,391,000 tons of shipping up and down the river's placid surface. This translated into 35,625,809,000-ton miles.

The U.S. Army Corps of Engineers, therefore, needed no persuasion to construct nineteen high dams to replace most of the original structures. The river has survived these great changes which not only enabled the use of larger tows but raised the water level so that placid creeks and minor rivulets were converted into vast bays and inlets. The new dams are located near Markland, Cannelton, and Newburgh, and Uniontown (Ky.), and as they were completed, engi-

*Left to right*: Mead Johnson Terminal, a river-rail-truck terminal on the Ohio River, Evansville, 1945. ◦§Southwind Maritime Centre, Mt. Vernon, Indiana's first riverport. ◦§Indiana's first state house, Corydon.

neers blasted out of the water the lower dams that stood near Rising Sun, Markland, New Boston, Leavenworth, Rome, Owensboro (Ky.), Newburgh, Henderson (Ky.), and Uniontown (Ky.).

Since Mead, Johnson & Co. at Evansville opened a rail-river terminal as the 1929 canalization was completed, others have taken the cue and riverports now exist or are in the planning stage at numerous points. The busiest is the state's Southwind Maritime Centre near Mt. Vernon, where coal, grain, and other commodities flow by land in a never-ending stream to barges waiting to complete the journeys. Traffic has outpaced projections and the terminal, opened in 1977, shipped 3,538,421 tons in 1981. Mt. Vernon also has manufacturers which produce chemicals, roofing, and agricultural products. The state also is planning a terminal at Jeffersonville, the city of Madison Port Authority is attempting to develop a river-rail terminal that will assure the future of the city-operated Madison Railroad and two barge terminals are planned at Utica, upstream from Jeffersonville. A large coal-loading dock is busy dumping coal from railcars near Yankeetown.

Pollution began to jeopardize the Ohio's waters as early as the turn of the century, and as cities grew and industry and coal mining expanded, the problem intensified. In 1948, eight basin states signed the Ohio River Valley Water Sanitation Compact to coordinate water quality improvement efforts. Significant progress has been made since that time.

The prosperity born of navigation has been a mixed blessing. The Ohio is no longer considered a river in the classic sense but rather as a series of connected lakes which provide a highway for barges and a cooling water source that encourages power generating plants to emerge like mushrooms after a spring rain. Predictably, conservationists took to the warpath as smokestacks arose at nearly a dozen locations scattered from Aurora to Mt. Vernon. But nothing stirred them like the controversial nuclear generating plant projected at Marble Hill below Madison. Marches, protests, finger pointing, and whistle blowing impeded progress, caused blood pressures to rise precipitously, names to be shouted stridently, and construction to be halted intermittently until the project was abandoned after $2.3 billion of an estimated $7.7 billion had been expended.

In a day when "progress" is measured in kilowatts just as it is measured in miles of paved highway, the Ohio has undergone great change, but the basic beauty discovered by the Iroquois Indians and the French explorers remains in the serrated hills and the winding, shimmering thread of water.

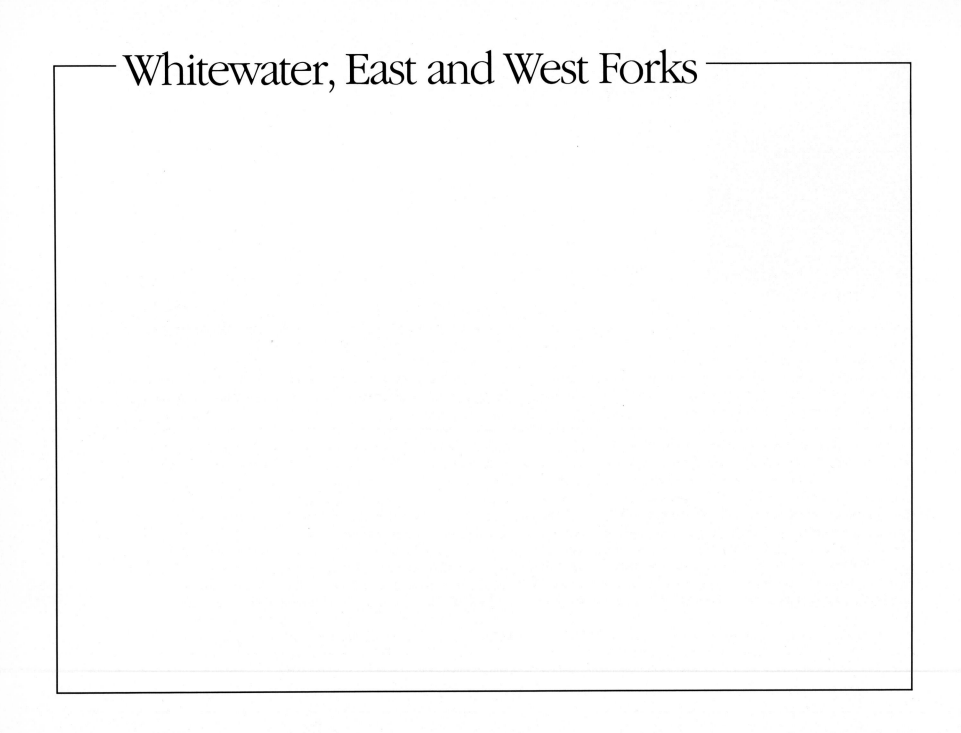

# Whitewater, East and West Forks

There is something about the majestic, wooded hills of the Whitewater Valley that draws men to them as a magnet attracts steel filings. It has been thus for centuries, going back to the earliest Indians who lived in the valley and left burial mounds behind them on the highest, most scenic hills. The Whitewater also attracted modern men who found it a convenient pathway to the state's unsettled interior where they could find a new home in the wilderness, a refuge for the seeker of social justice, or a haven for the outspoken exponent of free speech and thought. To others it has been a political springboard or a creative inspiration for art and literature.

To all of them the valley has been a place of great and enduring natural beauty, a small area that shaped men and events all out of proportion to its size. It is an old valley—geologically, architecturally, commercially, and culturally. The river is a river apart, differing from any other in Indiana. It is the state's swiftest flowing stream, rising on its highest land.

Unlike most rivers, whose characteristics differ from one locality to the next, the Whitewater Valley is a cohesive unit bound together by its scenery, the national origins of its people, and its transportation and commerce. To speak of any part of the valley is to speak of the whole. The earliest settlers, seeking to migrate beyond the Ohio River, found the valley an inviting notch through the forbidding hills that form the state's southern boundary. Before 1800, which is nearly the beginning as Indiana reckons time, men were settling in the valley.

The river they followed northward descended directly from the glaciers which had covered the Midwest 15,000 years earlier. As the warming sun caused it to shrink, the great ice sheet sprouted huge streams that flowed away toward the present Ohio River. Among these were the two forks of the Whitewater—East and West—which flow in deep, parallel valleys scarcely ten miles apart until they reach Brookville. Here they unite and, dashing over a shallow, rocky bed, speed toward the Great Miami River, which the Whitewater enters only a few miles above the former's junction with the Ohio River.

Although a peek up the valley disclosed a long, green trough sloping between the crouching hills, the early settlers found the river deceptively treacherous. Then, as now, it was swift, shallow, rocky, often narrow, and subject to destructive flash flooding. Yet it was easier to travel through the hills than over them and settlers quickly filled the valley from mouth to source. The influx was so great that by 1820 Wayne was Indiana's most populous county, by 1840 Richmond was Indiana's fourth largest city, and by 1850 Wayne was the leading manufacturing county.

The countryside was full of wonder to the settlers who migrated upstream. It was pleasing country and they could overlook the fact that only a thin mantle of soil sometimes covered the Ordovician bedrock, oldest exposed deposits in the state. Kentucky farmers, accustomed to scratching their existence from rocky ground, arrived first, followed by Carolinians, both North and South. It was one of the great migrations of America.

These people were the first of three groups to fill the valley. Their arrival marked the beginning of the Quaker migration that moved like a spring tide up the river, denuding North Carolina of their denomination and enabling Richmond to replace Philadelphia as the orthodox Quaker capital of the United States. As a result, the Indiana Yearly Meeting of Friends came to extend from western Ohio to the Pacific Ocean and for thirty-seven years Richmond was its headquarters. The Quakers were pacifistic, conscientious, and outspoken. As early as the War of 1812 some of their members had been fined and suffered seizure of property for refusing to serve in the

The Whitewater Canal (now a state
memorial) was once Metamora's
main street.

armed forces, but they stood by their beliefs and broadcast them boldly and fearlessly.

Most Quakers migrated in search of greater economic opportunity, but others so intensely loathed slavery that they packed their belongings, loaded them on wagons, and set out for Indiana as for a promised land. One of these was Levi Coffin, known as the president of the Underground Railroad. Coffin settled in what is now Fountain City, where he would shelter in his home at least 2,000 runaway slaves as they were being surreptitiously spirited northward to freedom. Many a day his house, which is now a state memorial, echoed to the shouts of angry slaveowners in hot pursuit of human property which had scarcely moved out of sight in hay wagons or other camouflaged vehicles.

Following the Quakers, the Germans became the second great group to settle in the Whitewater Valley. The Irish followed, many of them arriving as canal laborers. The Germans left an indelible imprint on the valley with their many villages which clustered about high-steepled churches in the European manner. Oldenburg in southwestern Franklin County is the most notable. Its substantial homes stand close to the quiet streets and the spires of its numerous massive buildings pierce the sky and can be seen for miles around. Down through the years, not only the Holy Family Church but the convent, academy, and monastery have served a population that is nearly 100 percent German Catholic.

With such a large population in the valley, the demand arose for improved transportation. As early as 1818, two years after Indiana attained statehood, Jacob Whetzel had blazed his famous trail from Laurel on the West Fork of the Whitewater to Waverly on the West Fork of White River. It was probably the first important road into the interior from eastern Indiana, but it did little to solve the problem of valley settlers who desperately needed a satisfactory means of moving their crops out and manufactured goods in.

Completion of the Erie Canal in New York threw the nation into a spasm of canal fever that could be abated only by digging ditches wherever the clamor arose. As early as 1823 men had talked of a canal down the Whitewater Valley, and a few years later when the National Road was surveyed across the East Fork at Richmond and the West Fork at Cambridge City, visions arose of a vital travel junction that would give access to all directions.

Great joy swept the valley in 1836 when Hoosiers committed themselves to a vast $13,000,000 state internal improvements program geared mostly to canals. Because of the area's large population, the Whitewater Canal work began first, and within three years boats entered Brookville.

*Left to right*: Once vital transportation systems have now become tourist attractions: The Whitewater Canal, with its rare covered bridge aqueduct, here parallels an abandoned New York Central branch, now used as a seasonal steam line. ◄§Levi Coffin sheltered many fugitives in his home at Fountain City, a station on the Underground Railroad.

Yet all was not well. The overly ambitious program, which represented one-sixth of the state's wealth, soon ground to a halt, and the Whitewater Canal was completed only after it had been turned over to private companies which extended it to Cambridge City and Hagerstown. Lawrenceburg was the Ohio River terminal, although the state of Ohio later built a branch to Cincinnati. Backers of an East Fork canal from Richmond to Brookville fortunately learned from the experience and stopped digging before they impoverished themselves.

At best the canal was a wandering ditch that followed the base of the hills for a while, then would shoot off, in a straight line across level bottomlands, only to reappear along the hills where it was least expected. It skirted some towns, ran adjacent to the main streets of others, curved with the riverbank, and took its water supply from likely locations along the stream.

The planners had not allowed for the quirks of the mischievous river. Almost as quickly as they built, floods washed out banks, carried away aqueducts, destroyed locks, and breached dams. The river wore out the patience of legislators. It stranded the hopes and vessels of boaters. Despite every effort to tame it, the encircling, tumbling, contrary river dashed on, destructively unsubdued.

Transportation was still needed by the valley, and as the seventy-six-mile canal lay dying, progress brought that new annihilator of space, the railroad. Purchasing the canal as the Civil War ended, the Whitewater Valley Railroad laid its tracks on the towpath. Hopes ran high for the railroad, just as they had for the canal. For a time it contributed to a through passenger service between Fort Wayne and Cincinnati, then it degenerated into a Cincinnati commuter service and finally into a Penn-Central freight line connecting Connersville's numerous industries with Cincinnati. Now the upper section is a steam-operated tourist line that carries eager passengers through some of Indiana's most beautiful scenery. Once again it is named the Whitewater Valley Railroad. The lower section is an independent freight line that connects Brookville industries with Cincinnati. The little town of Milton illustrates the transportation dreams of the valley. At various times it has been connected to Cambridge City, less than two miles distant, by the canal, two railroads, and an interurban line that ran only to that city.

Although the two largest cities, Richmond and Connersville, stand as gateways to the valley, Brookville, at the junction of the forks, is more typically a Whitewater town. Perched on a narrow, scenic ridge between the two rivers, it retains the flavor and appearance of its earlier days. Long before most of Indiana had been cleared of forests, it was an important commercial and banking center and location of a government land office.

Bustling with activity, Brookville attracted an amazing array of talented men. The roster of great names here is a long one, including three successive governors who headed the state from 1825 to 1840, two successive U.S. senators, and numerous state supreme court justices and U.S. representatives. President Ulysses S. Grant chose a postmaster-general, James N. Tyner, from Brookville, and the Prohibition party named a presidential candidate, John P. St. John, who was carrying on the Whitewater tradition of embracing social causes when he proposed the first constitutional prohibition of liquor.

Author Lew Wallace was born at Brookville, and artists T. C. Steele and J. Ottis Adams settled there as they re-created some of Indiana's best landscapes on canvas. Brookville College, founded before the Civil War, was one of the state's earliest higher education institutions, and Little Cedar Grove Baptist Church is Indiana's oldest church standing on its original site. Education and religion, as well as arts and letters, were rooted early in the valley.

Although Brookville has remained primarily an agricultural community, Connersville became an important industrial city and produced at least ten makes of automobiles, including the Auburn, Cord, and Lexington. After the auto industry vanished, it became known for the manufacture of home appliances, automotive parts, and industrial equipment. The town was founded by John Conner,

who operated a trading post in the Whitewater Valley after coming to Indiana with the Delaware Indians. He was a state senator in the first General Assembly that met at Corydon and also served as a state representative in the first General Assembly that met at Indianapolis.

Richmond, standing astride the National Road and near the East Fork headwaters, has been the principal city of the valley since it was founded as Cox's Settlement and attracted the Quakers of North Carolina. The cultural fountainhead of the valley is Earlham College, which the Quakers established in 1847.

The Whitewater, shallow, rocky, and tumbling, remains an invitation to adventure. The pioneer who braved its wilderness is gone, succeeded by the canoeist who seeks thrills and spills on the state's swiftest stream. The river winds and folds back on itself like a ribbon, trying the limits of its prison and touching first one wall and then the other while scooping out its own flat bed in the glacial fill.

As in the early years, the wild beauty of the panorama in the Whitewater Valley appeals to every nature lover. In contrast to the rugged beauty of Brown County, the scenery has a settled, sedate look. Little alpine valleys crown many hills; orderly forests clothe others. Hoosiers have preserved some of the best scenery at 1,710-acre Whitewater State Park near Liberty, where they absorb its beauty, and at Mary Gray Bird Sanctuary near Connersville, where they enjoy its wildlife. A fourteen-mile canal section between Laurel and Brookville, restored as a state memorial, once again flows past the mill at Metamora and carries visitors on a canalboat replica through the fascinating covered bridge aqueduct. A village from canal days, Metamora is now given over to shops which reflect that earlier era when the canal and the railroad successively were the main street. It lies between two of the many locks of tailored stone that line the length of the valley.

The years have been good to the Whitewater Valley. Now that I-74 has removed through traffic from U.S. 52, there is time to view leisurely some of its wonders. Spires of churches built in the European manner still dot the lower valley, and the Little Cedar Grove Baptist Church is adequately designated and well cared for. Federal-style and stately Greek revival homes remain the hallmark of the valley, testifying to the affluence of early settlers. Centerville, with its row houses and arched entrances, tells the story of an early culture. Richmond, the early manufacturing center which now produces school bus bodies, tools, wiring, closures, and cabinets, along with Connersville, has brought much industry to the valley and provided jobs for its people.

But change has come. The Brookville Reservoir on the East Fork of the Whitewater drowned forever villages such as Fairfield, which gave us Maurice Thompson, author of *Alice of Old Vincennes*, and other notable persons. When the gates clanged shut in 1974, the river's swift flow slowed to a halt and the water spread itself into a $40,000,000 lake which covers 5,260 acres. It is the state's deepest man-made lake, the third largest and at fifteen miles, one of the longest. The dam is designed for flood control, but the roll of thunder still brings apprehension to the people of the valley just as it did in canal days. For thunder means rain, and raging torrents often washed out highways and bridges, breached the feeder dam at Laurel, and left the canal dry. Present and past flow together through the valley, and the river on occasion feels compelled to issue a reminder that it is master of both.

# Land of Lincoln

Patoka

Indiana's third longest completely Hoosier river is a geological blunder and shouldn't exist at all. Its valley is too broad, its flow too small, and its basin too tiny. Most of its course closely parallels a much larger river to which its waters rightfully belong, yet it exerts an influence all out of proportion to its size. This river is the Patoka.

Like the river itself, the name is a puzzle. Some authorities say it derives from Indian words which mean "the crooked river filled with logs" or from the Miami word for "Comanche," a tribe whose members were sometimes taken slaves by the Miami. Other versions attribute the name to an Indian word meaning "How deep?" or to a Fox chief named Pah-ta-ko-to.

The river begins on a narrow, tortuous ridge southeast of Paoli, where a shallow brook tumbles down a grassy hillside. Forming a lonely highway between rows of trees, it flows westward through country alternating sharply between rugged hills and level plains until it reaches the Wabash opposite Mt. Carmel, Illinois, at a point known as Hell's Neck. Its valley varies in width between one and five miles. Its mouth is one mile below that of White River, which crowds the Patoka Valley on the north for more than fifty miles and limits its watershed.

Men who read the rocks say that the Patoka originally was four short, disconnected streams. Three flowed into White River; the fourth entered the Wabash. They would have remained that way except for the glaciers. They came crunching out of the north with all their devastating coldness 300,000 years ago, overspreading most of Indiana. Hundreds of feet high they came, grinding up forests, leveling the land, blocking streams. Rivers and creeks stopped flowing, their waters piling up against the face of the huge ice sheet. One such body, which geologists named Glacial Lake Patoka, backed the water up over northwestern Dubois County and part of Pike County. As the waters rose, they topped low divides which had separated the four Patoka ancestors until they united into a single stream.

When the southern sun checked the glaciers' progress at last and the huge silent task of melting billions of tons of ice was completed, the Patoka flowed westward for nearly 200 miles in a series of tumbled rapids, incredible curves, and placid meanderings. It forms the liquid spine of four counties as it extends a slender, searching finger toward the Wabash, to which it once rushed headlong with little self-control and in a destructive passion. Hemmed in tightly by larger rivers, it drains a basin of only 860 square miles which nowhere exceeds twenty miles in width.

The Patoka's appearance contrasts remarkably in its different stretches. Sometimes it flows through a long green trough between gently terraced or sloping hillsides. Then, with a sudden show of resolution, it batters at stone bluffs whose walls, in their forbidding aloofness, tower like fortresses over the water. Steep palisades and rock-lined gorges are vigorous testimonials to its rugged, determined current. Again, it crosses plains so level that the view is for miles and the sluggish river is impossibly crooked. From start to finish of the Patoka, nature puts on one of her best shows, ranging from the grandeur of towering, 400-foot hills to a sideshow of limestone caverns and grotesque rock formations.

There are still primitive wonders along the Patoka, cherished by those who seek them—the solitudes of its continuing woods, the sounds of its dashings, the awe of its hills, the tangle of its jungle that extends for several miles on either side. Along the upper Patoka, the hills are rugged, the ridges and bluffs steep, and the valleys deeply dissected. Limestone caverns honeycomb the headwaters around Valeene. Tributaries are short and steep with rapid runoff that makes the adolescent Patoka a troublesome youngster. This is a country where the land dominates mankind.

In every direction, the landscape is a sweep of awe-inspiring beauty and luxuriance. The alternation of hill and valley makes for varied and impressive scenery, which is best exemplified near Dubois where beauty takes on one of its more spectacular forms. Approached from the east, the village, with its neat rows of dwellings and towering steeple makes the scene a transplant from Europe. For a moment, it is a world away from the world, charming and dreamlike. In this region, beauty sports her whimsical nature, creating unusual formations such as Pilot Knob and Indian Kitchen; Blue Bird, Raven, Hanging, and Wildcat rocks.

The surroundings change suddenly near Jasper where the river enters the flat bed of Glacial Lake Patoka, which covered dozens of square miles. The stream wriggles across flats underlaid with 150 feet of silt and sand, flowing twenty-seven miles to gain thirteen.

The restrictive hand of the hills again crowd the river before it embarks on a devious route of many windings and bendings, folding back on itself like a ribbon, lying sluggish in the sun. In eastern Gibson County, the way is rugged once again. The ridges are sharp and narrow and their sides slope steeply. One of the best known is Bald Hill which rises 130 feet. Tributaries occupy V-shaped valleys separated by sharp divides and their descents are steep in their upper courses. In its final miles the Patoka flows through the flat Wabash Lowland, a serene pathway between the fresh green of the fields on either bank.

Prior to construction of Patoka Lake, the Patoka was deceptive. Sometimes it had plenty of water for all; other times, in a season of little rain, it failed lamentably in strength, depth, and width. It was a river of mischievous quirks. When the hills gathered up their rainfall and poured it into the tributaries, the Patoka became an arrogant stream of water. There was nothing yielding about it, nothing submissive, nothing that could even be called considerate.

It spread over lush bottomlands like a lake. In Jasper, it closed industries periodically. Circling, contrary, unsubdued, it clawed at bridges and roads, remaining a wild river while civilization stood back in timidity and fear. Onrushing currents roared irresistibly through narrow channels and set stubbornly against rocky ledges, falling back below the riverbanks and sinking into the rich earth with the coming of summer. It was a river strong enough to tear acres from the land and lose them forever in the flood. In a single year the river would crawl past Jasper during an October drought with no perceptible flow, but during an April flood might roar by at 670 million gallons a day. The April deluge at Princeton has been measured at 150 times the October flow.

To meet the Patoka's demand that man spend time and energy to deal with its eccentricities, the U.S. Army Corps of Engineers built Patoka Lake. Orchard and shade trees joined the funeral pyre of bulldozed farm homesteads on more than 27,000 acres between the dam in eastern Dubois County and the headwaters west of Valeene in Orange County. Eighty-eight hundred acres were scrubbed clean and drowned by the time the lake was completed in 1980.

The dam was designed to control the willful strength of the Patoka so that it would never again race through the valley, clawing and rending the land. Early results indicate that it is succeeding and that it will leash forever the fury of the river's springtime floods and prevent the sluggish currents and low water of late summer. As an added bonus there are facilities for fishing, camping, boating, and swimming.

The buffalo first discovered the Patoka country and used it as their favorite route from the western plains to the Kentucky and southern Indiana salt licks. Early travelers told how endless herds of bison broke paths through tangled forests impenetrable to man and how "a salt spot several acres in size was so much trodden down and grubbed up that not a blade of grass can grow and the entire woods are for miles around quite bare."

Recognizing the buffaloes' instinct for following direct lines and the easiest grades, pioneers adapted their path for the first road from Clarksville to Vincennes. They called it the Buffalo Trace, and it became one of early Indiana's most famous thoroughfares. In 1908 when the Southern Railway built a line to tap the rich passenger traffic to French Lick, it used the Buffalo Trace, crossing the Patoka seven times in fourteen miles to keep to the easiest grades.

George Rogers Clark used the trace during his Revolutionary

War expeditions, and by 1800 U.S. mails were hauled over it to Vincennes, the trip requiring four days. Elihu Stout, Indiana's first newspaper publisher, hauled his press and newspaper supplies to Vincennes over the trace. The countryside was beautiful but desolate, and Constantin Volney, a Frenchman who covered the route in 1795, told of journeying 120 miles without seeing a single human habitation or hearing a bird sing, although he made the trip in July. Thirty-five years later, the Lincoln family no doubt used the trace as they emigrated from Indiana by way of Vincennes to Illinois.

During the Civil War Captain Thomas H. Hines led a band of Confederate raiders to the Patoka at Valeene. Hines's men were well on their way north, posing as Home Guards, when some sharp-eyed Valeenian spread the alarm. The raiders were forced into headlong retreat and pursued south where they were captured on an Ohio River island.

Pioneers found the Patoka a strange combination of contrasting moods. In its upper, adolescent reaches a clear, brawling, boulder-strewn hill-country stream, it drops more than 300 feet during the first twenty-five restless miles of its life, flowing through superb but often hostile land. But its lower course is so crooked that anyone attempting to lie along its banks would risk developing curvature of the spine. West of Winslow, the muddy meanderer wanders like a lost child and when it was dredged and straightened in the 1920s, a thirty-seven-mile channel was reduced to eighteen simply by cutting through the loops on a straight line. Prior to its straightening, the lower Patoka was so stagnant and unhealthy that John Collett, assistant state geologist, described it as "naturally a foul, stinking, rotten river—in summer a solution of decaying vegetable matter . . . thick enough to bear up small animals."

Despite the hazards of its twisting course and the thickness of its surface, the Patoka was the pioneer's great water highway, and each season hundreds of tons of flour, pork, grain, hides, staves, and vegetables traveled the moody, muddy waters on flatboats. Perils of the Patoka were so numerous that a fast trip to the Wabash from the head of navigation at the boat-building center of Jasper required five days. Steamboats churned the water as far as the town of Patoka, and in a single winter 1,000,000 pounds of pork left the docks there.

Competition arose when the Wabash and Erie Canal, the continent's longest artificial waterway, reached Evansville from Toledo, Ohio, in 1853. It drained off the Patoka's westbound tonnage and turned it south, radiating dreams of prosperity that rivaled those of a western gold rush. Towns such as Dongola sprang up, complete with public square and six-lane streets, but died with the canal and all traces disappeared.

*Left to right*: Surface coal pits and tipples are found in Pike County. ∾Dubois County is a national leader in turkey production.

In addition to carrying boats, the Patoka also floated logs from the dense forests of Dubois and Pike counties to the hungry sawmills that whirred along its banks. From Newton Stewart in the headwaters to Patoka near the Wabash River, mill wheels creaked and groaned. Dubois, Winslow, and Jasper were water-powered milling centers. Jasper's Enlow mill came to bask in the fame of an early patron, Abraham Lincoln, and it survived until quite recently. A desk exists that Abe's father made to pay a milling debt. The mills are gone, but that other reminder of pioneer days—the covered timber bridge—remains. One still carries traffic across the Patoka, near Wheeling.

Since its early days the Patoka country has been a blend of North and South, Europe and America. Tobacco fields once were sprinkled through southern Dubois County at the same time vast cornfields, shimmering in the heat of summer, supplied a distillery along the river. Negroes settled the village of Lyles, but it was Germans who mingled with Kentuckians to settle the middle Patoka country. They chose a county named for a Frenchman, Toussaint Dubois, and settled largely in Jasper, which had grabbed the courthouse from poorly located Portersville.

The Germans turned their woodworking skills loose on the region's vast forests, and soon established so many furniture factories that Jasper proclaims itself the "Nation's Wood Office Furniture Capi-

tal." Rambling brick buildings of more than two dozen factories edge the city, turning out a prolific number of products ranging from school to executive's desks, from chairs to pianos, and from veneers to kitchen cabinets. More than twenty additional woodworking plants are scattered throughout Dubois County, mostly at Huntingburg and Ferdinand, but also at such unlikely villages as St. Anthony and Dubois. Jasper names like Gramelspacher, Uebelhor, Stenftenagel, Sermersheim, Schneider, and Schwartz vividly testify to the community's German traditions, while the presence of the German-American Bank reminds visitors that the entire background is predominantly European. A local dialect, spoken by older residents and understood by nearly everyone is called "Jasper Dutch."

Predominantly Catholic, Jasperites point to St. Joseph's Church and proudly describe the parish as the largest in central and southern Indiana. In earlier days, Catholic orders also operated Jasper College and St. Benedict at nearby Ferdinand. The magnificent buildings of the Convent of the Immaculate Conception continue to rise in hilltop splendor at Ferdinand. Vincennes University now operates a regional campus at Jasper, and farther down the river the Baptist-supported Oakland City College operates in its namesake community.

Jasper, whose cleanliness is obvious, achieved a degree of dis-

tinction when it became the nation's first city to outlaw the garbage can. Since 1949, long before it was fashionable to battle pollution, every new or remodeled home has been required to have a sink disposer. Husbands who had been carefully trained to carry garbage pails to the curbs sighed with relief when the rumble of the disposer replaced the rattle of can lids.

Ferdinand, which grew up without a railroad, displayed typical German industry when it constructed its own to connect with the Southern Railway at Huntingburg, 6.4 miles away. Aptly named The Ferdinand Railroad, it is historically the shortest independently owned line in Indiana.

Industrious Dubois County farmers began draining the Patoka's swamps about 1850, including part of the 700-acre Buffalo Pond. By 1890 Germans were farming much of the county. Some farmers eventually wearied of attempting to scratch a living from the hillsides and turned to poultry farming with gratifying results. A recent study placed Dubois County eighteenth in the nation in turkey production, fifty-third in total value of poultry products, and eighty-seventh in hogs sold.

Farther downstream, watermelons grow so thick on the sandy soils that Gibson County became the nation's fiftieth ranking producer. Oil also has gushed from beneath the valley floor from Oak-land City to the Wabash, bringing the corn and watermelon growers an additional cash crop.

Scattered ore deposits brought early hopes of iron mining and gave such an unlikely name as "Iron Mountain" to an area northeast of Jasper. But the big wealth beneath the soil lay in coal beds which underlie the valley from Dubois to Princeton. Shafts, which once contaminated the river with their foul discharge, were followed by strip mines, which left bare and gutted hillsides in their wake. Conservation and anti-pollution practices now lend more respectability to the industry, which produced nearly 6 million tons from Indiana's second-ranking Pike County in 1984 and 654,542 tons from Dubois County. Efforts have been under way recently to revive the industry at Princeton, seat of Gibson County, which was once an important coal producer and home of King's Station, the state's largest underground mine.

Much of the Patoka country remains in its wild state, and near Winslow it has been preserved in the 2,914-acre Pike County State Forest and the 6,889-acre Patoka State Fish and Wildlife Area. Drainage, channeling, and impoundment have left their mark on the Patoka, but much of the valley's best is being preserved in its natural state.

Anderson

Few rivers in the world are as much the property of one man as is southern Indiana's scenic Anderson River. Like New Salem, Springfield, and Hodgenville, the Anderson belongs to Abraham Lincoln and it bears the stamp of his great, rugged character and his independent spirit.

After the Lincoln family left Kentucky, they first trod Indiana soil at the mouth of the Anderson. When they settled in their new home, they were near the Anderson Valley. When Thomas Lincoln and his young son, Abe, took grain to be ground, they went to a mill powered by the Anderson. And when Abe launched his first business venture, it was at the mouth of the Anderson. His first taste of legal action arose from an incident there.

Leaving Hardin County, Kentucky, in 1816, the Lincolns traveled by wagon toward the Ohio River, where they looked across that wide stream to the promised land of Indiana. Near this point, a tiny river thrust itself into the Ohio from the Indiana side. One hundred feet wide and fifteen feet deep near its mouth, it began its race to the Ohio twenty-five crow-flown miles to the north, perhaps twice that far by river, in an obscure, tangled ravine in western Crawford County. An extremely short river by Indiana standards, a narrow river and a shallow river, it is for much of the year a poor trickle of water. Yet it has cut a deep swath before it as it makes its way south, tumbling restlessly over a rock-strewn bed backed by wooded hills of primitive, unspoiled beauty.

Troy, at the mouth of the Anderson, was the Perry County seat during the Lincolns' first years in Indiana, and young Abe gravitated there, taking a job at the age of seventeen. With two friends, he cut wood for passing Ohio River steamers, receiving 25 cents a cord, which sometimes was paid in merchandise. Nine yards of cloth he once received contributed to the first white shirt Lincoln ever wore.

Not far from the place where Lincoln cut cordwood, James Taylor operated a ferry across the Anderson. Taylor offered the muscular young Abe a job as ferryman and he spent the summer setting travelers across the stream for 6¼ cents apiece. He also slaughtered livestock for Taylor—a job he detested—for 31 cents a day.

Lincoln used a flatboat to ferry his passengers, along with their teams or livestock, and powered it by pulling on a cable anchored to trees on the bank and run through pulleys on the ends of the boat.

When traffic was light, he used a rowboat. As an added service, the enterprising Lincoln carried passengers to midstream in the Ohio to meet passing steamboats and on one occasion his two passengers each tossed him a half-dollar for fare.

The incident stamped a lifelong impression on the teen-aged Lincoln and years afterward he related at a cabinet meeting how the fare was beyond all expectation; he had never before seen so much money. But as he contemplated his good fortune, one coin slipped from his grasp and sank into the water. "This," he told William H. Seward, his Secretary of State, "was a most important incident in my life. I can see the quivering and shivering of that half dollar yet as it sank out of sight."

Lincoln's enterprise also brought him face to face with the law and into his first legal action. Who was the defendant? Abraham Lincoln. Two Kentucky brothers named Dill held an Ohio River ferry license near the mouth of the Anderson. When Lincoln answered the ferry bell on the Kentucky side, they attacked him and attempted to duck him in the river. A fistfight followed and Lincoln was taken into court charged with operating a ferry without a license. Lincoln argued successfully in his own defense that he did not set passengers across the river, but only halfway, meeting boats in midstream and, therefore, did not operate a ferry. The judge, impressed with Lincoln's handling of his own defense, acquitted him and then urged that he study law.

Lincoln's storytelling talent was nurtured at the Anderson ferry, and he founded a reputation there that stayed with him his entire life. At Troy, which was the area's social and business center, he would often be encircled by children listening intently while he recited stories from *Aesop's Fables* and other books he was known to have read as a Hoosier youth.

At age nineteen, Lincoln and a companion loaded produce aboard a flatboat at Rockport and started down river for New Orleans about the end of December, undaunted by the prospect of winter's low temperature. For the first time he saw slavery in the Deep South and legend has it that he declared, "If I ever have a chance to hit it, I'll hit it hard."

The ground Lincoln trod as a boy is well memorialized. The 1,747-acre Lincoln State Park and the Lincoln Boyhood National Me-

morial, both adjoining Lincoln City, include a replica of the Lincoln cabin hearth, the graves of Lincoln's mother and sister, and a Baptist church built on the site where the Lincoln family worshiped. An unusual Trail of Stones presents the Lincoln biography from the birthplace cabin at Hodgenville, Kentucky, to his tomb in Springfield, Illinois. Each authentic and set firmly in concrete, they form a wooded trail that inspires the awe due a great president. The park provides campgrounds, hiking, and bicycle trails and lakes for swimming, fishing, and boating.

Although Troy no longer is the county seat, it wears a look that could be considered similar to Lincoln's day. Stone buildings remaining along the river look much as they did when Troy was an important river port. Across the Anderson, part of the Taylor farm was dedicated in 1939 as the Lincoln Ferry Park to perpetuate the memory of the pioneer youth who worked there.

As the years passed, life took on a pattern in the Anderson Valley—a pattern of small clearings in the flat river bottoms, of long, laborious days tuned to the slow change of the seasons, of tobacco to be cultivated, grain to be harvested and wagons transporting it to Huffman's mill, about ten miles up the river. The Lincolns, father and son, used both Huffman's mill, which was closer to their farm, and the Enlow mill on the Patoka. Huffman's mill was established in 1815,

the year before the Lincolns arrived in Indiana. The mill is long gone, but a rambling southern-style house with a two-story gallery marks the site where the Lincolns stayed overnight on their trips to the mill.

The last remaining covered bridge on the Anderson, built in 1864, stands at the mill site, forming a physical link with the president's lifetime. The river in summer is narrow and tranquil, barely moving through a lane of trees whose leafy branches meet overhead. Continuing upstream, the alternation between the wide, flat bottomlands and the high, bold line of hills that elbow close to the river make for varied and splendid scenery.

Suddenly there is St. Meinrad, which gives the visitor the startling impression that he has penetrated into a foreign world. Although St. Meinrad is a village, established along the river in 1861, it is also an archabbey, which had been established seven years earlier by Benedictine monks. The archabbey stands in the best European tradition on the crown of one of Spencer County's cone-shaped hills. The drive winds up the hill in a series of switchbacks and the massive sandstone Romanesque buildings, topped with spires and turrets like a medieval fortress, swing into view. It is said that Benedictines love the mountaintops—they're the monks who made famous St. Bernard dogs with brandy casks—and when they came to Indiana they chose the best the state had to offer in mountaintop real estate.

Monks laboring in nearby quarries, built the original structures.

The archabbey is a self-sustaining city and many trades are carried on within the walls. The brothers operate carpenter, blacksmith, shoe, and tailor shops and a printing plant which employs up to 300 persons. Products of the monastery's dairy, meat packing plant, bakery, farm, and forest also serve the 310 students and their faculty in the liberal arts college and the seminary. A $10,000,000 expansion, completed in 1983, consists of a triangular-shaped monastery and a library inserted in the hillside. With traditional attention to self-sufficiency, the monks have converted its flat roof into a garden. St. Meinrad at one time operated its own coal mine, one of many along the Anderson. Iron oxide, used in the manufacture of paint at nearby Ferdinand, also was a mineral product of the valley.

Midway between St. Meinrad and the Lincoln homesite, the never-never village of Santa Claus grew up in the rolling Spencer County hills. The story is that the villagers applied for a post-office under the name of Santa Fe, which the government rejected because of a duplication. A town meeting held during the Christmas season brought the suggestion of "Santa Claus," and that's how Santa Claus came to southern Indiana's hills.

The village eventually became the processing point for the nation's Christmas mail, and in time a park, Candy Castle, Enchanted Forest and Wishing Well, all under the pleasant eye of a huge Santa statue, gave the village a year-round purpose. A newer development, however, moved Santa Claus Land down the highway a short distance, where not only is the mail dispatched, but an amusement park and replicas of fairy tale scenes dear to a child's heart were developed.

Back at the river, the Anderson pushes among nameless folds in the hills as it descends from its wilderness source. Geography and history combine to slow the time scale of the region. The stream is a tiny trickle now, since few tributaries share its progress south. The country grows progressively wilder. There is much forest, few cultivated fields. Farmhouses are sparse and scattered. Hills are long, steep, and frequent. Trees snuggle up to the rural roadside, casting shadows on a summer day that interlace with splotches of sunshine.

More than 7,600 acres along the upper Anderson now form the Ferdinand State Forest, which provides water recreation, picnicking and camping facilities. Above the State Forest, the Anderson flows through a remote valley, far wider than required by the present hesitant stream. Finally it leads to an embankment of the Southern Railway. A steep, high, cinder-covered fill crosses the head of a deep ravine. From its foot, in a tangle of trees, brush, and briars flow the most remote waters of the Anderson. The scene is as untamed as the Anderson country Lincoln knew.

# Rivers of the Heartland

# White, East and West Forks

When the General Assembly appointed ten men in 1820 to locate a new state capital, they met in central Indiana to search for a river. Rivers were immensely more important in those days. They were the bright wedges which carried civilization into the uncharted forests. They were the first highways, and people moved with them, not across them as they do today. They gave men power to use, and they created trade. The new capital, obviously, had to stand on a riverbank.

Finding a qualified stream was no problem. White River—the Wapihani of the Indians—flowed diagonally across the open-to-settlement portion of Indiana. Gliding quietly past the doorstep of William Conner's trading post near Noblesville, where the commission met, it could not escape their attention. The search for the new capital site quickly resolved itself into finding the most suitable location on White River. For nearly forty miles the commission inspected the riverbank seeking the most advantageous site. Finally, they found it. They located the capital where Fall Creek entered the river. It was the geographical pivot of the state, and in time it would become the political, social, cultural, recreational, financial, commercial, and transportation center as well.

Believing the river to be navigable, the commissioners retired, confident that they had placed the capital on a water highway that would stimulate its growth and extend its influence. But the majestic waterway envisioned by the commissioners was not to be, for the White was navigable only on paper, not in fact, and the few steamboats that would dare to churn its waters were halted abruptly, sometimes disastrously, by the caprices of the anemic stream.

Yet the commissioners had chosen better than they knew. For the White River typifies Indiana, more so, perhaps, than the Wabash. It is the chain that binds the rural to the urban, the farm to the factory, and the fringes of Indiana to its heartland. It is a workhorse river: a river of power, industry, water supply, and abundance. The White River is indeed Hoosierdom's capital river. Four of the state's ten largest cities lie within its basin, as did the U.S. Center of Population from 1890 to 1930.

White River, in reality, is not a single stream, but twins, and they have much in common. Headwaters of both forks rise in the eastern Indiana plateau country, not far from the Ohio state line. West Fork, after some hesitation about the direction it will take, heads west, then southwest, eventually linking the industrial cities of Anderson and Muncie with the awakening giant that is Indianapolis. East Fork, on the other hand, immediately flows southwest, and by nomenclature rather than geography its source is considered to be the junction of Driftwood and Flat Rock rivers at Columbus. Where Big Blue River and Sugar Creek meet, the river that flows south is named Driftwood. Geographers argued for years that Big Blue River actually is the upper East Fork of White River, but local custom in names has prevailed notwithstanding their contentions.

Although West Fork is longer, it drains a smaller basin. Yet it is more visible because central Indiana's three largest cities—Indianapolis, Muncie, and Anderson—lie along its banks and Indianapolis is moving to spotlight the river in a sort of permanent world's fair to be called White River Park. West Fork flows 353 miles; East Fork more than 300 from the Big Blue River headwaters, or 203 if local nomenclature prevails. From their junction near Petersburg, they flow another 50 miles to the Wabash. West Fork collects rainfall from 5,300 square miles; East Fork from 5,700. Together, they drain nearly one-third of Indiana and they take their waters from its heartland.

West Fork begins as a lazy pastoral stream, sliding over murmuring shallows, gliding past hardwood forests, and winding through prairies and meadows. Cattle drink contentedly from its waters. Grain ripens along its banks. The easy days of its infancy are short-lived, however, for after flowing northward for ten miles, it suddenly runs headlong into the Union City moraine, a glacial-built ridge running halfway across the state. Unable to penetrate this barrier, the river turns abruptly west, bumping against the moraine's edge for more than thirty miles before giving up and turning southwest, never again to do battle with a force so much more powerful than itself.

Shortly beyond its west turn, West Fork arrives at Winchester. The seat of Randolph County lies on the riverbank, a geographical selection pointing up the pioneers' high esteem for its waters and duplicated in nearly every county through which it flows. Both a farm and a factory town, Winchester manufactures glass containers and re-

William Conner House at
Conner Prairie, West Fork
of White River.

lated production equipment in profusion, a reminder of the days when the land blazed with natural gas wells and factories rushed in to utilize the cheap fuel.

Muncie, its neighbor to the west, likewise grew up with the gas boom, riding to fame with Ball Brothers, the fruit jar kings, and a sociological study of the '20s that produced the "Middletown" books and was echoed in a 1982 TV series. In the gas-discovery decade, the population more than doubled. Subsequent growth has brought it to 77,216 which makes it the largest White River city next to Indianapolis and seventh largest in the state.

Although automotive parts and electrical equipment have stolen the industrial spotlight from fruit jars, the pervasive and philanthropic influence of the five Ball Brothers is felt everywhere in Muncie. There is no escape from this fact, whether the impression is gained from a taste of campus life at the mushrooming, 17,600-student Ball State University, the soothing touch of a nurse's hand in Ball Memorial Hospital, a visit to the Ball Department Store, the sight of the Ball family mansions spreading down to White River along Minnetrista Boulevard, or the throbbing sounds of a diesel locomotive on the Ball-owned Muncie and Western Railroad. Railroads are a familiar acquisition with the Balls. George Ball, almost single-

handedly, at one time controlled a $3-billion empire whose rails spread for 23,500 miles through twenty states and one Canadian province. Today it comprises major segments of the Chessie, Norfolk Southern, and other systems.

Long before the white man produced glassware at Muncie, the Indians had found the abundant fish and game of the valley to their liking, as had their ancestors, the Mound Builders. These aboriginal people have left their imprint near Anderson, where huge earthworks as much as 9 feet high and nearly 400 feet in diameter are preserved in Mounds State Park. Anderson, like Muncie, is an automotive city, dominated by General Motors and its parts plants. The city's population is 64,695. The Church of God has its Anderson College and its headquarters located here.

At Noblesville, producer of rubber products and castings, the interurban which once dominated Indiana travel, has made a miniscule revival. One may travel in a restored electric traction car at the Indiana Transportation Museum, which stables a fleet of old-time equipment ready to carry riders seeking fun and nostalgia.

By the time the river reaches the Conner Prairie Pioneer Settlement, where the capital's site was decided, it has widened from the strength of countless brooks and has changed from farming rural to

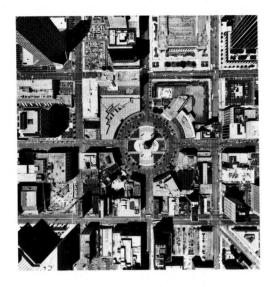

suburban rural. But urbanization also has sapped much of the river's natural beauty as the stream attempts to drain and dilute the waste from city after city. The valley's tributaries are being impounded at a quickening pace in an effort to satisfy the rapidly growing thirst of its cities. A half-dozen major reservoirs supply Indianapolis, Muncie, and Bloomington. To them the White is as much a lifeline as the Nile is to Egypt.

In Indianapolis the West Fork loses its pastoral character completely and becomes a winding thread stitching together sections of the city which calls itself the "Crossroads of America," and once was known as the nation's largest inland city. This is the city that steamboat captains vainly attempted to reach during the early days. One succeeded, but success became a mockery when the *Robert Hanna*, first steamboat to reach the capital, foundered on the return trip and spent the summer lodged sullenly on a sandbar. Had it made the round trip, there might have been no "largest inland city" title.

Since the imposing water highway envisioned by the commissioners never materialized, the West Fork became content to gaze on rail lines entering the city from sixteen directions and on more interstate highways than in any other city. Thirteen traction lines once entered Indianapolis to make it the interurban capital of the world.

Its early population predominantly German and with intense cultural interests, Indianapolis remained a rural trading center for sixty years. Then industrialization took hold and the population jumped 40 percent in the '80s and another 65 percent in the '90s. It carried on a brief romance with the budding auto industry but lost out to Detroit and settled on becoming a parts manufacturer, a leading producer of pharmaceuticals, electrical equipment, machinery, and glass, as well as becoming a metal producer and fabricator, food processor, and telephone supplier to the nation. When the city reached maturity, the German flavor was diluted, although the influence is still felt in such institutions as the Indianapolis Symphony Orchestra, which is one of the nation's greatest; the Athenaeum, whose Greek name belies its German origins, and the annual German-American picnics.

Indianapolis no longer is the easy, mellow city of Booth Tarkington's *The Magnificent Ambersons*. Instead, it is newly dynamic, ever reaching for new horizons which are reflected by its downtown business plaza and projected downtown mall, high-rise office and apartment complexes and new hotels that are sprouting everywhere, the Convention Center and Hoosier Dome Stadium, Market Square Arena, the gay festival that honors the 500-Mile Race, and vast re-

The Rivers of Indiana

*Left to right*: Aerial view of the Circle, Indianapolis, 1983. ◆⁵Indianapolis in 1820. ◆⁵The 1913 flood: wreckage of railroad bridge over the White River, just south of Washington Street.

gional shopping centers which help make the capital, more than ever before, the center of Indiana. Its population of more than 700,000 places it thirteenth among the nation's cities.

Yet with all the changes, the Soldiers and Sailors Monument, that grand piece of sculpture that John Gunther in *Inside U.S.A.* called America's second ugliest monument, dominates the downtown. It has been cleaned up, lighted, surrounded with outdoor cafes in summer and ice skating rinks in winter, and ringed with brick paving blocks to place Victorian charm side by side with twentieth-century dynamism.

Not far away, Indiana University-Purdue University Indianapolis, founded in 1969, serves 23,000 students and is home of a sports complex that Indianapolis hopes will help it become the national center of amateur athletics. Expansion also has been significant at its two private universities, Butler, known for its striking Clowes Hall for community professional entertainment, and Indiana Central. The Lilly Endowment, established by the pharmaceutical family, has encouraged and liberally funded many contemporary projects.

While the city has changed, the river has not, except where man has attempted to control it. Usually so shallow that it could scarcely drown a midget, the river nevertheless occasionally roars, bares its

teeth, and shows its ugly side. It did this most disastrously in 1913. Rain fell unceasingly for four days on Easter weekend, and the usually placid White exceeded flood stage by seventeen-and-a-half feet. It caused enormous damage, left thousands homeless, and brought loss of life. The flood swept away most major bridges and isolated the west section of Indianapolis. The city's answer, after the waters subsided, was to enlarge levees and build boulevards on top, widen channels, and encase the river in concrete banks.

Leaving Indianapolis, the West Fork takes on a new face. Hurrying over vast deposits of glacial outwash, the river spreads over sand and gravel beds that supply building materials for the changing city. The valley broadens and the stream, almost like a lost child, wanders over the glacial fill of its basin. The land changes. Communities, such as Martinsville, Bloomfield, and Washington, are located up to three miles from the channel, yet they occupy valley areas that spread far behind them. Especially near Martinsville, once a nationally famous spa, the hills are far in the distance. In Owen and Greene counties, the valley narrows with a spectacular beauty. Then the river broadens again, bordering the rich Indiana coalfields and watching the luscious watermelons and cantaloupes spring from the sandy soil.

Generating stations border the West Fork and the main stream

and use its waters to help produce nearly 3,300,000 kilowatts of power, which are channeled throughout Indiana. The largest plants are located at Indianapolis, Centerton, and Petersburg, supported by smaller facilities near Noblesville and at Edwardsport.

There are both similarities and differences on East Fork of White River. Unlike West Fork, which is a rural stream turned urban, East Fork is an urban stream turned rural. Its valley is often narrow and rugged, rather than broad and flat. Although it parallels West Fork which travels only through glaciated country, East Fork must fight its way largely through the rugged rocky barriers of a land the glacier never visited. Its valley is more picturesque, wilder, and often spectacular.

East Fork, according to the popular nomenclature, begins at Columbus, hub of south-central Indiana and architectural trailblazer of national repute.

Above the city, the continuation of the East Fork is known as Driftwood River for the sixteen wooded miles upstream to the mouth of Blue River. During World War II, the army operated Camp Atterbury here where 9,000 men a month said "hello" to military service and a total of nearly 600,000 said "good-bye." The 40,351-acre camp also held 15,000 prisoners of war. Much of the land is used today as a fish and wildlife area and for other state purposes.

Downriver from Columbus, East Fork flows through the flat reaches of the Scottburg Lowland, whose rich soil helps make Jackson County a national leader in sweet corn production. The stream is broad and sandy, lazily swinging through the valley until it approaches Seymour, known as the site of the nation's first train robbery and until recently the farthest east point in the United States reached directly by a railroad from the Pacific Coast. As a manufacturer, Seymour produces apparel, containers, pharmaceuticals, plastics, and furniture.

From here the river veers west and prepares to leave the easy travel of the plain. It experiences a taste of things to come as it battles its way through a notch in the Knobstone Escarpment, which rises as much as 360 feet above water level. This range of rugged hills is Indiana's most dramatic topographic feature.

East Fork is fortunate to receive here the Muscatatuck, its largest tributary. For nearly forty miles beyond, it flows across the Mitchell Plain, a sinkhole area where few surface streams reach the river, preferring to flow underground where they carve scores of exotic caverns. Some streams, like Lost River, disappear and reappear before reaching East Fork.

The river borders Bedford, producer of world-famous limestone which has gone into such buildings as the Empire State, Pen-

tagon, Washington Cathedral, and Chicago's Prudential Building. Nearby Mitchell, a cement manufacturing center, was the home of Astronaut Virgil Grissom, whose exploits live in a memorial at Spring Mill State Park. The park contains a fascinating blend of rugged scenery, underground adventure, and a working water-powered mill and village which provide a trip through time to pioneer days. Bloomington, which straddles the divide between the river's two forks was a backwoods settlement in 1820 when it became the location of the seminary that became Indiana University, now home of more than 30,000 students. By impounding nearby Salt Creek, Monroe Reservoir, the state's largest body of water, was created. It extends into Brown County, Indiana's great haven for artists and magnet to tourists.

East Fork soon fights its way through rugged Martin County, where towering bluffs and bizarre formations give Indiana some of its most dramatic scenery. Near Shoals, the Pinnacle is a ridge that towers 180 feet above the water. Where one end has become separated, it leaves Jug Rock, a forty-two-foot column topped by a flat sandstone slab that extends on all sides beyond its supporting column and looks for all the world like a finely balanced table which might teeter and drop off at any moment. Numerous mineral springs,

bursting forth in malodorous splendor, gave rise to a once-thriving spa industry complete with rambling hotels filled with health-seeking guests.

In one final spectacular burst of energy, East Fork tumbles over Hindostan Falls, a six-foot sandstone ridge. Shortly it reenters the glaciated area, where the vast ice sheet of 20,000 years ago ground down the rocks and filled the valleys. The river now has much less work to do; its fighting days are over.

Now the East Fork exchanges spectacular scenery for abundant agriculture. Daviess County, whose southern border it forms, ranks forty-fifth among the nation's 3,070 counties in turkey production and sixty-third in horses, due, perhaps, to an extensive Amish population. Below the junction of the two forks near Petersburg, the sandy soil creates one of the country's most prolific watermelon-producing areas. Knox County ranks twenty-first in the United States and Gibson ranks fiftieth. Knox also is known for peaches.

The two White Rivers are now one as they roll relentlessly toward the Wabash, fifty miles beyond. The waters that went their separate ways on the Randolph County plateau are united at last.

Big Blue

Knightstown School was famous for its rooftop globe and telescope; Charles A. Beard, the well-known historian, was one of its graduates.

High on the rim of eastern Indiana's plateau region, a tiny stream issues from a roadside field drain and begins its search for a valley. Although most streams carve their own valleys, this rivulet seeks one that is ready-made, and for six circuitous miles it fights its way alternately across treeless fields, among rounded hills, and through dense forests, wandering aimlessly and changing direction abruptly. Then, suddenly, its birth pains over, Big Blue River bursts from between the rising hills onto the floor of an unbelievably rich valley that is table-top level, a mile wide and a hundred feet deep. Obviously, this is no ordinary valley.

The beauty of the panorama that unrolls here calms the mind and it is immediately clear that the story of Big Blue River is not alone the story of a river but also the story of a valley—one that is a vast tapestry patterned by black blankets of earth, green oases of corn and soybeans, and the gray, rectangular plots of small cities. For approximately 100 miles, Big Blue River flows southward through this ready-made valley, growing from the delicate springtime of its life to a show of willful strength when floodwaters fill its banks. Yet today's Big Blue River is a mere trickle of water compared with the great rushing ice-filled torrent that originally carved this lush green trough through the land.

In the beginning Big Blue River occupied the valley's entire length, but in some obscure period a small northward-bound stream, flowing at a lower level, stretched a slender, threatening finger toward Big Blue. Eventually it captured the upper river, turned the stream in the opposite direction and carried it away. This is the supreme indignity a river can suffer. Geologists call it "stream piracy."

Thousands of years later, the river, now a beautiful but lonely highway between walls of trees, attracted a tide of settlement up the valley. Like waves upon the sand, the tide spent itself at such points as Edinburgh, Shelbyville, Knightstown, and New Castle, where the principal towns were established. Quakers marched in the vanguard, settling in the Carthage area in 1821 and establishing at Spiceland an academy which for four decades was synonymous with scholarly thoroughness.

The academy's most distinguished alumnus was Dr. Charles A. Beard, one of the handful of men who brought fame to the valley through political science, literature, and agriculture. A Knightstown native, Beard gained national repute as an outspoken and often controversial historian and political scientist.

However, it was a Shelbyville lawyer, Charles Major, who made Big Blue River a familiar name to all Americans. He did it in 1901 with

Maxwell cars were manufactured in New Castle by the Maxwell-Briscoe Automobile Company in the early 1900s.

his instant-hit novel, *The Bears of Blue River*, perhaps the best loved of his many works. Major's story carries the reader back to pioneer days when bears, deer, and wild turkeys filled the valley, and the primary tasks were to push back the forest and to plant the first corn crop.

Over the years, producing prize winning corn crops became such an ingrained habit in the valley that Shelby County alone gained a near monopoly of International Corn Kings and Princes, outpacing every other county in the United States. It came as no surprise, then, that when President Richard M. Nixon looked about for a secretary of agriculture he turned to the Blue River Valley and chose Clifford M. Hardin, a native of Knightstown.

Even before the valley gained distinction for its prize winning corn crops, its people envisioned it as a great natural trade route into the interior of the infant state. Long before most Hoosiers were concerned with getting from here to there, they flirted with railroad building, laying the state's first experimental tracks and later pushing two continuous lines from Edinburgh up the valley as far as Knightstown, where the National Road, today's U.S. 40, crossed. The dream burst like a bubble when it became obvious that Indianapolis, rather than the Big Blue River towns, was the gateway to beyond, and that

the valley, as a transportation route, really didn't lead anywhere. The state's first railroad, a one-and-a-fourth-mile experimental strap-iron affair built at Shelbyville in 1834, was nothing more than a brief interlude, and the two lines up from Edinburgh were dismantled long before the Civil War.

Despite the lower valley's efforts to grow through transportation, New Castle, near the river's upper limits, was to become the largest city. It was back in 1823 that Ashael Woodward climbed the heights on the left bank, marveled at the pleasing panorama before him and decided that this was the spot. The settlement he planned as a typical pioneer farming center grew slowly until 1907. That was the year the Maxwell-Briscoe Automobile Company, producer of comedian Jack Benny's favorite conveyance, chose to build its cars in New Castle. Almost overnight, 6,000 persons rushed in, tripling the population within three years. The next decade brought an additional 50 percent increase. About the same time the present New Castle State Hospital, which has grown into a self-contained city, was established nearby. The growth rate was heady stuff, but New Castle clearly had bitten off more than it could chew.

By the 1940s the narrow, cramped streets, which once had offered hitching space for every farmer's buggy, were strangling the

surging automobile traffic that the city's largest industry—now a part of Chrysler Corporation—had helped to create. Thoroughly concerned, New Castle selected the eminent planning firm of Saarinen and Swanson to blueprint the solution. In a study that attracted national attention, the planners came up with a proposal to develop New Castle into a group of independent, yet related, areas spread like a huge wheel around the core of the city. Although movement has been slow, it is interesting to note that American cities today, with their outlying shopping centers, parks, and residential developments, have grown swiftly in the direction which was recommended for New Castle two generations ago.

New Castle's growth, in fact, pushed it far afield and residential developments which crown the high, bold line of the hills are not a bit inaccurate when they adopt such street names as "Skyline Drive." In the new downriver areas it is impossible to build a home without a view. Realizing the valley's scenic appeal, New Castle had established Memorial Park across the valley from the city early in its history and filled its wooded, rolling acres with chains of attractive ponds tenanted by swans and ducks. Motorists along the park's drives see the distant city, dominated by the tall courthouse tower which provided Ross Lockridge, Jr., with the setting for his famous novel, *Raintree County*.

Below New Castle the valley broadens to as much as three miles as it approaches Knightstown, where the National Road (now U.S. 40) was surveyed across the river in 1827. Perhaps because it failed to develop into the vital transportation hub that some predicted, Knightstown today wears a settled, comfortable look emphasized by several ornate Gothic, Italianate, and French mansard homes. But more unusual than its homes is the school that Charles Beard attended; a giant telescope and a huge globe, visible for miles, surmount the school's twin towers to signify heaven and earth. The Indiana State Soldiers and Sailors Children's Home stands on the highlands at the edge of the valley. A short distance below Knightstown and farther on is the town of Carthage with its sprawling Container Corporation paper mill. Not far away is the site of Beech Settlement, an antebellum black community that mothered similar settlements elsewhere.

Below Carthage the valley, now banked by wooded hills, grows progressively broader and more beautiful. The river flows on its serene pathway with a pride of ownership as great as if the stream itself had carved out the great trough through which it runs.

There are beauty spots at every bend and reminders of the part the river played in the settlement of the valley. A pleasant, wooded ripple above Morristown marks the site of an early Shelby County

*Left to right*: Machines at Carthage produce paper. ⌇Nearly every railroad in the country used message delivery forks made by The High Speed Delivery Fork Co., Shelbyville.

mill, built in the 1820s. At Freeport, five miles downstream, a double dam, separated by an island, marks the scenic site of a later mill. The river, flowing still and deep, makes the village a pleasant boating and fishing resort. Tradition has it that Dr. Richard Gatling, inventor of the machine gun's forerunner, had a casting made here for his first weapon. He believed that his invention would make warfare too destructive to contemplate.

The river at last reaches Shelbyville, which Major's book made the capital of the Big Blue River Valley. In addition to Major, Shelbyville was the home of Thomas A. Hendricks, governor, U.S. senator, vice president, and a presidential candidate during the fragmented election of 1872. Little Blue River joins the Big Blue here.

Since the river is flanked by dense hardwood forests, it was natural that the furniture industry should take root in the valley. When it did, Shelbyville became the center. In recent years the city also has been important for production of fiberglass, heat-treating devices, paper products, plastics, and industrial equipment, as well as such unusual items as snaths and railroad message delivery forks. Cabinet producers represent the once-great furniture industry.

Although the Big Blue River is known for the cool clarity of its water, there was an amazing day in 1870 when the water turned hot, and Shelbyville might have become a competitor of such a famous

spa as Hot Springs, Arkansas. Wells within a four-mile radius of Shelbyville suddenly began to produce warm water, which eventually reached 86 degrees as it came from the ground. Since the owners were interested only in household water supplies, they abandoned the wells and the thermal waters became a matter of history.

Below Shelbyville the valley's liquid backbone is the chain that binds the valley into a single, interrelated unit. For half a county, few bridges span the river and the flow of traffic is with the stream, as in early days, instead of across it.

At last the Big Blue reaches Edinburgh, once busy with nearby Camp Atterbury but now a plastics and veneer manufacturing center. Although the river soon joins Sugar Creek to form Driftwood River, such local businesses as Blue River Savings and Loan Association, Blue River Products, and Blue River Cablevision perpetually remind Edinburghers that when the scenic, wandering stream reaches the end of its trail, it belongs to them.

# Flat Rock

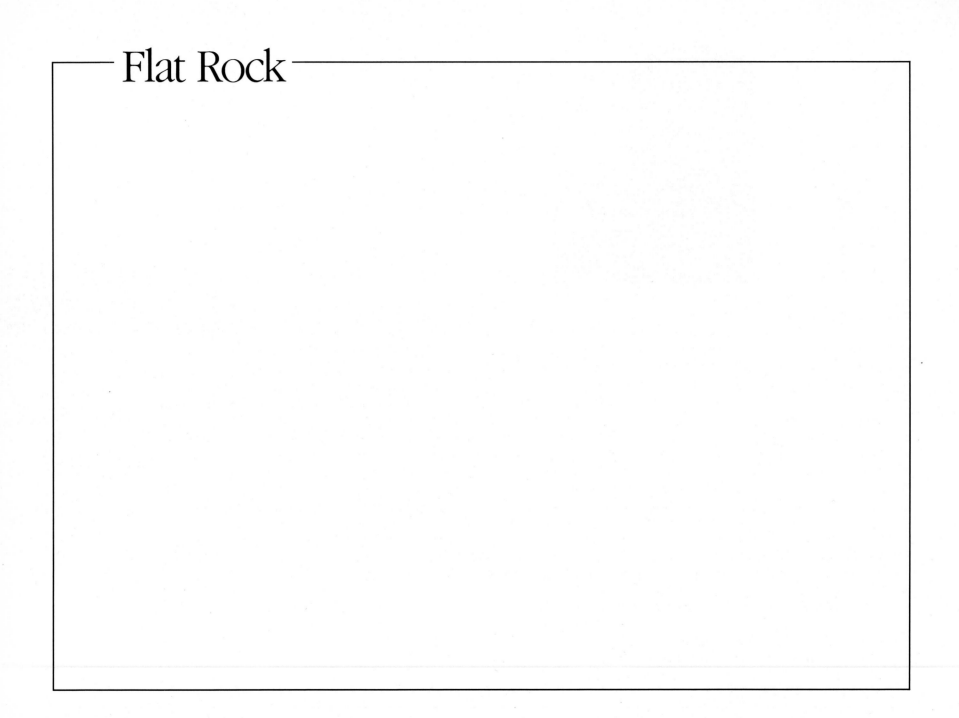

If any Indiana stream could be singled out as typical, Flat Rock River would be a leading contender. Flat Rock is a common denominator, all-American stream—the river country counterpart of apple pie, the freckle-faced kid next door, or Main Street in the Middle West. It is typically rural, uncomplicated and placid, folksy and as unattractive in its beginning as a growing child midway through the awkward age. Yet it has its moments of striking beauty and occasionally brushes elbows with men and events distantly removed from the simplicity of the valley and far ahead of their time.

How a purely agricultural stream which traverses some of Indiana's richest and deepest topsoil came to be named "Flat Rock" appears something of a mystery and you must travel half the river's eighty-eight-mile, five-county course to discover the reason. To some of the eighteenth-century Indians who dwelt along the wooded banks, the stream was *Pack-op-ka*, and to others *Puchk-achsin*. To the nineteenth-century white settlers, it was Flat Rock, which is a literal translation of the Indian word. Sometimes it is spelled as a single word and in truly democratic fashion, there is a lively difference of opinion about the correct designation. The early settlers, however, did agree that the waters bounding down from the eastern Indiana highlands would provide abundant power for their mills, so they built approximately fifty along its banks.

To early twentieth-century residents it was the "home ground" for men who dared to accomplish the spectacular in transportation and politics and to achieve superiority in agriculture. And to contemporary residents it is the river that leads to Columbus, "Athens of the Prairie," the twentieth-century city with the twenty-first-century architecture.

The humble beginnings of the Flat Rock River are found a few hundred feet behind an isolated farmhouse site two miles northeast of Mooreland in Henry County, where a small tile field drain empties into the head of an ugly, insignificant open ditch. Cattails and rushes crowd the spot, but the trickle of water slowly pushes its way through and the river is born.

Moving sluggishly, Flat Rock etches its way ever so slightly into the thick mantle of rich topsoil, and a barely discernible valley appears in the level farmland. It is strictly a rural river as it glides past flat prairie landscapes rich with cornfields that lean against the sky and invades the remnants of the vast hardwood forests. Soon it becomes a pleasant meadow stream, wandering and charming, as it courses down the rim of the eastern Indiana plateau where it started.

Although early settlers found Flat Rock to be quiet and well behaved, they soon discovered its strength as a millstream and by 1840 had built more than sixty mills in its 532-square-mile basin. Like the fertile soil of its valley, Flat Rock's mills produced essential ingredients for pioneer living. Their wheels, turning to the cheerful mutter of the stream, ground grain, made flour, sawed lumber, and produced woolens in a day before modern manufacturing was known. The mills are idle now, or have long since disappeared, but numerous dams, ponds, and races linger on and at least one mill building stands at its original site as a reminder of the river's importance to early life. Communities such as Rushville, Moscow, and St. Paul owe their existence to millsites.

Rushville, the only city above the river's mouth, is the county seat of Rush County, one of Indiana's richest farm areas and a national leader in corn-hog production. Since early days, Rush County has been known for the abundance of its crops and the quality of its livestock. The term "corn-hog" describes not only a view of the landscape but the backbone of the economy. It ranks in the upper 3 percent of the nation's counties in value of hog production.

In spring Rush County is a neat checkerboard of light green and chocolate brown. The rich earth, freshly plowed for the summer's corn crop, stands darkly against the bright green of wheat and oats pushing from the soil. In summer the heat shimmers over vast stands of rustling corn. The Flat Rock, flowing diagonally across the county, divides the level lands in the northwest from the slightly undulating regions in the southeast.

The skill and diligence of Rush County farmers have brought numerous International Corn King, Prince, and Princess titles to the banks of the Flat Rock. Any man who tills the Rush County soil finds himself batting in the big leagues.

It is of more than passing interest that Wendell Willkie, presidential nominee in 1940 and a staunch advocate of a "One World" policy, called Rushville his "home." In strong contrast to the rural, isolationist background in which he grew up, Willkie pressed for a total United States involvement in world affairs and traveled interna-

*Left to right*: Mill building northeast of Rushville. ꝏBirthplace of Wilbur Wright, co-inventor of the airplane, near Millville.

tionally to expound his views. When he campaigned for the presidency, he established headquarters in Rushville, taking over the Durbin Hotel, which went on to become an institution whose reputation grew completely out of proportion to its size or the size of Rushville. Two Durbin sons went on to top executive positions in the Marriott and Sheraton hotel chains.

Willkie was not the only famous person attracted to the Flat Rock country. To the river's headwaters came the Reverend Milton Wright, later a bishop, with his family shortly after the Civil War and here his third son Wilbur was born in 1867. Wilbur went on, with his brother Orville, to become co-inventor of the airplane. A simple state memorial marks the birthplace site, two and one-half miles northeast of Millville in Henry County. The Wright home, rebuilt after the original burned, portrays their simple family life and a mounted F-84 fighter plane symbolizes their contribution to mankind. Memorial plaques complete the story and a picnic area provides relaxation from the fast-paced age the Wrights helped to create.

Local residents have engraved the Wright story on the map with no less than a half-dozen names related to the airplane. In addition to Wilbur Wright Creek, which is a tributary of the Flat Rock, Wing Branch, and Flight, Propeller, Tail, and Wind Runs find their way to the Whitewater River.

Despite the world acclaim of its best-known sons, the Flat Rock remains obscure and completely rural. Not only the mills but numerous covered wooden bridges mark it as a gentle, rustic stream. Most of the valley's fame as a covered bridge center belongs to A. M. Kennedy and his sons, whose creations were among the most artistic examples of the builder's art. Four spans remain across the Flat Rock, two a short distance northeast of Rushville and two in the Moscow area. Three were built approximately a century ago, but they carry modern traffic and attest to the Kennedy's skillful workmanship.

Below Rushville the Flat Rock flows on its idyllic way, a placid water highway between comfortable rows of trees. However, at Moscow in southern Rush County extensive limestone quarries along the banks indicate the reasons for the river's name and push aside, for the first time, the Flat Rock's strictly agricultural character. After a short journey through deep and beautiful valleys in the corner of Decatur County, the Flat Rock arrives at St. Paul, where it slides over a rugged limestone bed which edges completely across the stream and shows clearly in the shallow water. The secret of the river's name comes out at last.

The scenery turns spectacular before your eyes and the wild, panoramic beauty of rugged cliffs, limestone caverns, and rocky canyons replaces the gentle contours of the upper river. This is the coun-

*Left to right*: North Christian Church, Columbus, designed by Eero Saarinen. ❧Jim Durbin, Marriott Hotels president, and Bob Durbin, Sheraton Hotels executive vice president, at the family hotel, Rushville. ❧Four Kennedy bridges remain on the Flat Rock.

try marked by sparkling water tumbling over picturesque dams and narrow stream-side roads, which bring the river to your feet. Dams near Geneva in Shelby County raise the water level to make it suitable for shallow boating and a small riverside resort colony establishes the unquestionable magnetism of the river's beauty.

Then the land changes slowly, returning to the gentle, level reaches of its upper course. The huge load of gravel gathered in nearly 100 miles of wandering is deposited in bars as the river, now broad and shallow, nears its junction with the Driftwood River to form the East Fork of White River at Columbus, the seat of Bartholomew County.

It is a curious terminus for a river occupied with the simple, rural life, for Columbus is an eager-beaver city of 30,614 busy producing some of the nation's best-known products. Its industries, many home-grown and home-owned, turn out prodigious quantities of diesel engines, automotive parts, furniture, and castings. The industrial diversity also includes plastics, foods, paper products, and motor components.

The city has attracted so much national attention to its striking architecture that it has earned the title "Athens of the Prairie." In fact, Columbus is so star-studded that it has arranged a thirty-one-point tour to conduct visitors past its architectural wonders. J. Irwin Miller, chairman of the Cummins Engine Company and first layman to be elected president of the National Council of Churches, is the driving force through the Cummins Engine Foundation, which provides architects' fees. Designers of the city's startling collection of churches, schools, public buildings, and a shopping mall come from three continents and ten states, in addition to Indiana. Eliel Saarinen, the famous Finnish architect, first broke the conventional barrier when he created the controversial First Christian Church in 1942 but the explosion did not erupt until the '60s. The men who followed assured Columbus of outstanding talent through their designs of the John F. Kennedy Memorial, Kennedy Memorial Library, and John Foster Dulles Airport, Washington, D.C.; Memorial Arch, St. Louis, Mo.; Rockefeller Institute, New York City; Independence Mall, Philadelphia, Pa., and the Finnish National Museum in Helsinki. The result has made the mouth of the Flat Rock a striking contrast to the idyllic countryside that marks the river's journey.

# River of Mystery

French Lick

Lost

Indiana's most spectacular vanishing act is the mysterious disappearance of Lost River. Done on a scale so massive that it would defy Blackstone the Magician and make Houdini envious, the river disappears gradually, quietly, and completely. It is unique among Indiana's major waterways.

For nearly three-fourths of its seventy-eight-mile course, the Lost flows as a conventional and usually a beautiful stream. But the other fourth in the upper central section is a twisting, tortuous, totally dry bed that carries water only during occasional floods. The true river in this area flows completely underground—out of sight, out of earshot, out of mind except to those who know it best: the geologists. These men who read the rocks have traced the invisible channel from its gentle, gradual disappearance southeast of Orleans to its dramatic reappearance as a giant spring three-quarters of a mile south of Orangeville. From that point, it flows normally, hugging the hills and skirting the valleys of spectacularly beautiful Orange and Martin counties. For scenery, it is unsurpassed in Indiana. For mystery, it is unsurpassed anywhere.

But Lost River is more than a textbook example of a sinking stream. It is a colorful valley that bounces back amazingly from blows that would have flattened a less resilient and determined region. It has lived many lives and, like a gyrating gypsy dancer, has performed against many backgrounds. It is many things to many people.

To naturalists, the valley is a classic example of a sinking stream and they have fought all comers in their determination to keep it that way.

To soil conservationists, it is an arrogant, high-spirited watercourse which periodically unleashes the full fury of springtime floods on thousands of valuable farm acres. They were equally determined but lost the battle to dam its waters and subdue its floodtime destruction.

To the resort set, it is the tributary Springs Valley, where Victorian opulence lingers in the huge French Lick Springs Hotel, now known as the French Lick Springs Golf and Tennis Resort.

To students, it is the end of the Northwood Institute era in which they learned such diverse subjects as hotel management and the performing arts taught in the bygone splendor of a onetime lavish resort hotel at West Baden.

Lost River rises by several forks in northwestern Washington County near the village of Smedley, and it is apparent in the first mile of its rock-strewn course that this is no ordinary river. Unlike most rivers, which barely scratch the surface in their placid youth, Lost River develops a valley with surprising swiftness. Five miles from its source, it flows seventy-five feet below the uplands. In the first eleven miles of its restless life, the Lost drops a vertical distance of more than 200 feet, knifing through the thin soil and limestone hills. This is the springtime of life for the Lost.

Growing from springs that rise from crevices in the limestone bedrock, it begins its race to the sea, tumbling restlessly and unceasingly over its rock-strewn bed. It scampers, like a boy who has raided a neighbor's orchard, behind boulders and under cover of thickly grown woodlots until it is well away from its pursuer.

As the gentle contours of the land change swiftly into rugged, isolated valleys, the river gathers the fine, spidery lines of its tributaries and various branches join forces with their sisters to form the main stream. For the next few miles, Lost River glides gently over shallows, the soft mutter of the stream giving no hint of the disappearing act to follow. Fishermen take possession of the picturesque banks, and the alternation of hill and valley makes for strikingly beautiful scenery. The river becomes a placid, scenic highway between green rows of trees.

By now Lost River has gained respectable size, flowing serenely past grassy pastures toward the point where it makes an astonishing change of direction from westward to downward. The river fades so gradually that it is difficult to discover where it has gone. A lonely highway normally flowing forty feet wide between dense rows of trees, it slows nearly to a halt, feeding successively smaller shallow pools which rotate slowly in the streambed. Each has a vortex which whirls lazily like water draining from a bathtub. A little water escapes each pool, fragmenting into rivulets that disappear beneath bankside rocks. The channel continues, but the water disappears completely.

Most of the year, no ponds, no puddles, no moist spots lie below the sinks. For the next twenty-two miles the dry riverbed coils among the hills, and those farmers who are willing to gamble against the river's mischievous quirks sow their crops and pasture their livestock in its bed. But to a greater extent than most streams, Lost River

The Rivers of Indiana

is more than water flowing between two banks. It is a changeling with the seasons and a March ribbon which disappears before your eyes may overflow the swallow holes and boil into an April spate, destruction-bound, through its dry bed. The enormous deadfalls of large trees and crop debris give mute evidence of the willful power of the current. At these times, it roars irresistibly through the narrow surface channel until the underground system is once again able to accept the entire load.

Lost River's behavior has a simple geological explanation: Its middle course flows across a porous limestone region that resembles a gigantic sieve and carries water with about the same degree of dependability. One square mile of the valley, for instance, contains 1,022 sinkholes. Over thousands of years, the water table continuously dropped and the river, seeking the lowest level, entered tiny joints and crevices in its limestone bed. The water, which is weakly acidic, dissolved the underlying limestone. As more water poured in, the reaction increased until it bored a complicated underground system of tubes, channels, and caverns. As short, disconnected segments merged, they captured all the river's water.

Any waters overflowing the sinks enter the first principal funnel, which is a short distance east of the Ind. 37 bridge and three miles south of Orleans. Waters that meander lazily, if at all, in the dry heat of summer may rage madly eight feet deep in the spring through a crooked, 120-yard connecting channel. If this outlet becomes overloaded, the water sweeps downstream to the Turner swallow holes, a short distance west of Ind. 37. About forty funnels line a short connecting channel there. If the water exceeds these inlets' capacity, it races downstream three miles to a 565-foot underground connection with the subterranean Lost River through a small cavern system.

As a benevolent gesture to appease the curious, nature created Wesley Chapel Gulf two miles southeast of Orangeville. Somewhere in dim ages past, the entire roof of Lost River's underground home collapsed and created an eight-acre box canyon up to ninety-five feet deep. It is like a huge picture window which gives a frustratingly brief glimpse into the river's eight-mile-long underground system. Boiling out of a pit fifty feet deep in the canyon floor, the stream appears briefly on the surface. Then it flows into the limestone cliff on the opposite side of the gulf and disappears. An opening leads into a

maze of dark passages that can be followed for nearly a mile past a spectacular display of stalactites, flowstone and underground ponds, rapids and waterfalls.

Describing his Lost River explorations, the late Dr. Clyde A. Malott, Indiana University geologist, wrote: "This miserable little stretch of the underground river route gives us but a tantalizing glimpse of a mighty cavern, whose main channel length cannot be less than eight miles. Inadequate as it is, it is a sample of a big cavern in the making . . . coursed by a dangerous river. It presents a forbidding, mysterious, fearful picture to the senses and it is impressive only when conceived as the underground conduit of a large stream more than eight miles in length and 60 to 150 feet beneath the upland surface which feeds water to it through . . . nondescript inlets."

Two miles west of the gulf, Lost River ends its underground journey by bursting to the surface as a huge spring. Three-quarters of a mile north a similar spring flows from under a limestone ledge at Orangeville at a maximum rate of nearly six million gallons a day and joins Lost River. Fluorescein dye tests prove this to be a tributary, although it has erroneously been called the rise of Lost River. Blind fish swim about in the water-filled cavern that feeds the spring. Lost River now flows among lofty hills, serene and unfettered, until it reaches East Fork of White River, forty-eight miles away. Declared a

*Preceding page*: French Lick Springs Hotel. *Left to right*: Lost River headwaters. The first sink; water flows beneath the surface. South of Orangeville, Lost River resumes its normal flow.

navigable stream, it carried the produce of this isolated region and its waters turned a mill at the mouth of Orangeville Rise. Its lower course was a water highway over which the pioneer shipped his staves, hams, bacon, and sawlogs to a waiting market.

Many Lost River wonders would have been lost permanently during the early '70s when the U.S. Soil Conservation Service planned to construct a sixty-three-foot dam two miles north of West Baden. The resulting 957-acre lake would have drowned the two rises under fifteen feet of water and destroyed forever unusual flora, wildlife, and geological phenomena. The threat sent chills down the spines of nature lovers who fought it to extinction and saw the Orangeville Rise become a National Landmark.

The wonders of Lost River, however, are not as well known nationally as the twin spa towns in its tributary Springs Valley, French Lick and West Baden. Long before the white man arrived, the Indians knew about the mineral-laden waters that oozed from the ground, and before the Indians, thousands of buffalo wore a well-trodden path to the waters as they migrated between the Great Plains and the Kentucky salt licks.

Like much of the Lost River basin, Springs Valley has endured its share of controversy, punctuated by a colorful boom-and-bust econ-omy. The mineral waters which built the towns might have remained only a foul-smelling nuisance were it not for Dr. William A. Bowles, a maverick physician, minister, and Civil War insurrectionist. Recognizing their therapeutic value, he built a hotel at French Lick in 1840, catering to health seekers. A hotel later went up at West Baden, and Springs Valley was launched on its career as one of the nation's four or five great spas.

Eventually Thomas Taggart, Democratic kingmaker and U.S. senator, acquired the French Lick Springs Hotel and thrust the valley into its greatest era. He expanded the hotel continuously until it soared seven stories and sprawled in all directions. It became the tail that wagged the dog, carrying the town with it. Taggart also built politics into the French Lick tradition, and for many years state and national Democratic leaders made it their mecca. Republicans used it too. Vice presidential candidate John Bricker kicked off his campaign there in 1944.

French Lick lies in a valley so secluded that it easily can be passed by unnoticed and so steep that driving its streets imparts the feeling of climbing a sheer wall by car. But despite its unlikely location, the wealthy and the mighty streamed in by the trainload for decades, traveling on the twenty trains that arrived and departed daily.

The Southern Railway, unhappy with the thought of letting the Monon enjoy the entire pie, cut itself a slice when it climbed a ridge and bored a costly tunnel nearly a half-mile long to enter the valley. Today the Monon line is gone and the Southern branch has become a steam tourist line.

As the valley's fame spread, other hotels sprang up until there were fifteen or twenty, including the incredible West Baden Springs Hotel, opened in 1903. All capitalized on the mineral water, which was taken both internally and externally. Pluto, the laxative water that made French Lick famous, was bottled in a separate plant and hauled to the nation's drug counters in special boxcars emblazoned with the Pluto trademark.

Many of the nation's great relaxed regularly in the atmosphere of well-seasoned opulence in the hotels. Registers carried the names of Colonel Jacob Ruppert, the brewer who owned the New York Yankees; song writer Irving Berlin; novelist Mary Roberts Rinehart; and heiress Barbara Hutton.

Springs Valley became synonymous with fun and relaxation. The French Lick Springs Hotel built an eighteen-hole golf course and later added a second one along with skeet and archery ranges, swimming pools, bowling alleys, and tennis courts. Spinning roulette wheels and whirring slot machines also made the valley famous until the lid was clamped on in 1949 and such famous casinos as Brown's were forced to close their doors.

Even though they were practically within walking distance of each other, a streetcar line was built to connect the French Lick Springs Hotel and the fabulous glass-domed palace at West Baden. Six stories high, its 708 rooms surrounded the granddaddy of all atriums, a 200-foot diameter unsupported glass dome which covered a courtyard so large an entire circus once played in it. Fifteen hundred diners could be served with ease. The dome was claimed to be the largest in the world at the time, and the building was trumpeted everywhere as the eighth wonder of the world. In 1974 it received just recognition when it was placed on the National Register of Historic Places. The 1929 stock market crash, however, sent the guests scurrying home to assess the wreckage. The hotel limped along hopefully until 1932 looking for a brighter day that never came and in midyear it closed permanently.

Two years later, much to the chagrin of the townspeople, who longed for the hotel boom days, the idle building was donated to the Society of Jesus (Jesuits), who renamed it West Baden College. The massive lobby was converted into a chapel and guest rooms became

West Baden Springs Hotel later became a college and is now a health spa.

libraries and classrooms. An awesome, monastic quiet descended on the once-gay structure.

Thirty years later, the Jesuits vacated the building and once again it stood mute. While government agencies funded surveys to see what could be done, Mr. and Mrs. Macauley Whiting of Midland, Michigan, purchased the hotel and donated it to Northwood Institute, a private college with other campuses in Michigan and Texas. In 1967 Northwood opened its doors to students. Lively classes in the performing arts, retailing, automotive marketing, and hotel management replaced the monastic atmosphere of the Jesuits.

Not only did Northwood offer a highly specialized community college service but it pumped in new blood at a time the valley was fighting for its economic life. Loss of the resort industry—only the French Lick Hotel remained and it had gone through a receivership—a general lack of industry, and an unruly French Lick Creek that lapped periodically at the hotel doorstep combined to strike cruel blows.

Northwood, however, like other valley institutions was only an interlude. After sixteen years, it closed its doors and the hunt for a new tenant began. It was the mid-'60s all over again, but by this time a scattering of industry turning out such items as organs and furni-

ture was present to ease the economic pain. History turned full circle, however, when a buyer was quickly found who would revive the grand structure as a hotel and add a health club.

French Lick Creek flows into Lost River, which becomes a stream of primitive and unspoiled beauty backed by the high, bold line of the rugged hills. Its valley indulges in gracious and expansive moments. The sides pile up their heights to 250 feet, looking almost mountainous compared to the scenes that have come before. It plows its deep bed through nameless folds in the Martin County hills, and the wild beauty of the panorama unrolls at every bend. Settlements are tiny and sparse and you feel as if civilization is in another world.

Finally, Lost River enters the level floodplain of White River's East Fork. It is now a serene pathway between the fresh green of the trees on either bank. Its water is clear and cool as the valley spreads out into a rare and beautiful landscape. Nature's great sleight-of-hand performance at last has reached the end of its act.

# *Wilderness Rivers*

Muscatatuck

Point your finger at any of a whole handful of streams on the map of southeastern Indiana and you are pointing to the Muscatatuck, for unlike most rivers, the Muscatatuck is not a single stream but a collection of rivers. It is Indiana's good fortune that the river comes in multiples for the Muscatatuck, in all its branches, is an invitation to adventure. Few Hoosier streams match its ruggedly beautiful scenery, its romantic history, or act as such a lively companion to water-sports lovers and fishermen.

The name, not nearly as formidable as it looks, is accented on the second syllable: Mus-CAT-a-tuck. The Indians called the river *Mosch-ach-hit-tuk*, which is translated variously as "clear river" and "stream flowing through swampy land." Either would be correct, depending on which part of the Muscatatuck's changing course you are viewing.

The Muscatatuck is by turns a swift little stream plunging over rapids and cascades; a wild jungle pathway full of rugged mystery and uncontrolled passion as it races past groves that have never known an ax, and a placid water highway flowing between level, endless fields where the summer heat shimmers over the rustling corn. Its tributaries rush madly into the valley in spring but meander lazily in the dry heat of summer.

The valley is a blend of the north and south, where in spring tobacco seedbeds peek from beneath their white muslin covers and in fall the long, brown hands of the plant may be seen curing from the rafters of tobacco barns. Pioneers once raised cotton and indigo where modern farmers produce corn. But mostly the Muscatatuck country is too rugged for productive agriculture, and many associate the valley with hunting, fishing, and other outdoor sports. At least twelve state or federally protected nature areas border the river, ranging from tiny public access sites to the vast 7,202-acre Muscatatuck National Wildlife Refuge.

The main stream begins in northwestern Jefferson County near Paris Crossing, where ardent mapmakers arbitrarily decided to print the name "Muscatatuck" at a creek junction. Old-timers will argue till daybreak that the upper section is properly called "East Fork," but whatever its name the stream wanders fifty-three fascinating miles westward, often through a primitive and unspoiled country, until it ends its journey at the East Fork of White River south of Medora.

Despite this designation of the main river, the Vernon Fork, which rises east of Greensburg, is much the longer, flowing seventy-seven tortuous miles in a series of sinuous curves, tumbled rapids, placid meanderings, and steep-walled canyons that defy both the imagination and the compass. Eventually it combines forces with its mother stream west of Austin. Other principal branches in the Muscatatuck's 1,110-square-mile basin are known variously as Graham Creek and Otter Creek, although before action by the Indiana Board on Geographic Names there was a confusing collection that included North Fork, East Fork, and South Fork—there were two of these.

The Vernon Fork which to many is THE Muscatatuck, gathers its first waters from a gently sloping pastureland six miles east of Greensburg. Then it flows south along the border of a forest, emerging as a drainage ditch before crossing a field and slipping beneath I-74, a mile away.

Trickling south, growing stronger, the infant Vernon Fork is now a pleasant meadow stream, cutting briefly into bedrock near Smyrna and flowing between a rising corridor of banks as it approaches the German Catholic village of Millhousen. Millhousen is one of those quaint story-book villages that doesn't belong in Indiana at all. Yet when its founder, Maximilian Schneider, arrived from his native Germany in 1838, he chose an area so remote that to this day it has escaped the mainstream of traffic and has matured in a kind of splendid isolation which preserves its original appearance and special European flavor. The towering church looks down on a winding main street flanked by Federal-style and Greek Revival-style brick buildings set flush with the sidewalks. Schneider would know his village instantly if he could return to see it.

A short distance away from Millhousen, the Vernon Fork now etching its way beneath the high, bold line of the hills, jerks you back to the reality that this is, after all, Indiana. It brawls noisily over a rocky bed as it cuts its way toward North Vernon, the largest community on its path. The way is wild and remote; the palisades dark, grim, and majestic. Highways, where there are any, thread their way along a valley backed by wooded hills or cling to the brow of steep bluffs which drop suddenly down to the clear, brawling, boulder-strewn stream. The land is rugged, quiet, and lonely. There is a feeling that civilization, somehow, has overlooked the entire area and that the wild beauty of the panorama answers the river's need for a relationship with nature in her unviolated innocence.

The river emerges but once from its loneliness and that is at Muscatatuck State Hospital and Training Center where nearly 1,000 mentally retarded residents reside and work in approximately forty modernistic buildings scattered over a 3,200-acre area. For many years both the hospital and the city of North Vernon suffered from an acute water famine. The hospital, upstream from the city drew its supply first, purified the waste, and returned it to the river. This gave rise to the story, perhaps apocryphal, that signs appeared in the restrooms reading, "Please flush the toilets. North Vernon needs water."

After many years of going their separate ways, the state and city united to build the 167-acre Brush Creek Reservoir along the edge of the hospital grounds. The river which for much of the year was a poor trickle of water, began to flow in summer, so that North Vernon not only could slake its thirst but could inform any roving industry looking its way that water was among its assets. North Vernon, a city of 5,768, stands at the head of a series of remarkable bends where the river flows six miles to cover a crow-flown route of less than a mile and a half.

Vernon, the seat of Jennings County, stands on one of the four narrow, high peninsulas the river carved, surrounded by spectacular scenery and improbable geography. It is Indiana's smallest county seat and destined to remain that way. The town might have grown to impressive size if Colonel John Vawter, who founded it back in 1816, had kept his head and not been carried away by the spectacular scenery. A government surveyor, Vawter was a practical man, yet when he discovered one of the state's most impractical townsites he promptly discarded his better judgment and chose the quarter-mile-square, twin-peaked plateau which the looping Muscatatuck nearly encircled. He then offered a free courthouse site and $300 in cash, and what board of county commissioners in 1816 could turn down such a generous offer?

So Vernon was established on this island in the sky. True to Vawter's predictions the first railroad to connect the Ohio River with Indiana's interior passed through Vernon, crossing what is locally described as the first viaduct west of the Alleghenies. It also was the head of flatboat navigation and the junction of two forks of the Mus-

catatuck. The future looked rosy. But once the county seat had spread itself over the head of the peninsula it had no place to go and was effectively choked off by the river. A 130-foot-high razorback ridge, wide enough for only a single wagon road, connected Vernon to the "mainland."

"As a site for a medieval castle, with a cluster of cabins around it, designed primarily for defense, it is unrivaled," an assistant to the state geologist wrote eighty-seven years ago. "As a site for a modern commercial town, it is a failure." But he added that "its quaint charm and picturesque beauty give it a charm which no smart business town can possess."

When an important railroad pushed westward from Washington, D.C., to St. Louis, Missouri, in the 1850s, Vernonites smugly assumed that it could not afford to miss their town. But the rugged geography turned the tracks to a point two miles north where Colonel Hagerman Tripp speedily platted the city that today is North Vernon. Here it crossed the Madison and Indianapolis Railroad, and when a third line arrived, the city's future was assured. The ample transportation helped attract industries that today produce auto parts, rugs, forgings, and plastics.

Vernon, meanwhile, retained its charm undisturbed. In 1976 the entire town containing more than a hundred residential, commercial, and religious structures was designated a historic district and placed on the National Register of Historic Places. Greece and Rome have left their imprints everywhere and a leisurely trip through the streets is an architecture lover's delight. Nearly half the dwellings are substantial brick or stone structures. More than twenty buildings predate the Civil War, eight going back to the 1830s. A log cabin believed to have been built by Vawter, the Vernon Normal School, and ruins of the Tunnel Mill are added to other examples of a town that retains its nineteenth-century character. The 1859 vintage courthouse of Italianate architecture sports a Tuscan tower, and the local story is that it would have been moved to North Vernon long ago if the connecting ridge had been wider.

Not only the architecture, but the town government is an anachronism. Incorporated under a special charter issued by the state legislature in 1851, Vernon elects its officials every two years in March, instead of every fourth November, as other communities do. Until a

*Left to right*: Italianate courthouse, Vernon, 1859. ❧Tunnel Mill ruins. ❧North Vernon was an important railroad town until 1950s. ❧Flocks at Muscatatuck National Wildlife Refuge.

few years ago, it also collected its own taxes but later turned this prerogative over to the county treasurer.

The most exciting day in Vernon's history came in 1863 when General John H. Morgan's Confederate cavalry swarmed along the edge of town and demanded its surrender. But after extended parleying his troops rode off, sparing the town. For a few years it claimed the distinction of being connected to North Vernon by one of the state's shortest interurban lines.

From the edge of Vernon's plateau you can look out as from an airplane over the twisting Muscatatuck going through its meanders, folding back on itself like a ribbon. Leaping joyously downward toward the sea, it slides over rocky shallows squeezed tightly between steep palisades and rock-lined gorges as much as ninety feet deep. They are vigorous testimonials to a determined current fighting valiantly against the encroachment of stubborn hillsides. Tumbling restlessly and unceasingly over its rock-strewn bed, the river drops fifty-five feet in six miles.

Although the Vernon Fork's bed is rock along most of its twisting course, immediately below Vernon an undaunted Ebenezer Baldwin chose it as the site to build his famous Tunnel Mill in 1824. At the foot of a steep ridge where beauty takes one of its most spectacular forms, Baldwin chiseled a tunnel approximately 300 feet long and nine feet wide through solid limestone. Where the onrushing current flowed stubbornly along the ridge, he diverted the water through his tunnel, and at the far end he built a three-story stone mill. Ruins of the building still stand in the secluded hollow, mute evidence of the power of the Muscatatuck.

Upstream from the dam the former Muscatatuck State Park, known for its winding foot trails, deep ravines, and steep bluffs, occupies another of the river's famous loops. It is now operated by Jennings County. Crosley State Fish and Wildlife Area stretches into another loop, occupying 4,084 acres of rugged upland purchased from the late Powell Crosley, Jr., who once owned professional baseball's Cincinnati Reds and manufactured the Crosley car. The area is comprised principally of woodland tracts which provide deer, pheasant, quail, and rabbit hunting and fishing from small lakes.

Other upstream recreation areas include the 352-acre Selmier State Forest and the 1,841-acre Brush Creek Fish and Wildlife Area, but largest of all is the Muscatatuck National Wildlife Refuge, only such Federal property in Indiana. Established in 1966 astride the Jackson-Jennings county line southeast of Seymour, it contains 7,702 acres of water, marsh, timber, and crop lands. Stars of the refuge are the flocks of migrating waterfowl and many resident wildlife species. Observers have cataloged approximately 230. Walking and motor

trails fan out from the Visitors Center to photography sites, nature study trails, and the refuge's five lakes and marshes. Flocks of migratory sandhill cranes, resident Canada geese, and nesting wood ducks make Muscatatuck an outdoorsman's delight.

Nearby the Vernon Fork leaves the Muscatatuck Regional Slope, which it has worked so hard to cross, and enters the Scottsburg Lowland, where the terrain changes rapidly from rugged to flat. West of Austin, in Scott County, the Vernon Fork joins the main Muscatatuck, which begins at the junction of Graham and Big creeks in the northwest corner of Jefferson County, near Paris Crossing. In summer and fall it is a gentle stream flowing past broad, fertile bottomlands that now and again are elbowed close to the riverbank by the steep hills. But in spring, when the hills gather up their waters and pour them into the tributaries, it bursts forth in wild paroxysms of terrible rage, seeking to destroy all that stands in its way and leaving in its wake huge tangles of fallen trees. The hills are steeply rolling and in fall are carpeted with colors brilliant enough to make Brown County jealous. The land is rugged, and the soil thin, ragged, and worn through by limestone hills.

After receiving the offerings of Vernon Fork, the Muscatatuck, now the boundary between Washington and Jackson counties, winds lazily across the rich, flat lowlands, threading through ever-widening

bottoms which produce thousands of acres of grain. Agriculture in the lower Muscatatuck is such big business that Jennings is the nation's twenty-ninth ranking chicken-producing county, Scott ranks seventy-ninth in sweet corn yield, and Jackson stands in the upper 3 percent of both. Austin, in Scott County, is known for tomato packing. It is difficult to believe that the Muscatatuck crosses this flat country so effortlessly after fighting with such difficulty through the rugged hills.

Up from the Ohio River stretch the Knobs, Indiana's most spectacular physiographic feature. Approaching the Muscatatuck at right angles northeast of Salem, the hills abruptly turn to the west as if they feel that the river has struggled long enough, and then allow the widening stream to slip without effort through a nameless notch among them. The Muscatatuck, as though putting indecision aside, meanders no more. Boats appear on the water and youngsters canoe on what is one of Indiana's finest water trails. Vacation cabins line the banks. The Muscatatuck now meets its mother stream, the East Fork of White River. The state provides a public access site here so that the river ends gloriously in the service of some of its most ardent admirers—the outdoorsmen.

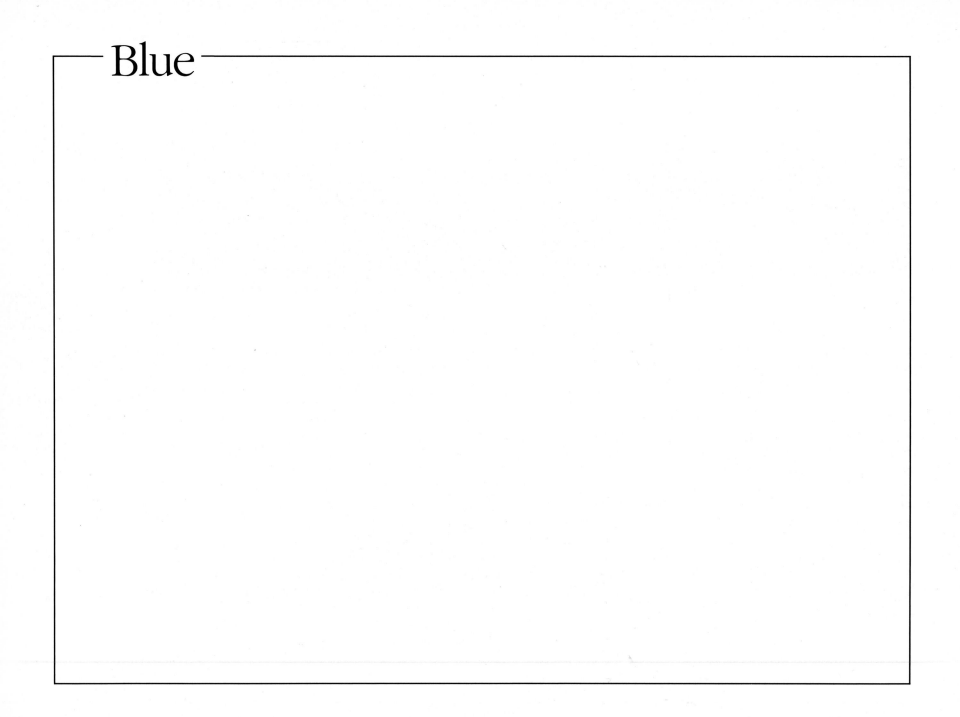

Blue

Rivers everywhere have their stories to tell and among the Ohio's tributaries, where settlement first came to Indiana, the stories are measured more by accomplishments of the men who settled the riverbanks than by length and girth of the waters. A good example is the Blue River. Flowing little more than ninety miles from its farthest headwaters northeast of Salem to the point near Leavenworth where it injects its sometimes murky flood deep into the side of the Ohio, it may appear an unpretentious stream. It has never served as a water highway that can recall a vital role as a barge carrier or romantic days of steamboat racing. It has no bustling industrial cities along its banks. Its rich bottomlands are few.

Yet the Blue is no insignificant river. It served the earliest settlers well as a route into the interior, where they established the Washington County seat of Salem and made it an outpost of culture and commercial activity. In addition, the valley distinguished itself as a producer of notable Americans, the home of the tallest men in the Union army, the terminus briefly of the first Hoosier railroad to reach Lake Michigan from the Ohio River and, at the river's mouth, host to a rare inland naval battle. The first woman graduate of Indiana University, Sarah P. Morrison, came from Salem.

Many spacious caverns dot Blue River's countryside. Under-ground streams steal its rightful waters, yet the outflow of huge springs balances the loss. One of Indiana's few remaining water-powered mills stands in its valley, which is the central artery of a region merging Southern culture into Hoosier.

Like the rugged pioneers who settled along its banks, Blue River personifies the American tradition of independence and self-determination. Rather than silver buckles on its shoes, it wears buckskin on its sinewy arms. Perhaps because geography and history have combined to slow the time scale of the region, the Blue remains unpolluted and natural. In earlier days, they called it the Great Blue.

Although its past makes it a cradle of Hoosier settlement, its future will be as a recreational stream and the state government views it with this in mind. The Blue—forty-five and a half miles of it, from Fredericksburg to the Wyandotte Woods Recreational Complex—was the first river to be protected under Indiana's Natural Scenic and Recreational River System Act of 1973. Its waters swift and its banks rugged, it is considered one of the state's most scenic rivers and among its most unspoiled. Whether it is edged with the light green reflections of spring or sporting the bright garments of autumn, it is picturesque every moment of the year. Canoeists who brave its waters will find adjoining the river the 25,618-acre Harrison-Crawford

*Left to right*: Beck's Mill, southwest of Salem  ⇜Morgan's raiders pillaging at Salem, July 10, 1863.

State Forest, the 2,000-acre Wyandotte Woods and the 1,200-acre Wyandotte Caves area.

Following the Blue on the map is only a matter of seconds, but following the twisting stream across the land and between the rugged hills is quite another matter. It rises near the crest of the Knobs, the astonishingly high, rounded, scenic escarpment that enters Indiana near New Albany and extends toward Brown County. The river has several branches, but the farthest distant, known as West Fork, rises in a grassy hog lot nine miles northeast of Salem.

To find it, you climb a roadside fence and push your way through a field to a willow-bordered depression sometimes filled with muddy water and fine silt. From its pools, when there is sufficient rainfall, the Blue hesitantly begins its race to the sea. Look to the southwest and you easily follow the outlines of a broad, gentle valley. Here in the springtime of its youth, the stream quickly cuts into bedrock and trickles southward, growing stronger with the springs that flow from among the limestone strata.

The Blue becomes almost instantly a scenic river, brawling restlessly and unceasingly over a rocky bed worn between the fresh green of the hills on either bank. In its first nine miles, the Blue tumbles down approximately 160 feet of rocky hillsides, a clear, boulder-strewn stream subject to sudden freshets. The hills grow steeper and higher as the adolescent river rushes toward its first contact with history at the Washington County seat of Salem.

When Indiana became a state in 1816, Salem already was established. Settled by Quakers, who are well known for the high value they place on education and religion, Salem had assumed an unusual wilderness stability by the time the first railroad on the western side of the state pushed its way up from the Ohio River. Salem was its terminus and the builders gave the town a brief fame by naming their road the New Albany and Salem.

Over the years Salem has been home to many distinguished persons and the best known is John Hay, who was secretary and biographer to Lincoln and Secretary of State to McKinley and Theodore Roosevelt. The roster of great names here is a long one—William L. Batt, vice president of the World War II War Production Board; Washington C. DePauw, a pioneer plate glass manufacturer for whom DePauw University was named, and various prominent college presidents, missionaries, evangelists, governors, and Civil War generals and admirals. The Blue River country's contribution to the Civil War was unique. Many of the Union army's tallest men came from this region, including the giant of them all, who stood just under seven feet.

He belonged to a company in which 67 of 101 men exceeded six feet. One Washington County family contributed three men who exceeded six feet six inches.

While the Washington County giants were away fighting the war, Morgan's mercurial raiders slipped into town, spreading more fear than damage, although they did manage to burn the railroad station, water tank, and bridges before speeding eastward on their horses. Legend has it that the Home Guard, determined to resist the invaders, loaded a small swivel cannon on the courthouse square and stood ready for battle. As one of their members, assigned to discharge the weapon, stood poised with a hot coal, he nervously dropped it into his boot. By the time he had regained interest in his weapon, it was too late.

But this was not the Blue River country's first taste of war. A year earlier, Captain Thomas Hines had led a cavalry unit, masquerading as Home Guards, across the Ohio. Hines's men advanced to Valeene before Hoosier un-hospitality turned them back toward the Ohio, where they hoped to find a safe haven. But Home Guard units forced them onto Blue River Island, which stood in the Ohio opposite the mouth of the Blue. They decided to stay and fight it out but when a small steamboat, the *Izetta*, hove into view and fired a single shot

from her six-pound cannon, the Confederates hoisted the white flag of surrender, and Indiana's only Civil War naval battle was over after a single shot was fired.

Above Salem, the hills gather up their waters and feed them into the fine, spidery lines of West Fork's tributaries, but below, its feeder streams are larger, successfully competing for floodwater with the tentacles of streams flowing eastward from the crest of the Knobs. Flushed with the contributions of its sister forks, the river finally becomes one and heads south, sometimes edging past ragged soil worn carpet-thin by the limestone hills. Lanes of trees, whose leafy branches meet overhead, and muslin-covered tobacco seedbeds issue reminders that this is southern Indiana.

The river now invades Indiana's cavern country and underground streams pop into view, supplying power for such industries as Beck's Mill, one of several which once dotted the valley. Built in 1865 on a millsite dating to 1808, it snuggles against a wooded hillside and is powered by a sizable stream that is ponded as it flows from a cave. A conduit drops the water to an overshot wheel which seems to await the signal to rumble into action. Beck's Mill is idle now and closed to the public, but Mrs. Estel L. Allen, the owner, lavishes fond affection on the fascinating building and attempts to keep it repaired, and equipped, ready to operate again on short notice if conditions should become favorable. The mill's last commercial duty was to grind cornmeal which the Monon Railroad (now Seaboard System), successor to the New Albany and Salem, gave to its friends as Christmas gifts in 1953. Occasional grinding was done for neighbors, however, until the early '70s. The mill's scenic setting any time of year delights a photographer's soul and the pleasant music of the stream adds a special romance.

South of Fredericksburg, the Blue becomes a remote, wilderness stream, folding back on itself in a series of rugged curves and hiding among nameless folds in the hills. The wild beauty of the panorama that unrolls here is totally unexpected for Indiana. It is an area hospitable only to the outdoorsman and reached by twisting roads that cling to tops of the ridges and lose themselves under summer arches of dark, green forests. Recreation, Unlimited, a private camping area, best tells by its name the story of a region that cherishes its wildness while civilization rushes across it or away from it.

The Blue's long meanders lengthen its journey by many miles, but at last it reaches Milltown, passing one of the state's few locations where limestone has been obtained from underground mines rather than from open quarries. Below Milltown, the outdoor clan has taken possession of the riverbank, lining it with fishing cabins. Hillsides become steep and wooded and beauty takes on some of its more spectacular forms.

Following a devious route of many windings and bendings, the Blue reaches Rothrock's Mill. Above the dam, the stream is green and still, with splendid reaches where huge trees dabble in the silent water and bass leap abundantly. The abandoned mill, now state property, stares with vacant eyes at fishermen who wet their lines, eagerly waiting to pull in bluegill, catfish, bass, or crappie. Below the dam, the Blue fights valiantly against the encroachment of stubborn hillsides. Elbowed close to the river, the floodplains encourage picnickers and beckon to campers to take possession.

Tributaries in this region are few because of the abundant underground streams which have carved some of America's largest and most beautiful caverns. Marengo Cave, four miles west of Milltown, contains an endless procession of fantastic formations and is open to the public with such refinements as colored lights and concrete stairways.

Wyandotte, acquired by the state in 1966, includes the small, colorful, and spectacular Little Wyandotte, which is simply an appetizer for the main course. Wyandotte has many miles of passageways

Wyandotte Cave is one of the country's largest.

and claims the world's largest underground mountain, which was formed eons ago when the ceiling collapsed in a room a quarter-mile in circumference. The cave, among America's largest, abounds in rare helictites, rock formations which seem to defy gravity.

Just as the subterranean rivers rob the Blue of some of its rightful waters, they also add to the stream. Harrison Spring, named for President William Henry Harrison who built a mill there in 1807, gushes startlingly out of a flat field at the average rate of 18,000 gallons per minute, flowing from a pool thirty-five feet deep. The waters rush away to join Blue River above a village with the enchanting name of White Cloud and near the Interstate 64 crossing.

Near White Cloud, the Blue turns west and begins the last lap of its race to the Ohio, cutting an ever-deepening swath that changes from tree-crowned valley to rugged canyon. U.S. 460 threads through the canyon as the Blue gives itself over completely to beauty.

But the Blue is as treacherous as it is beautiful. Freshets far up the valleys wreak havoc below and spring floods have pushed the water over a bridge that stands fifty feet above normal level. There is further evidence of the willful strength of the Blue as it rushes toward its mother stream with little self-control and a destructive passion. A marker far out of reach up a utility pole shows the water level during the granddaddy of all floods, the 1937 rampage. Since the pole juts from a prominent hill, the flood is nearly beyond comprehension.

Until now the past and the present have flowed together in the Blue, but this is the region where the river enters its future. Recreation is the name of the game. One observer calls the Blue the most natural stream of its size he has seen in the state. Another, writing from the vantage point of a float trip, occasionally sees a house or barn: "Otherwise, we could have been a thousand miles from civilization, such was the stillness and impression of solitude along the river." The area is becoming a major recreational complex where adventure on the water awaits the canoeist, on the land awaits the camper, and underground awaits the avid spelunker.

# Rivers of Nature

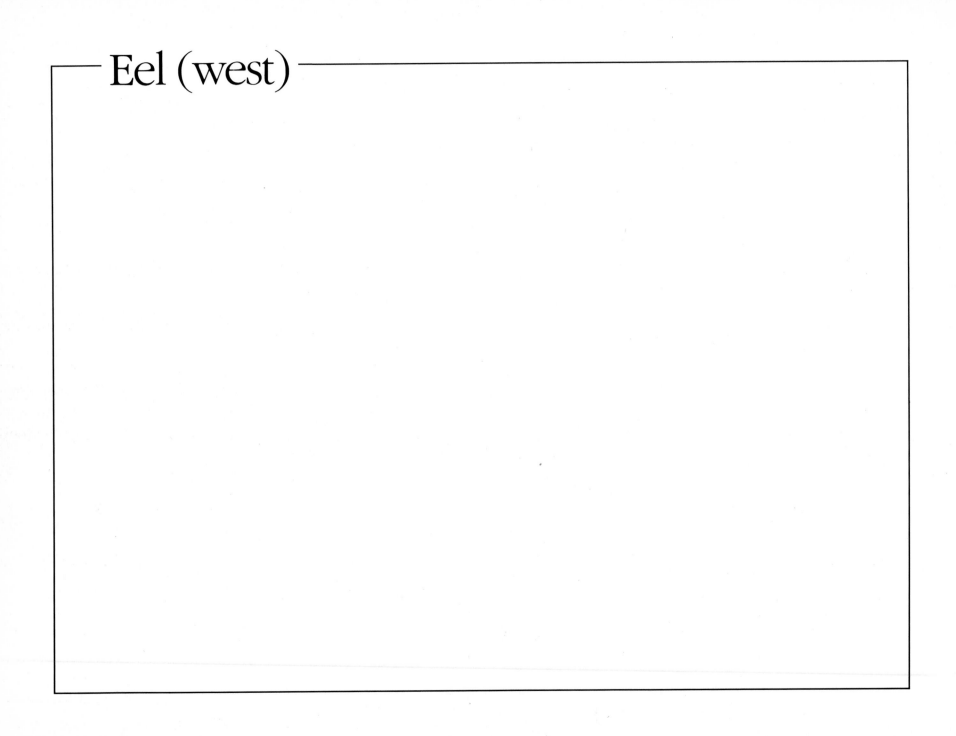

Eel (west)

Western Indiana's Eel River is a river of contrast, contradiction, and controversy. In its 115-mile journey from the rich farmlands of Boone County to the hills of Worthington, where it thrusts its upland flood deep into the side of the West Fork of White River, the Eel goes through a thousand changes in size, width, depth, surface, pace, mood, and surroundings. It is a bold river but it is also indecisive, having trouble making up its mind about its correct name and exhibiting a fuzzy sense of direction. Its bankside fields have yielded a wholly unlikely combination of crops for a state so far north, and its wild flowers and forests are equally unlikely for a state so far south. It has witnessed many turbulent events in history—big or small history.

During the early 1970s the Eel became at once a river of both yesterday and tomorrow, the prize in a fierce struggle between naturalists who were determined to keep it the way it was and the Army engineers who had decided to harness it, spread it into a vast lake, and give it the look of tomorrow. Those who love the Eel more as it is than as it might become battled to a standstill the full strength of the U.S. Army Corps of Engineers, which was determined to scrub clean and drown nearly 5,000 acres of breathtakingly beautiful valley which includes a unique natural area.

The battle, however, was but a replay of the Reservoir War of 130 years ago. The cast was new but the plot was similar. Now, as then, the Eel appears to be the winner, defying man's efforts to transform its valley, except on the river's own terms.

For all its brashness and bravado, the Eel is hesitant and timid about its name. It is known both as Eel River and as Big Walnut Creek, the answer depending on whose map you read and which portion of the stream you consider. If you hold the larger view, the Eel begins its journey to the sea four miles southwest of Lebanon where three field drains converge at a highway culvert to flow away to the southwest, straight as an arrow's flight, in a deep grassy ditch. Its birthplace is the flat, lush farmland where summer heat shimmers over rustling corn and the fields seem to lean against the umbrella of the broad prairie sky. It is a workhorse, harnessed to the task of draining the rich, black soil so that farmers can keep their fields tillable and productive.

Some consider the Eel to be only the lower section, yet the pioneers, who planted the names upon the land, designated a Hendricks County township as Eel River, so that historically the name applies to the entire stream. To the Indians the river was *Schack-a-mak*, which meant "slippery fish," and the translation to "Eel" has endured. The Indian name has been preserved by the state in Shakamak State Park, established in 1929 near Jasonville.

For many miles of the stream's early life it is serene, yet its appearance varies greatly in its different sections. Near the headwaters the valley becomes noticeable, ever so slightly, as the river, growing with dozens of field drains, begins gently to erode the land.

By the time the Eel reaches Jamestown, it shows a new face. Spoil banks of the dredged channel disappear and the stream winds through a deeper valley, sliding over glistening shallows that portend the personality changes to come. The waters run swiftly and the bed becomes rocky. Rising corridors of banks signal the approach of enchanting scenery. The gentle contours of farm fields give way to oak- and maple-clothed hills. The river indulges in gracious and expansive moments as the sides pile up their height as much as 135 feet, looking almost mountainous compared to the scenes which came before. Small tributaries plunge down stairways of falls to meet the river. Suddenly the Eel has become an invitation to adventure.

Out of sight of roads and power lines and enveloped in a stately forest there is a natural wonderland of primitive, unspoiled beauty northeast of Bainbridge that naturalists and conservationists guard against all comers. The federal government has taken strong note of the region's wonders, registering it as a National Natural Landmark. The river's steep palisades and deep gorges are vigorous testimonials of a rugged, determined current that tumbles restlessly and unceasingly over a rock-strewn bed. Here, more than anywhere else, the Eel is adventurous and challenging; its charms are never-ending and those who see its glories can never forget its beauty.

Botanists report that vegetation in this area is at least 5,000 years behind the times and 200 miles farther south than it should be. Fifty centuries ago this central Indiana wilderness was like today's New England in climate and vegetation, but as the great Wisconsin glacial sheet retreated and its weight disappeared, the land sprang back to a slightly higher elevation, the streams cut deep, entrenched valleys, and the climate became warmer. Most of the Canadian yew and hemlock retreated 200 miles to a colder climate and cooler, more moist soil, but some of it remained and dug a toehold on the steep, shaded, north-facing slopes.

Somehow this little enclave of two square miles, with its groves that have never known an ax, remained untouched. Fortunately, people who appreciated its wonders and guarded them jealously owned the land until much of it passed safely into the hands of The Nature Conservancy. Leaves and twigs from monsters such as two of Indiana's largest sassafras trees, one of the world's two or three largest sugar maples, and a thirty-two-inch-diameter hemlock that probably is Indiana's largest carpeted the forest floor and made it soft and springy underfoot. The tract is a veritable who's who of the forest. It consists of oak-maple and beech-hickory types with enough sycamores scattered about to make you wonder if you are standing on the banks of the Wabash, far away.

Any alert youngster can come up with newts, salamanders, skinks, frogs, and turtles, as well as mussel shells, in the cool ravines and along the stream. Beaver, rare in Indiana, have been reported. Deer, opossum, raccoon, fox, and rabbits roam the uplands.

Flowers, including many rare species, carpet the woods. Sweet William, swamp buttercup, and yellow violet crowd the paths and moisture-loving ferns spring from the cool north slopes. Orchids, snow trillium, Indian cucumber root, and bishop's cap are common. The area's 1,300-plus plant species make it a welcome laboratory for students of four nearby colleges.

Naturalists have cataloged at least 120 species of birds in the enclave. The most arresting feature is found in a grove of eighty-foot-tall beeches which have formed Indiana's largest great blue heron rookery for at least seventy years. As many as forty nests can be counted at one time, and it is fascinating in spring to watch as the graceful, long-legged water birds wheel overhead, repeatedly alighting, then taking off with neck outstretched and legs extended.

Man has made only slight changes and these in keeping with its natural surroundings. Boundary roads cross the stream on covered bridges, which impart the feeling that the whole area is fenced off from time and progress and that entrance is only through timbered tunnels to yesteryear. A sturdy stone house that dates to 1831 was occupied until recent times. It had no electricity and no phone, and it depended on an adjacent spring for water. A nearby log cabin further tightens the tie to the pioneer past.

This is the Big Walnut Natural Area the Army engineers set out to inundate. Not that they would have flooded the entire tract. The uplands were safe and some of the rare plant areas in this living library would have been flooded only intermittently. The implication was a greater threat than those who love the river could endure. The Izaak Walton League, headed by its then national president, Roy B. Crockett of Marion, mounted a determined attack. A Wabash College botanist, Dr. Robert Petty, pleaded eloquently in Washington that a book torn in half is destroyed, even if half remains.

The Department of the Interior listened and offered to save the natural area by moving the dam three miles downstream to a location one mile north of Greencastle. Subsequently, pressure forced cancellation of the entire plan, which, as nearly as can be determined, is relegated to the storehouse of unfulfilled government projects.

Below the Big Walnut Natural Area the valley broadens, turning spectacularly beautiful before your eyes. The stream becomes a placid highway through the forests as it sweeps gently southward, growing from the strength of a thousand brooks. Canoeists love to glide its quiet waters and fishermen take possession of its banks.

The river pauses momentarily to leap a dam at the Greencastle waterworks and pass the only city along its entire course. When it isn't resounding to the activities of DePauw University's 2,200 students, it busies itself producing metal stampings, capacitors, and cement and distributing business machine supplies.

Below Greencastle's urban interruption the stream again becomes rustic, spanned in its 115-mile length by seven sturdy covered bridges, largest number on any Hoosier river. Bankside back country roads capture the beauty of alternate hills and valleys as the unspoiled scenery spreads into rare and beautiful landscapes. Near the rugged southwest corner of Putnam County, Big Walnut joins forces with its sisters, Mill and Deer creeks, at a point where geographers of all persuasions agree on the name "Eel."

In 1948 the Army engineers pounced on Mill Creek and converted it into 1,400-acre Cataract Lake, which backs up to the foot of Cataract Falls. To reach the falls, Mill Creek waters churn furiously for three-quarters of a mile against the restrictive hand of steep, stony bluffs that crowd both sides of the narrow gorge, then plunge eighty-one feet into a turmoil of froth over the rocky bed beneath.

The upper falls is a series of giant steps which terminates by sending the stream crashing down forty-five feet into a swarm of boiling water that is picturesque every moment of the year. A 109-year-old covered bridge, like a brooding giant, stands guard above it. A short distance downstream the lower falls sends the water hurrying into Cataract Lake and past Lieber State Recreation Area, which memorializes the founder of Indiana's state park system.

As it flows southward, flushed with the contribution of its principal tributaries, the Eel passes the village of Bowling Green, where Clay Countians built their first courthouse in 1827. The river was more important then, having been declared a navigable highway, but it gave little service and after fifty years of hopeful waiting for boats that never came, Clay Countians transferred their seat of government to Brazil.

Below Bowling Green the Eel swings through an unbelievably flat valley that eventually stretches in table-top terrain to a width of six miles. The banks seem a monotonous extension of flatness, above which, at a respectful distance, thread the watchful levees. The river wriggles in the same southwest direction it has followed from its source until it swirls against Old Hill, one of the infrequent bluffs it encounters in its lower, shifting passage and is swung about to a surprising left face, to flow southeastward.

At this point, five miles west of Clay City, the Eel first encountered that grandiose fiasco of yesterday, the Wabash and Erie Canal, which was elbowed close to the riverbank by the formidable hills. A 464-mile transportation ditch which various interests periodically attempt to reincarnate, it connected Lake Erie at Toledo, Ohio, with the Ohio River at Evansville, and it etched a colorful chapter into the history of both states. Along the Eel, however, it lit a slow fuse to some highly combustible tempers and wrote a page known as the Reservoir War.

There was no great problem in pushing the canal, which was the continent's longest artificial waterway, from Toledo to Terre Haute, but the jump from the Wabash Valley into the White produced the greatest water supply problem on the entire route. Between the two rivers the canal climbed the summit and was forced to rely on the

undependable water supply of the shallow, shifting Eel. Engineers solved the problem by building two immense reservoirs, totaling more than 5,000 acres, on Birch Creek near Saline City and on Splunge Creek, west of Clay City. River water, impounded by a dam and conducted to the canal through a long feeder, supplemented the reservoirs. The dam had been constructed in 1839 during Indiana's great internal improvements fever, but the quirks of the mischievous river had washed around one end before the canal got around to being completed eleven years later.

Laborers worked like beavers—1,215 of them in the summit section—while local residents watched with wary eyes as the water level rose, though not every far. Certain that the reservoirs bred disease which menaced their life and health, they pressured Governor Joseph A. Wright into sending a task force of five physicians to examine the situation. They reported all well and returned home, pointing out that the natural, pre-reservoir condition of intermittent flooding was more dangerous to health than the permanent flooding which followed.

The residents were not satisfied with the report. Their cup of endurance was full to overflowing and they took matters into their own hands. On a warm June night in 1854 a mob cut the Birch Creek

dam and later burned the feeder canal discharge weir and attempted to burn the wooden Eel River dam. They effectively drained the canal, halting through traffic for 150 miles and causing a $20,000 loss in physical damage and anticipated tolls. Governor Wright countered by offering a reward for capturing the vandals. The state then set out to move 2,900 cubic yards of earth, every shovelful by hand, to restore the dam and agreed to remove all standing timber. Opposition leaders said they would interfere no more.

But the anti-canal forces only grew bolder. At noon on May 10, 1855, a mob of 100 men, armed and with their faces blackened, drove off a construction crew, burned the Birch Creek aqueduct, and wielded pick and shovel until they had breached the dam.

Governor Wright quickly ordered a militia company up from Evansville. Strong-arming their way through the ranks of canal opponents, they stood guard for a month, fraternizing with the natives and protecting crews sent to repair the $10,000 act of vandalism. Things went well under the militia's watchful eye, and the canal resumed its intended place as a busy artery of commerce. Cumbersome canalboats, able to load bulging cargoes on their backs, again paraded to and fro.

Now that all was quiet on the waterfront the militia returned

*Left to right*: Manufacturing ceramic and drain tile and brick, Brazil once called itself the "Clay Products Center of the World." ✒The river quickly enlarges itself in the headwaters area near Jamestown.

home. The next day the dam again was mysteriously breached, and the gurgling water rushing through the break sounded the canal's death knell. It rendered the entire section south of Terre Haute useless, and the trustees realized they had lost the war.

All through navigation was abandoned within three years, and local commerce south of Terre Haute ceased by 1860. The bawling "canawleers," shouting at the mules, untangling towlines, drinking and swapping yarns, disappeared. Thus the Wabash and Erie Canal story ended, not with a bang but with a whimper.

Perhaps it was just as well. Progress, by this time, had brought the railroad to supplant the canalboat and that new annihilator of space, the iron horse, entered the valley. As inevitable as the fact that pushed wheels roll, the skittish creature was coaxed along the former towpaths, and navigation became a topic for antiquarians. Eventually the railroad tied together Terre Haute and Evansville by a circuitous route twenty-five miles longer than an existing direct rail line but deemed practical because of the valley's economic potential.

Both the canal and its iron successor cut a path through Indiana's richest mineral area. The rail line, recently abandoned, hauled millions of tons of coal from fields in Greene, Clay, and Owen counties to heat the Midwest's homes and power its factories and generating

plants. The rich traffic also tempted the Monon (now Seaboard System), which thrust a branch through the valley for fifty miles into the same fields. When iron ore was discovered, it brought high hopes of an industry to rival that of Pittsburgh, but after a few blast furnaces were built the dreams disappeared. Clay mining for brick and tile manufacture followed, making Brazil the world's clay capital.

The river, meanwhile, survived great changes as men, goaded by obstacles, fell upon it, removed its playful meanders, widened its banks, and deepened its channel. Now flowing uninterrupted through the wide, level bottoms, the Eel approaches its rendezvous with the West Fork of White River near Worthington.

There was once a grandiose dream here called Point Commerce. To be the new metropolis of the Midwest, it would stand at the mouth of the Eel where the Central Canal down from Indianapolis joined the Wabash and Erie and where White River would carry a busy burden of steamboats. But Point Commerce has long since disappeared—if it ever existed as anything more than a paper city. The steamboat traffic failed to materialize, the Central Canal was never built, and the Wabash and Erie lived only a short and fitful life.

The tempestuous Eel, in its last mile a serene pathway between

the fresh green of the trees on either bank, had another dream made by the people in its valley. Pioneer settlers grew corn and cotton side by side near the river's mouth and felt such confidence in the "southern" crop that they built a cotton gin to process it. But like many another enterprise along the changing Eel, it died in infancy.

When a party of 200 Indians who were paddling their canoes past the river's mouth in 1819 stopped to investigate a merry commotion along the bank, they contributed a comic opera touch to the lives of the settlers. Beaching their craft, they joined a festive pioneer wedding party, adding a colorful chapter that would provide many years of telling.

Few streams anywhere provide so many strong contrasts; fertile, level fields and rugged, hilly forests; vegetation displaced from the North and crops displaced from the South; agricultural wealth and mineral riches; men who built the key to a vast water transport system and the men who destroyed it; pastoral meanderings and spectacular waterfalls.

The Eel, it is evident, is a naturally uncommon river.

# Elkhart

The Elkhart, little known but greatly loved river of the Hoosier Northeast, is enjoying the last laugh. For more than a century and a third it has been chuckling softly to itself over man's futile efforts to harness it, re-route it, and transform it, but now the pendulum has returned full swing. A gentle river, gracious and inviting, the Elkhart has never-ending charms and any attempt to alter them, it should have been realized at the outset, never would succeed.

Over the years it has been both an easygoing, gracious, lake-fed meadow stream and a driving, hardworking body of water harnessed to provide energy for man. It has been at the same time an affluent, leisurely gentleman bent on fun and relaxation and a brawny blue-collar worker scarcely able to find a day's rest. Yet it retains throughout its course the grace and placidity of its upper reaches and the quiet lakes that create its headwaters. Nature is its chief characteristic.

Rising by two branches in Lagrange and Noble counties, the twin Elkharts follow their separate, winding, lake-strewn paths until they join forces at a remote spot east of Ligonier. This small city, once known for its large Jewish population and its three Jewish heads of local government, was the birthplace of Simon W. Strauss, who originated the concept of real estate bonds to finance large structures such as New York City's Chrysler building. After coming together to form the main stream, the waters head northwest, leaping dams and in bygone days powering factories and energizing hydroelectric stations until they meet the St. Joseph River in the heart of the industrial city of Elkhart, approximately sixty miles from their sources and thirty-eight miles from their junction. En route, the Elkhart drains approximately 700 square miles and provides outlet for nearly 100 lakes.

For a journey down this quietly beautiful stream, let's begin with the South Branch, which is being considered for inclusion in the state's Natural and Scenic River System. Typical of its way of life, the South Branch rises in a natural, isolated setting. It flows from Hawk Lake, a shallow, eighteen-acre body of water, hidden—as in the palm of a hand—among rolling hills. It is untouched by roads, sheltered from outside sounds and best known only to fisherman of the area who regularly pull from its shallow depths bass worth shouting about.

From the kidney-shaped lake, the Elkhart winds casually in and out of a series of small lakes and ponds. The lake shores are marshy, topped with thick stands of cattails and rushes and tenanted by kill-deer, red-winged blackbirds, and bank swallows. From headwaters to mouth, fishermen line the river, picnickers take possession of its banks, and small boats and canoes glide over its waters.

Coursing through an unnamed notch in the hills, the river continues southward through a grassy meadow before striking the Saginaw-Erie Moraine, which deflects it northward. This moraine, more than any other factor, determines the course and character of the Elkhart. Left by the great glacial ice sheets, it is a high, rolling ridge extending northeastward toward Lakes Huron and Erie. Both branches of the Elkhart wander down the moraine's slope seeking the gravel plain over which the lower portion of the river flows.

Turning northward, the South Branch gathers the waters of countless cool lakes, including those which form the liquid backbone of Chain O' Lakes State Park. Established in 1960, the 2,678-acre playland has become a favorite with the emphasis on camping. A beach on Sand Lake, however, offers water sports. Boats are permitted, although in keeping with the Elkhart's quiet heritage, gasoline motors are not. The call of the outdoors is strong here.

Like all the Elkhart River country, Chain O' Lakes is a child of the glaciers. As the ice sheet retreated it gouged in the hilly upland a four mile-long trough characterized by a group of sand knobs. The nine connected lakes, plus two others in the park, are scattered among the knobs, and the adjoining land rises fifty to sixty feet to make the area rugged even for the state's hilly lake region. Connecting waters are so lazy that less than five feet of elevation separate Miller Lake at the foot of the chain from Long Lake at the head. The Elkhart follows a marshy way here, and the infant river winds sluggishly across the land, its willow-lined banks punctuated by the outflow of clusters of cool, clear lakes.

Near Port Mitchell, where the Elkhart glides through a basin containing a quintet of lakes, man first attempted to harness the river and alter its course. The time was the 1830s and canal fever burned furiously in the state. One project was to connect Fort Wayne and

Lake Michigan, with the stipulation that the canal pass through Goshen and South Bend. This would have made it uniquely an Elkhart River canal, either paralleling the river or canalizing its channel.

Work was done sporadically, and Governor David Wallace reported in 1838 that seven miles of the Erie and Michigan Canal was under contract. Work also had begun on two reservoirs, one of which is now called Sylvan Lake.

This was the Elkhart's first bout with men determined to change its character. But the internal improvements bubble burst and all work was abandoned. Port Mitchell, which was established in the canal project's glory days and served as Noble's county seat and site of a woolen mill, became an inconspicuous scattering of modest dwellings, nothing more.

Below the onetime county seat, a road runs beside the river, providing easy access for fishermen before the Elkhart ambles off among the encroaching hills. The banks are low and the channel poorly defined, so that a slight rise in the water level sends the Elkhart expanding over acres of lowlands. One large area locally is called "The Spreads." Winding among lakes and around a mountainous moraine, the South Branch meets the North Branch west of Wawaka, birthplace of Ford Frick, former commissioner of professional baseball.

The North Branch flows from Messick Lake, lowermost of an extensive chain northwest of Wolcottville. It wanders eighteen scenic miles before it meets its sister stream. This is Amish land, where a drive through the countryside frequently turns up picturesque buggies, filled with bearded men and bonnet-topped women. It is the land of neat, prosperous farms, where electricity and power equipment are little known and the way of life is in keeping with the gentle simplicities of the river.

The first Amish settled along the Elkhart during the early 1840s, migrating from Pennsylvania. They found this to be pleasing country, rolling and fertile, and they sent word back east about their promised land. Others of their denomination followed until the Amish and the Mennonites from whom they sprang dominated the Elkhart River country. More than one of every five Lagrange County residents adheres to the Old Order Amish faith and when combined with the Mennonites comprise 30 percent of the population, more than triple the next largest denomination. In Elkhart County, the Amish and Mennonites nearly outnumber adherents of the United Methodist Church, which predominates Protestantism here as in most Indiana counties. The Amish influence, no doubt, is responsible for Elkhart ranking near the upper 2 percent of the nation's horse-owning counties. The Mennonite concentration along the Elkhart led to founding Goshen College in 1903, the outgrowth of an earlier institution located at Elkhart. It was the first four-year Mennonite college in the nation.

During its sluggish course toward its sister stream, the North Branch gathers in the waters of Sylvan Lake, the only canal reminder that stands intact in the valley. Sylvan, its irregular shores lined by beautiful wooded banks and its surface studded with picturesque islands, is entirely man-made. Conceived as a canal feeder, it was too beautiful to abandon when the project died, despite loss of the dam three times during the first sixteen years. For nearly thirty years, thousands swarmed to the Chautauqua programs at Island Park Assembly and to drink the mineral waters of nearby Kneipp Springs Sanatorium, which a Catholic order founded in 1895. More recently it has become the home of a Protestant group.

Nature lovers have crowded into the valley for years. By far the most famous was Gene Stratton Porter, whose writings influenced earlier generations of amateur naturalists. Her search for a natural setting to replace her beloved Limberlost, near Geneva, which disappeared under man's civilizing impact, led her to the wooded shores of Sylvan Lake. In 1914 she moved into her new fourteen-room cedar log home in Wildflower Woods and resided there until failing health caused her to move to California in 1923. The state now operates as memorials not only Mrs. Porter's home but also the adjacent woods, retaining much of the original appearance by allowing fallen trees to decay and return the nutrients to the soil.

More recently other naturalists have come. Purdue's Alton A. Lindsey, an author of the authoritative *Natural Areas in Indiana and Their Preservation*, listed no fewer than nine tracts along the Elkhart

that cried out for preservation in our increasingly industrial society. They ranged from the six-acre Porter Woods to the 600-acre Merry Lea Nature and Religious Center, where sharp-eyed bird lovers have observed 111 feathered species, and a thirty-acre marsh provides a specialized nature sanctuary. Dr. Lindsey rates highly Browand Woods and Olin Lake, which is believed to be Indiana's largest in a completely natural state, since it has no structures on its shores. The Nature Conservancy now controls the area. Quog Lake, whose name comes from a contraction of the words "Quaking Bog," is known for cranberries, tamarack, and the rare pitcher plant, which consumes insects it traps. Cattails, ferns, and yellow pond lilies grow from the marsh along the lake.

To naturalists the Elkhart country is unusually appealing. Two leading conservation organizations, The Nature Conservancy and ACRES, Inc., have placed under their protection eleven natural areas. ACRES was so imbued with the river's charms that it paid the supreme tribute of locating three of its first six areas and three-fourths of its total acreage along the Elkhart.

The river basin provides a complete variety of unpolluted habitat, ranging from the glacial demonstration plot that is Lonidaw Nature Preserve near Kendallville to the Long Swamp Woods near Wolf Lake, which contains the largest stand of yellow birch in Indiana and has been invaded by several species of Canadian plants. At Shoup-Parson's Woods in Goshen, where the Elkhart plunges over a sizable dam, Goshen College biologists found a handy study area where they cataloged 174 species of birds, the largest number found in any single Indiana area.

Willows line the river with a green fringe in summer and the white of dogwood glistens in spring. The sweet scent of honeysuckle fills the air and sumac, pawpaw, and spicebush enhance the botanic interest. Orchids carpet the forest floor, while hawks wheel overhead and woodpeckers send their rat-a-tat-tat resounding through the woods. A cattail swamp lines the river.

While the Elkhart country may mean nature to some, it means sports, summer or winter, to others. Wawasee, Indiana's largest natural lake, pours its waters into the Elkhart, but not before thousands have enjoyed its 2,618 acres for swimming, boating, water skiing, and fishing. Wawasee also means winter sports, particularly at Mt. Wawasee near New Paris. Enthusiasts flock to the slopes of a high morainic belt, selecting those for experts, intermediates, or beginners. Bright lights illuminate the runs for night skiing.

Below the Mt. Wawasee area the Elkhart first feels man's restric-

tions. In the 1920s The Northern Indiana Public Service Company built two small hydropower stations, one northeast of New Paris, the other west of Benton. Canals carry the water from ponds created by dams. Near Goshen, however, the river was forced into its hardest labor by the hydraulic canal built in 1868 to power mills and factories. At Waterford Mills, two miles south of Goshen, a flour mill was built as early as the mid-1830s.

In those early days people had navigation on their minds, and the Elkhart was described in 1842 as a "fine, boatable stream," that could be made navigable to a point three miles above Goshen. As a water highway, it already carried cargoes of flour, pork, and wines. Dams and bridges, however, impeded traffic; Goshen merchants once demolished a newly constructed bridge and threatened to remove all other structures.

As railroads appeared, boat traffic dwindled. Goshen, the county seat, became a metal and woodworking center and a producer of rubber products and control devices, but it lost its dominant position to Elkhart, which listened more to the snort of the iron horse than to the whistle of the boat.

Elkhart today is a manufacturing city of 41,303 where nearly 100 factories produce mobile homes, campers, or parts for them. More than twenty other plants give it the title of "World's Musical Instrument Capital." The city also is known for production of Alka-Seltzer, Anacin, and Dristan. Still other plants produce automotive and electrical components and furniture.

Obviously so much industry requires vast amounts of electrical power; and the Elkhart's small hydropower plants eventually became economically inadequate. In 1967 Northern Indiana Public Service Company donated its three power areas totaling approximately 1,000 acres to Elkhart County for public park use. Thus with a strong assist from industry this river of nature was returned to the boaters, fishermen, and conservationists for whom its placid waters are best suited.

Fawn

If one were to list Indiana's "wildest" rivers, an obscure little stream in the northeastern part of the state would be near the top. It's the Fawn River. Sportsmen have known about the Fawn for years. For more than a half-century the Fawn has been considered one of Indiana's most adventurous canoeing streams, and like the Pigeon River which parallels it a short distance to the south, it is strictly for the outdoorsman. In the words of no less an authority than "Bayou Bill" Scifres, *The Indianapolis Star*'s Outdoors Editor, the Fawn is "Indiana's answer to Canada."

A narrow, twisting, shallow marsh river only forty-four miles long, the Fawn lends itself completely to raw beauty and it more than compensates in charm, tranquility, and that wilderness feeling for its lack of size. It flows smoothly but the pace is often swift, as if the river were in a mad rush to gain substance and the fullness of maturity, something that it never quite attains. It is sort of an afterthought of the last glacial age, and nothing short of aeons will change it.

The Fawn rises at Orland and from source to mouth at Constantine, Michigan, where it joins the St. Joseph, there are no settlements larger than the tiny villages of Greenfield Mills, in Lagrange County, and Fawn River, Michigan. In between, there are woodlands and marshes and the stream meanders lazily through the meadow grasses and cattails so that it sometimes flows 400 wandering yards to move 100 yards west, or 200 feet to advance 20. However, above the milldams there is a good current and on the straightaways the quick-moving, smooth-flowing water gives a canoeist the feeling he is sliding downhill.

The Fawn rises from a Steuben County lake at the north edge of Orland, which Vermonters settled in 1834, and helps provide water for nearby Fawn River State Fish Hatchery. Twenty-two of the hatchery's forty-three acres are under water and each year the ponds produce fish by the millions. Many pike which lurk in the deep spots along the Fawn are among the 600,000 stocked in northern Indiana's waters from the hatchery's annual production, which also includes 49,000 catfish and 17,000 bass.

Although official edict places the Fawn's source at Orland, its headwaters rise about twenty miles farther east near Fremont and trickle west across Steuben County under the name of Crooked Creek, growing stronger as they drain nearly forty morainal lakes.

This keeps the Fawn's waters clear and constant, since each lake acts as a huge expansion tank for the wandering stream's tributaries.

In earlier days the Fawn and Crooked Creek waters turned mill wheels at such settlements as Nevada Mills, Fawn River, Greenfield Mills, and Orland. Although most of the mills long have been silent, the glassy ponds remain to add a picturesque touch to a river that emerges only occasionally from its wilderness hideaway and then slips quietly away into the marshes and meadows.

Nevada Mills, although abandoned long ago, has left a rich legacy to Hoosier vacationers. Its dam now controls the water level of the Jimerson-James-Snow Lake basin and it assures visitors to Pokagon State Park that the water level will remain adequate for boating, fishing, swimming, and water skiing. In years past, many persons enjoyed a pleasant boat trip from Potawatomi Inn at Pokagon across James and Jimerson lakes and down the Crooked Creek channel to the dam. Lines of rowboats were attached to motorcraft and pulled gently through the pastoral stream where cattle came to drink and suspiciously eye the processions gliding over their stream. Park visitors disembarked to enjoy box lunches delivered from the inn and consumed to the pleasant gurglings of water dashing over the dam.

A short distance below Nevada Mills, Crooked Creek receives its only important Indiana tributary, drainage from a chain of lakes that extend as far as Angola, seat of Steuben County, home of Tri-State University, and a resort center in northeastern Indiana. The largest body of water in the chain is 802-acre Crooked Lake.

Along the shores of that lake once ran the St. Joseph Valley Railway, a sort of comic opera transportation system. In its final days, two trains collided at Inverness, killing two passengers and injuring twenty-five. Investigation of the crash involving passenger and freight trains revealed the following: The conductor was so busy helping the women passengers off that he failed to protect the rear of his train. Besides that, a rear warning light was missing, the train carried no warning torpedoes, and the conductor didn't know where the warning flares were kept. The number of passengers on the train was three and one-half times its seating capacity. The freight train which thundered out of the darkness and struck the standing passenger train probably couldn't have stopped in time anyway; the locomotive brakes had gone out during the day. The fireman hadn't bothered to read the train orders and running on schedule was difficult because there was no standard clock on the entire railroad. This incident on the Valley Line, which connected Angola and Orland before it crossed into Pigeon River country, was one of the few incidents to interrupt the Fawn River area's tranquility, although there are places today where the roar of trucks on the Northern Indiana Toll Road disturbs the calm.

At the village of Greenfield Mills there is a water-powered mill which has operated continuously since 1846. There is a special route to the mill—north on Lagrange County road 1100 East from Ind. 120, then left on county road 700 North—that is sort of a time machine in reverse. It provides an easy transition from the twentieth century back into the nineteenth. For a few hundred feet the road winds through a dense forest. There are no ditches, no fences, no cultivation, no houses. It is a "time tunnel" between lofty branches which meet overhead in summer. Then suddenly the forest ends and the millpond lies dead ahead. The mill, at the far end, forms the backdrop. Although originally operated directly by waterpower, the mill now uses water-generated electricity to run its machinery and to create a surplus that it sells to a utility company.

From Greenfield Mills the Fawn wanders like an undecided child, crossing the Indiana-Michigan border five times before permanently turning away from its Hoosier birthplace. Fishermen who cross the boundary must be licensed by both states.

Michigan's counterpart of Greenfield Mills is the village of Fawn River, which grew up around a glassy millpond and the willow-lined stream that issues from it. The mill building, quietly aloof, formed part of the Fawn's rich heritage.

Back in Indiana while mills were in their prime a fascinating group flourished and withered in the Fawn River country. This was the Congregation of Saints, founded in 1843 as "the perfect solution to mankinds's social ills." This experiment in communal living was one of about thirty such communities that sprang up across the United States before the Civil War. The Hoosier colony was located at Lexington, now Brighton, where Ind. 3 and Ind. 120 now intersect.

The problems of the time were simply some of today's problems in a simpler setting. The colony's constitution spoke of the "innumerable evils which afflict all classes of society, and despairing of deliv-

erance through our present social and political systems. . . ." It pointed out the need for "ample provisions for the aged and afflicted" and described society as "little else than a pandemonium." As a result, the Congregation of Saints agreed "to unite in association, and to purchase and cultivate a domain of from 2,000 to 6,000 acres of land; to prosecute such branches of commercial, mechanical, scientific, agricultural, and horticultural employments as shall be conducive to our good; to divide the produce of labor among ourselves on a discriminating scale, by which each shall, as nearly as possible, reap what he may sow; to abolish the distinction of master and servant; to preserve individuality; to secure the rights and extend the privileges of women. . . ." The Saints' plan didn't work out, however, and the congregation broke up shortly after it was organized.

Through the various changes and events that have occurred in Fawn country, the river has not changed. It still remains a river of nature and "Indiana's answer to Canada."

*Above*: Greenfield Mills has operated on water power since 1846.

Pigeon

*Left to right*: A series of dams control water level. ✑Howe Military Academy was established in 1884.

Among the undulating moraines of northeastern Indiana, the quiet waters of two streams unite to form a glassy millpond at a Lagrange County village with the engaging name of Mongo, which is shortened from the Potawatomi *Mongoquinong*, meaning "Big Squaw." Waters issuing from the pond bound over the dam to dash themselves into a frenzy of sparkling foam on the rocks below. Then they sweep out of sight around a willow-lined bend and begin their quiet journey to a rendezvous with the St. Joseph River, thirty-six miles away. This is the Pigeon River, named for Chief White Pigeon whose Potawatomi braves hunted its banks and fished its waters in the long ago.

Then the white man came and cast a long shadow that portended change in the unspoiled character of the Pigeon. The change came, and the Pigeon, finding the shackles of civilization not altogether to its liking, reverted after a time to its former self—the river of the hunter and angler. With a strong assist from the Indiana Department of Natural Resources, the Pigeon returned to its original character and mile for mile and drop for drop it is doubtful whether any river in the state can exceed it today for fun, recreation and natural, unspoiled beauty.

Yet the Pigeon was not an uncomplicated river. It is true that early visitors would have encountered the simple, idyllic life of the Potawatomi, but they also would have come across a web of ideas and convictions that led to intricate social philosophies, complex industries, advanced educational institutions, and fantastic transportation dreams that flourished for a little while and then went away. Today's river is once again wandering and charming, mirroring the swift, powerful flight of the kingfisher, echoing the quack of the mallard, providing a comfortable home for thousands of trout, giving a warm spot in the sun to countless turtles, and carrying the silent traffic of endless numbers of canoes.

Modern nomenclature has the Pigeon beginning at Mongo, although above the village the stream is known as Pigeon Creek, and it flows nearly as far above Mongo under that description as it does below Mongo designated as a river. From the extreme headwaters, its length is about seventy miles and its Indiana drainage is 350 square miles. The entire Indiana portion of the river lies in Lagrange County, but the lower fourteen miles winds through Michigan, although it is never more than two miles above the Indiana line.

Pigeon Creek rises in the extreme northeast corner of Indiana in what once was called Cedar Lake, but now, having succumbed to the advance of cattails and swamp grasses, is called Cedar Marsh. For nearly twenty miles the stream flows south, hugging the eastern face of a morainic belt left by the great glaciers of 15,000 years ago. Then

at Pleasant Lake it abruptly turns northwest, slices through the moraine in a deep channel and arrives at Mongo after flowing over a gravel plain marked by many lakes, large and small.

More than fifty lakes drain into the Pigeon and act as expansion tanks which control the flow and clarity of the water. The river valley is shallow and narrow, averaging less than a half-mile wide. Where it chooses to spread out, the land is often swampy and wild. Hugging the moraine as it does, it receives no tributaries from the north and is paralleled on that side for more than half its length by Fawn River, which approaches within a mile at one point but does not join it.

The Pigeon first showed signs of returning to its primitive self when the state opened the Pigeon River Fish and Wildlife Area in 1956. Beginning with a modest lowland area bordering the river, it has grown to 11,500 acres and stretches along seventeen miles of waterfront, with Mongo in the center.

Above Mongo, two miles of dikes seven feet high control floods and create a shallow lake where a Canada goose flock keeps company with other species. It is a land of shallow marshes and meandering streams interspersed with low sand ridges and gravel hills.

This is a veritable sportsman's department store where any man can shoulder a gun and expect to come home with his share of the hunt. During the 1984 season, nearly 18,000 hunters carried home deer, pheasant, rabbit, squirrel, quail, ducks, and woodcock.

But the Pigeon is not alone for the hunter. The Indiana Department of Natural Resources produces 50,000 trout annually at its Curtis Creek Station near Mongo, and in 1984 10,000 found their way into the Pigeon's cool waters, alongside the northern pike and bass that make it one of the state's best fishing streams. Anglers favor the region between Mongo and Ontario, where ponds back up behind three abandoned power dams, as well as the Scott Public Access Site at the location of the former Scott Mill dam.

The upper reaches of the Pigeon are safely wadeable but sportsmen favor canoes in the lower part, and they find a ready supply of rentals and auxiliary equipment maintained by the state. As a float stream, the Pigeon is among Indiana's best. Campgrounds are well spaced along the way.

Long before the sportsmen re-discovered the Pigeon, the river had its brief romance with industry. Flowing through an area settled largely by thrifty, industrious New Englanders, the river found itself harnessed to turn numerous factory wheels. This led to a running duel between the adjacent towns of Lima—since renamed Howe—and Ontario. These were great days for both towns. Lima gloried in being the county seat and took on importance when a forge was established to work iron ore which was discovered nearby.

In the meantime Ontario residents dammed the Pigeon and used the power at various times to operate grist and flour mills, a woolen factory, a tannery, and factories producing boots, shoes, gloves, potash, and wood products. Ontario reached the ultimate in industrial dreams when Carlo Jenks, a local resident, envisioned it as a silk manufacturing center. He gave substance to his dream by planting mulberry trees and importing silk moth pupae to feed on the leaves. But neither the trees nor the moths flourished and the Hoosier threat to the Japanese economy died a quick death.

The Howe-Ontario feud continued in education. Chief prize here was the Lagrange Collegiate Institute, which was dangled over the heads of both towns until Ontario finally landed it. The Institute went into receivership about 1881 and Ontario has found more lasting educational fame by being the birthplace of both Dr. Charles L. Doolittle and his son, Eric, who became internationally famous astronomers while on the University of Pennsylvania faculty.

The feud ground to a halt when both towns encountered greater problems. Lima lost the county seat to Lagrange, and Ontario declined until today it is little more than an open square bounded by scattered dwellings, a church, and vacant lots which indicate that busier days have been enjoyed there.

The last educational plum went to Howe, however, when it became the home of Howe Military School in 1884. With ties to the Episcopal Church, it serves 275 pupils in grades 5 through 12 on its 135-acre campus. The architecture of its more than twenty buildings ranges from the ornate Italianate mansion, which serves as the administration building, to the modified Norman-style St. James chapel, which is described as one of the nation's most beautiful school chapels.

Federal and Greek Revival architecture mark the Pigeon River country. New Englanders and New Yorkers—who imported the Yankee assets of thrift, ingenuity, and industry—people the valley and brought the distinctive architecture and its modifications which separate the far northern fringe of Indiana from the remainder of the state. Immigration here was overland from the East or by canal rather than down the Ohio River or across the mountains as it was through southern and central Indiana.

Below Howe the valley widens, at times becomes swampy, and it drains large lakes such as Shipshewana and the Twins. As it progresses, it becomes more primitive, more beautiful.

Although the Pigeon never has served as a water highway, one of the state's most unusual transportation chapters was written across its

valley. This was the St. Joseph Valley Railway, the pampered plaything and tightly ruled personal empire of Dr. H. E. Bucklen, who had made his fortune selling Arnica Salve. Dr. Bucklen dreamed of his line as a middle link in a Chicago-Toledo, Ohio, interurban system. Looking on the map for all the world like an undecided roller coaster, the Valley Line began at Elkhart, ran up to Bristol, down to Middlebury, across to Lagrange, up to Mongo and Orland, down to Angola, and across to Columbia, Ohio. There, at something approximating nowhere, the whole thing ended.

Best known for one of the oddest assortments of motive power in America, the Valley Line was part electric interurban, part steam train, and the remainder an incredible conglomeration of gasoline-electric cars, storage-battery units, and chain-driven gasoline cars. On one type of car the motorman inserted a shotgun shell in a chamber over a cylinder and struck it with a ball peen hammer. This started the car. If the motorman was successful, it started on the first try. Another car suffered from a chronic power deficiency, which was overcome by progressively adding equipment. After a time there was no room left for the passengers, so a trailer was attached to accommodate them.

The Valley Line crossed the Pigeon River millpond at Mongo where the weathered bridge piling remains clearly visible from Ind. 3 as a sort of ghostly reminder of the dream that died with the doctor in 1918. Mongo's principal claim to fame, however, preceded the Valley Line. This was the Lagrange Phalanx, one of about 30 Fourierist communitarian settlements which sprang up over America prior to the Civil War.

Organized in 1844 under a charter granted by the state legislature, the Phalanx was a sort of latter-day New Harmony in which all members lived under the same roof and ate at the same table. At its peak, 120 persons from northern Indiana and southern Michigan had been convinced that communitarian socialism was the most effective instrument to deal with problems of the times. Activities centered about a two-story building 210 feet long and were supervised by councils of industry, commerce, and education. All personal efforts were contributed to the community and property was held in common. But, like similar experiments earlier and later, it failed and after four years of questionable success, the Phalanx disbanded. A similar colony at Brighton, a few miles away, ended in the same failure.

But the islands in Lagrange County's social stream have not disappeared. Old Order Amish comprise more than one-fifth of the population. Their buggies, moving at a steady pace behind the klipklop of horses' hooves, are as familiar to anyone who travels the area as are the bonneted women or the bearded men beneath their broad-brimmed hats. Use of electricity, automobiles, and farm machinery are as rigidly forbidden as are colorful clothing or posing for photographs, the entire system being based on Amish biblical interpretations. Due in large part to the Amish, Lagrange ranks ninth among U.S. counties in number of horses. It also ranks among the top 2 percent of counties in poultry and pig production.

Dreams of people like Dr. Bucklen and the communitarian socialists flourished for a little while and then went away, leaving behind proof that nothing is so permanent in the valley as the unspoiled beauty of the stream where Chief White Pigeon and his tribe had made their home. The Pigeon once again is a river where you can stand on the bank, watch the water glide silently by, and lose yourself endlessly in the vast outdoors. You can stand there admiring its quiet beauty, out of sight of cars and power lines and feel as if you've just discovered a scene that no man has ever viewed before. It is a world away from the world, a serene pathway, primitive and aloof, between the fresh green of trees on either bank. It is the special possession of those who love the Pigeon the way it is and believe that it should remain that way.

# *The Last Frontier*

Kankakee

As secluded as an elderly recluse in a cobweb-laced mansion and as filled with mystery and passion as a forbidding jungle pathway, the Kankakee River forms the sinuous thread binding together "The Land God Forgot to Finish."

Not alone a river or a drainage system as it wriggles across northwestern Indiana and eastern Illinois, the Kankakee River, since its discovery, has been a contradictory way of life. Its name, according to some authorities, was corrupted from the Potawatomi word, *Teh-yak-ki-ki*, which means "swampy country." Others say it comes from the Miami word, *M'wha-ki-ki*, which means "wolf country."

Following the Kankakee on the map is only the work of minutes but following the stream on the land is another matter. Unlike most rivers, which invite settlement and give man power for his mills, water for his villages, and transportation for his produce, the Kankakee repelled settlement and prevented expansion. A notoriously rambling stream, with 2,000 bends in its eighty-five-mile upper valley, it was a surly, snarling dog holding people at bay; the cantankerous brother among Hoosier waterways. Man, however, has attempted to subdue it—to change its personality, reform its lazy, slovenly habits, and transform its sullen disposition into one of sunny usefulness. The drama has continued for more than 300 years and each generation produces a new and often fantastic act.

The river has undergone four transformations. First it was the land of the Indian hunter and the French fur trader, then the domain of the frontier farmer. The recreationist and the stock farmer followed, only to be succeeded partially by the reclamationist and the sportsman. Sometimes man has adjusted to the river; other times, he has forced the river to adjust to man. The changes have been great, but the Kankakee has survived them.

By turns the Kankakee has been proposed as a water supply for Chicago, a navigational shortcut between the Great Lakes, or a vast sewage lagoon for points as distant as Milwaukee, Wisconsin. Conservationists have battled farmers over drainage schemes and channel clearance. Scientists in many fields have made it their target. If the Kankakee suffers from an inferiority complex, its frustrations have been understandable.

Geographically, the Kankakee is not one river but two. Viewed chronologically, it again is divided into two startlingly contrasting streams. Few rivers anywhere have exhibited a more contradictory personality or have been so set upon and manhandled by surgeons of the soil. Results have been upheaval of county boundaries, bridges left with nothing to span, an expensive Indiana-financed project that took place entirely in Illinois, and elimination of one of the world's great wildlife habitats.

The original upper Kankakee was more nearly a 500,000-acre sponge than a free-flowing stream. Throughout the area it followed its original channel, winding around, doubling back, in complete disregard of man's attempt to hurry rivers to the sea. Only the most determined braved its tangled maze of multiple marshes, which soaked up water in wet seasons and released it in dry. Sportsmen on two continents knew it for extraordinary hunting, rich trapping, and bounteous fishing which were embellished by spine-tingling legends and mysterious tall tales. This river and its valley are worth knowing.

At Momence, Illinois, nine miles across the state line, the Kankakee's character changed abruptly. A natural rock barrier blocked the river here and try as it might, the sluggish current could not wear it down. So the river surrendered and backed up. For nearly 250 miles it was lazy, sullen, moody, and antisocial, scarcely moving between banks of sandy hillocks, idling among tall reeds. In places and in season, the river widened to look like shallow lakes, the best known being the vast English Lake, where it received the contribution of the Yellow River. Thus the Kankakee remained a wild jungle pathway, cherishing its wildness while pushing civilization away from it. Anyone wandering into it had the startled impression of having invaded another world.

But once beyond the rock barrier the Kankakee ended its laziness, stopped its incessant wandering, and suddenly achieved maturity. It widened abruptly and dashed happily in full current, leaping over its rocky bed, gurgling among the stones and speeding between neat meadows and stately woods. There was no kinship of character whatever between the upper and lower rivers. One was mysterious and perverse; the other was open and gracious.

Chronologically, the change was equally startling. For two centuries man dreamed of straightening the channel and speeding its water toward the sea. Finally, goaded by obstacles, he fell upon the river, blasted open the barrier, removed the surly meanders of its youth, widened its bed, deepened its channel, shortened its course, and chained its flow between straight, ugly banks until it was no longer recognizable to those who had known it. It was like a six-foot man shrunk suddenly to midget size.

The Kankakee, like an unrepentant delinquent, must have laughed diabolically as it again became a battleground, this time between farmers and conservationists. The battles continued, but with different actors and a different plot. Men seemed determined to give it no rest.

Caught up in the early succession of empires, the Kankakee briefly served as a water highway and witnessed the human march between the Great Lakes and the Mississippi. Later its vast, mysterious fastnesses sheltered thieves, counterfeiters, and murderers. Flowing through the center of things, yet so isolated that no cities broke the willow fringe along its banks, it has traveled the full swing of the pendulum from medicine men to missile men. Between these two extremes flow 300 miles of river and 300 years of time.

The Kankakee first made contact with history when a lone explorer, lost overnight in a nearly impenetrable wilderness, pondered the direction to his bankside camp. He was the dashing Frenchman with the unwieldy name of René Robert Cavelier, Sieur de La Salle, and he was to leave his imprint indelibly on the Midwest.

Reunited with his twenty-nine-man expedition, La Salle discovered the St. Joseph-Kankakee portage and at its crest a small lake, which now bears his name. This was the river's source. Urbanization in South Bend, however, has now pushed the source ingloriously to a storm sewer outlet at the intersection of Meadow Lane and Lombardy Drive. It flows immediately into a broad, flat-floored valley famous for its rich coal-black soil which produces huge quantities of mint, potatoes, and other muck crops. Although the Frenchmen who followed La Salle have disappeared into the mists of history, they have planted their names permanently on the land at such places as Bourbannais, L'Erable, Papineau, and St. Anne in Illinois and La Crosse and Demotte in Indiana.

Carelessly, without hurry, winding 250 miles through Indiana to gain eighty-five miles toward the sea, the river set out to find the Mississippi. It was sluggish, meandering, doubling back in a continuous swirl of loops and oxbows, twisted bayous, and grass-choked sloughs; it lay like a giant snake in the mud and marshes, hardly stirring, torpid under the sun, sleepy, and satiated.

By land and by water men came to win the river. As late as 1831 a party reported traveling on the water an entire day and finding it only a lonely highway between walls of trees that scarcely took them out of sight of their starting point. Following a devious route of many windings and bendings, they found themselves surrounded by eerie, glassy stretches of water which mirrored tremendous, gloomy trees standing knee deep in the marsh. They found a jungle stretching up to five miles on either side of the river with the dark, lingering mystery of antiquity clinging closely to it. All night the party proceeded, unable to land and guided by fires they built in the prows of the boats. They had penetrated a world away from the world, primitive, aloof, and unspoiled. Where most rivers invite adventure, the Kankakee formed a fearful barrier.

Somewhere in the misty regions of prehistory, the Kankakee's story had begun. In glacial times, it had been a swift, devastating torrent up to ten miles wide fed by meltwaters from the vast white blanket. Racing westward, the swollen river swept everything before it and scoured out a broad valley below what is now South Bend. Gradually, as the southern sun melted the great ice sheet, new outlets appeared elsewhere and the Kankakee's floods dwindled to today's insignificant stream.

The river remained just as geologic ages shaped it and handed it over to the people who were to come—a lazy, surly, and unruly stream. It wound 250 miles from South Bend to Momence—which was eighty-five crow-flown miles—and for nine months each year, it covered an eight- to ten-mile-wide path up to four feet deep, inundating everything except occasional sand islands. About one seventh of the 5,300-square-mile basin lay in marsh or swamp.

Timber, which bracketed the river up to three miles wide, formed a natural defense for the Indians, but even though they were accustomed to forest living, they could not penetrate it. The settlers who followed could do no better. Up and down the valley they vainly poked the finger of exploration in an attempt to subdue the quirks of the desolate river.

Like the Indians, they dejectedly turned back except at one point south of Hebron, which was known successively as the Potawatomi Trail Crossing, Eaton's Ferry, and Baum's Bridge. Here they found the only point where nature had been kind to the traveler. A narrow, sandy tongue of land projected from the south side like a searching finger. It was the only crossing for 250 miles and when Indiana searched for a route for the vital Michigan Road, it eagerly pounced upon this location.

But the sluggish, stubborn Kankakee proved "too wet and impracticable," surveyors reported, and they went packing eastward, cautiously checking possibilities. Briefly they considered crossing at the outlet of English Lake, but they found the river 748 yards wide, deep and sluggish. They continued upstream, finally bowing to the impossible and detouring around the source via South Bend.

The Potawatomi Trail Crossing, however, was so inviting that George Eaton established a ferry there in 1836. Construction later began on a bridge three-quarters of a mile long, which was considered an engineering marvel of its day, and there was a comforting feeling that the ungracious Kankakee had been subdued at last. But the traffic had scarcely begun to contemplate the new convenience when the bridge burned. A successor lasted only a year until ice crushed it and flood washed away the remains.

Throwing a bridge across the defiant Kankakee was no ordinary feat, and the structures were no ordinary bridges. One of the best known is Dunn's Bridge, a graceful arched span near Wheatfield which brings to mind New York City's beautiful Hell Gate Bridge and the famous Sydney, Australia, harbor span. But it seems completely out of place in the Kankakee wilds. Widely-accepted stories that its structural members came from either the Ferris wheel or the Administration Building at the Columbian Exposition of 1893 seem to be without fact. The bridge was contracted for in 1895. Fire had destroyed the Administration Building in 1894. The Ferris wheel was operated as late as 1904 at the St. Louis World's Fair, after which it was dynamited.

Predecessors of the Seaboard (Monon) Railroad also conquered the river to make possible the first rail travel the length of the state. Horace Greeley, the famous editor and politician, traveled it in 1853 under circumstances that left him violently out of sorts and gener-

ated a lifelong hostility toward Hoosiers. Greeley missed a train in Lafayette that was to take him to a speaking engagement in LaPorte, and in desperation he commandeered a handcar and four men to propel it. On that dark, frosty night, the desolate wilderness of the Kankakee waited, eerie and silent.

But let Greeley tell his own story in bitter words tinged with frustration and anger:

> From Culvertown a prairie marsh stretches thirteen miles northward, and I think no building and hardly a cultivated acre was visible through all that distance. The dense fog, beaten down by the cold air, lay low on this marsh, and was heavily charged with prairie-smoke for a part of the way. We crossed on a pokerish bridge of naked timbers the slough-like bed wherein the Kankakee oozes and creeps sluggishly westward. . . . They say the Kankakee has a rapid current and dry, inviting banks from the point where it crosses the Illinois line, which might tempt one to regret it did not cross the line 40 miles higher up. . . . Bunyan might have improved his description of the Slough of Despond had he been favored with a vision of the Kankakee marshes.

Not everyone was so unhappy with the Kankakee. Sportsmen found it the wonderland of fur, fish, and fowl. Hunters and trappers bought and sold claims like real estate, although they held only squatter's rights to the tangled islands which existed before the high water annually fell below the banks and sank into the rich earth. During off season, they provided an ample farm labor supply.

Muskrats were the most plentiful, providing from 20,000 to 40,000 pelts annually in Lake County alone. Beaver were also abundant, providing skins for the tall hats of Europe's grandees. Otter, turkey, deer, and raccoon vied for food and cover with mink, skunk, opossum, and fox. Although prices ranged from an insignificant 3 cents to 10 cents apiece, game was so plentiful that trapping produced an estimated $3,750,000 during the most productive years. John Jacob Astor's powerful American Fur Company established a trading post to tap the valley's rich yield.

Although the valley had been overtrapped by 1855, it continued to act as a bountiful pantry for water fowl which arrived in sky-darkening numbers. Ducks and Canada geese, arriving during Febru-

The river at the Kankakee State Game Preserve, 1966.

ary, gorged themselves on acorns, smartweed, and wild rice. Sandhill cranes and brant followed, and then the snipe, rail, plover, and prairie chicken flew in to nest among the rushes, sedges, and lily pads.

By Civil War times, farmhouses could no longer accommodate the swelling army of hunters. Lodges sprang up in profusion near Baum's Bridge and dotted the winding riverfront near Thayer. Sir William Parker, who brought a party from England in 1872, built the twenty-three-room Cumberland Lodge near Schneider and embellished it with elegant walnut paneling and imported furnishings. The operation was strictly top drawer. A stately tallyho and four met patrons arriving by rail and transported them to the lodge with its wide verandas and broad center stairs. Surrounded by barns and kennels which housed horses and the baying dogs used in the hunt, the building stood for nearly seventy-five years.

Up and down the river other sportsmen built their lodges—the Pittsburgh Gun Club, which stood until 1966; Rockville, Terre Haute, Indianapolis, and Louisville clubs; White House and Valley Gun clubs; and the Columbia Hunting Club. Near Thayer stood the Diana Club House and Ahlgrim's Park, and near English Lake was that grand misnomer for the Kankakee flatlands, the Alpine Club House.

Prominent businessmen flocked in from Boston, New York, Philadelphia, Washington, and Chicago, tempted by reports of hunters who averaged 100 birds a day. No one could know who would show up next for a hunting trip, for club memberships included President Benjamin Harrison, James Whitcomb Riley, Lew Wallace, George Pullman, the Studebakers of South Bend, Potter Palmer, and "Bet A Million" Gates.

Lew Wallace vacationed near Baum's Bridge for forty-three years on a houseboat that he named *The Thing*. Tradition has it that he worked here on two of his most successful novels, *The Fair God* and *The Prince of India*. A Kankakee native, Don Lytle, told how a short, bearded man appeared as he rowed past Wallace's houseboat and asked Lytle to serve as his hunting guide. Only later did Lytle discover that his employer was Benjamin Harrison, who came to rest in seclusion after he had been elected president of the United States in 1888.

By that time, the Kankakee area had produced a bumper crop of fantastic legends designed to assault the ear and set the nerves aquiver. There was the curse thrown by the mysterious woman of White Woman's Island and the quest for the lost woman of Grape Island. Its Paul Bunyan was a man named Rol Gordon, who is said to have skinned buffalo fish covered with scales twice as large as silver dol-

*Left to right*: The river's source is a storm sewer outlet at the edge of South Bend. ✑Ruins of a dam below Kankakee, Illinois. ✑Commonwealth Edison built the world's first privately financed, full-scale nuclear power plant at mouth of Kankakee in 1960.

lars and who, on occasion, would look out his cabin window to see man-eating turtles waddling toward the front door. Fugitive criminals found the vast, tangled country made to order and the region is alive with stories of secret hideouts, buried treasure which has never been located, vigilantes riding off in hot pursuit, and men who swung from the gallows if they failed to cross county lines quickly enough.

Such legends go back many years along the Kankakee. More than 170 years ago a soldier of the Battle of Tippecanoe settled on Snake Island. He was never seen again. Subsequently a burning trapper's cabin on Grape Island yielded its owner's body, and waters off French Island yielded another when it floated free of the weights used to hold it down. The murderer was hanged.

Place names that dot the waterways hint at the richness of local tradition. A traveler might come upon Indian Garden, Goose Island, Skunk Knobs, Camp Six To Two, Frenchman's Slough, Deserter's Island, Prairie Straight, Windy Bend, Point Comfort, and Garden of Eden. Bogus Island received its name because of the counterfeiters captured there.

But the Kankakee produced something more tangible than engaging place names. Loggers arrived to thin the great forests that mantled the river and in spring, after straining teams of oxen had dragged the heavy logs across the frozen swamp, their rafts choked the channel. Although steamboats seldom churned the upper Kankakee, the Indian Island Saw Mill Company operated the *White Star* to transport logs to Momence, which was one-and-a-half days away by water.

Kankakee timber helped rebuild Chicago after the great fire, although marsh fires, always a threat, were particularly devastating during that dry summer and fall. Timber thieves added to the feverish confusion, but after Chicago was rebuilt, they disappeared and the timber supply was diverted to the furniture industry.

Agricultural interests now drew a bead on Kankakee's potential riches and the long efforts to skim the water off the land approached a climax. As early as 1848 the legislature called for straightening the Kankakee and draining the marshes. It took seventy-seven years to complete the project, and in the interim all sorts of wild and imaginative schemes were proposed. Many a man is made by a river, but the Kankakee is a river made by man.

The Kankakee Valley Draining Association got around to organizing itself in 1858 and proposed to dredge a perfectly straight channel that would have nothing in common with the romantic river of the explorers and voyageurs. It would cross the river twice and at

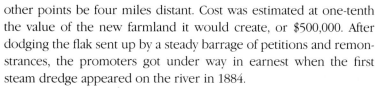

other points be four miles distant. Cost was estimated at one-tenth the value of the new farmland it would create, or $500,000. After dodging the flak sent up by a steady barrage of petitions and remonstrances, the promoters got under way in earnest when the first steam dredge appeared on the river in 1884.

For nearly a century the Illinois barrier had blocked Indiana settlement, and when it was removed, after decades of contemplation, conversation, and contention, Hoosiers footed the entire bill. In 1889 the Indiana legislature first appropriated funds to remove the rock ledge at Momence. This was the key to the lock that held the river in suspended animation. During the next thirty years it became uniquely a man-made river—a captured stream.

Typical of public works, the cost had catapulted from an estimated $500,000 at the beginning to $1,250,000 at completion. But it was a bargain. LaPorte and Starke counties alone pulled 150,000 rich acres from beneath the watery blanket. The 2,000 sinuous bends were reduced incredibly by cutting across the oxbows and sweeping curves. Channelization reduced a 65-mile section to 22 and 111 miles to 39. When the job was done, 85 miles of water flowed where 250 had been, and the stagnant five-inch fall per mile had been tripled.

No longer was the Kankakee the river that ran back through an-

other world, back through the centuries. Seeing the possibilities, speculators rushed in and opened the era of the great land companies. They gobbled up acreage by the thousands. The LaCrosse Land Company, for example, purchased 7,000 acres at an average price of $23.50 and eventually controlled 50,000 acres. Buying, however, was done on pure speculation since much of the land remained under water. The inside joke was that only here could land be bought by the gallon.

Dredging sharpened many tempers and brought great changes. As early as 1871, inventors of a peat mining machine snarled publicly at men who would drain the marsh, and as late as 1925, legislators busily rearranged county boundaries which had been deserted by the new channel. In between, fanciful schemes proposed to divert Kankakee water to supply the growing Calumet region or to canalize the river as part of a Lake Erie-Lake Michigan Canal.

The dredgers, however, won out and as a result bridges were left with no water to cross and new spans appeared over erstwhile dry land. Shifting boundaries switched bridge ownerships overnight and excess spans were moved about like erector-set pieces. Depending on the viewpoint, "The Land God Forgot to Finish" became a man-reclaimed area of extraordinary fertility or a manhandled marsh

*Left to right*: Arch bridge on the Porter-Jasper county line. ◄§Kankakee State Fish and Wildlife Area attracts hunters. ◄§English Lake rural post office, North Judson.

which substituted unproductive lands for one of the world's most ideally adjusted wildlife habitats.

As from the beginning, when Indians canoed it and explorers made it their road, the valley remained a transportation route. As early as 1869, the flat valley floor tempted railroad builders who pushed tracks from South Bend to beyond Kankakee. The New York Central promoted it as the Kankakee Belt Line which saved up to two days time by bypassing the congested Chicago yards. A run-through service with the Santa Fe sent nearly 12 million tons a year rolling over the rails, but it failed to fit into the pattern of Conrail, New York Central's successor, and is now being abandoned piecemeal.

Below Momence, where the river put aside its early indecision and meandered no more, the Kankakee follows a straight, business-like course which once was improved for navigation. Two dams and the remains of locks stand as reminders of the short-lived experiment. The Kankakee first begins to feel its power below the natural barrier at Momence and spreads into a broad channel, which falls as much as four feet to the mile.

Receiving the offerings of its largest tributary, the Iroquois, the Kankakee soon enters its namesake city, home of 36,000 persons who earn their livelihood largely by producing water heaters, stoves,

steel bars, pharmaceuticals, dog food, and furniture. Concerted efforts were made here to convert the unruly river into a dependable water carrier. Men set about to tame its rapids and shoals by locks and dams, to constrain its meanderings by dikes, and to mark its channel by navigational aids.

In 1847 the Illinois legislature chartered the Kankakee and Iroquois Navigation and Manufacturing Company, empowering it to improve navigation, build dams, and erect mills. The company completed four dams and companion locks before the battering of the river and financial reverses forced it into receivership in the 1880s. Small hydroelectric generating plants, since abandoned because of obsolescence, were installed at the dams in the 1920s.

While men were dreaming of navigation on the lower river, they were having second thoughts about what they had done to the upper river. Conservationists, spearheaded by the Izaak Walton League, opened a campaign in 1931 to return the marsh to its original state. Seeking 100,000 acres of submarginal land, the project would restore original conditions from English Lake to the Illinois line, including Beaver Lake, a shallow body of water which once rippled in the Newton County breeze.

As a result, the Kankakee State Fish and Wildlife Area came into

being on the triangle formed by the Yellow River and the Kankakee. Dikes were built to keep the water out of the river—not in it—and 2,300 acres were returned to exclusive use of the sportsman. There is still a primitive wonder in this region—a satisfying feeling of remoteness.

Recognizing the natural habitat's value, the Indiana Department of Natural Resources has scattered five additional wildlife and recreation areas up and down the valley from Potato Creek near the headwaters to LaSalle at the Illinois line. Jasper-Pulaski, east of Wheatfield, is a seasonal stopping place for sandhill cranes as the big birds make their semi-annual migrations. Lake County also has established the 850-acre Grand Kankakee Marsh Park and the state of Illinois established the scenic Kankakee River State Park in a rugged downriver area.

In spite of the "back to nature" pressures, the Kankakee now plays a dominant role in power production. Commonwealth Edison's Dresden Nuclear Power Station at the Kankakee's mouth was the world's first privately financed full-scale nuclear power plant, and it depends on the river for its cooling water. A second power station, coal-fired, is the first on the upper river. It has been constructed near Wheatfield.

The presence of power plants may have disturbed the Kankakee's tranquility and the clatter of ditching machines may have altered its appearance unrecognizably, but these are minor aberrations compared to the fantastic, character-changing schemes that surface periodically. One project would have incorporated the Kankakee into a Great Lakes-inland waterway system, but the idea died. Another would have cleared timber from the banks and riverbed. Conservationists fought it to a standstill. But it required the incredible originality of the U.S. Army Corps of Engineers to come up with the nerve-shattering C-SELM plan of the early 1970s. This would have piped waste from the entire southern end of Lake Michigan, from Milwaukee around to Gary, into lagoons along the river, converting thousands of productive acres into a vast sewer.

Farm owners and city dwellers alike rose in uncontrolled wrath and the din at public hearings became deafening. The idea died quickly but one can never be sure it has died permanently. For the Kankakee, accustomed to being pounced upon, realigned, disfigured, and abused, there is always the question: What new scheme will tomorrow bring?

Iroquois

Hazelden, George Ade's home.

In the heart of the great northwestern Indiana prairies, where the spaces are wide open and the cornfields lean against the sky, a field drain discharges its liquid contents at the base of a gentle moraine. Collecting in a tiny marsh at the edge of a green-carpeted pasture, the water pauses. Redwinged blackbirds and killdeer chatter noisily along the edge. Pheasants roam the upland and kingbirds and brown thrashers flit overhead. Then the water flows away in an arrow-straight ditch that forms the first few miles of the Iroquois River.

Named for the Indian confederation of six nations in upstate New York, the Iroquois is a creature of the open country, uncomplicated by cities, industries, or commerce. Like a bright tree of life, it runs through a land known for its unbelievably rich yields of corn, soybeans, and mint. It is quiet and rural, plain and unpretentious, little noticed and often disregarded. It is a Plain Jane among prairie rivers.

But to write off the Iroquois as colorless and unimportant is an error, for the lazy, muddy river, whose fall per mile is measured only in inches, has had its glittering moments in the limelight. Like the day William Howard Taft launched his presidential campaign and addressed thousands along its banks. Or the time the Indiana Society of Chicago ate its way through a colorful, history-making banquet. Or

the gala parties of humorist George Ade, whose guests alternated between the nation's great and his homespun neighbors.

Flowing ninety-four miles from source to mouth and draining 2,175 square miles, the Iroquois rises northwest of Rensselaer. Trickling due north, growing stronger, widening from the strength of a hundred field drains, it swings in a great circle toward Rensselaer, which is less than three crow-flown miles away, yet is twenty by the circuitous course of the river.

Once, in preglacial times, there was an ancient Iroquois River which flowed about two miles south of the present stream and occupied a valley up to 200 feet deep. But the glaciers ground up the rock and filled the valley with it so that today the land is flat and open. Yet there is a haunting grandeur about its emptiness, which in springtime turns beautiful before your eyes. It has all the lonely splendor of the prairie. In summer the country is a vast tapestry patterned by grain farms that individually number their acres far into the hundreds. Seas of corn, green oases of wheat, olive blankets of soybeans, and the refreshing fragrance of mint afloat on the breeze mark the country as one of America's richest farm baskets. In every direction the landscape is a sweep of luxuriance.

In the beginning the Iroquois basin was swamp intermingled with sand ridges. The flat, wet land discouraged settlement because of its poor drainage, the numerous sloughs filled with a rank growth of reeds and cattails, and toughness of the sod, which resisted the crude plows then in use. To break through the ribbed soil and convert the wild growth into a fertile cornfield was a superhuman job. As late as 1850, after most of Indiana had been inhabited, the land lay nearly untouched by settlers. Newton County was so sparsely settled that it was merged with neighboring Jasper County in 1839 and was not reestablished until twenty years later.

The Iroquois country was both the enticing gateway to the prairie and a discouraging obstacle. Consequently it lay in wait for men of vision, faith, and resources. The first was U.S. commissioner of patents, Henry L. Ellsworth of Connecticut, a man of high hopes, great perseverance, and a willingness to gamble. Ellsworth, whose daughter Anne, later chose the immortal first words to be sent over the telegraph, accumulated more than 124,000 acres, most of it in the Iroquois basin. To him this some day would be pleasing country, and he persuaded so many of his eastern friends to invest that they became known as the "Yale Crowd." No swivel-chair farmer, Ellsworth moved to Lafayette in 1845 and personally managed his operations. Most of the "Yale Crowd," however, which included Noah and Daniel Webster and Joseph S. Cabot of the Boston Cabots, were absentee landlords.

Ellsworth tinkered with advanced farm machinery, experimenting with a combination ditching and fencing machine, as well as with improved plows which he hoped would break the tough prairie sod. He published a book to promote cultivation of such exotic prairie crops as tobacco, sugar beets, flax, and hemp. His first commercial production, however, was hay which he shipped to southern markets. When Ellsworth died in 1858, he left nearly 11,000 rich acres to Yale University, which for many years was a principal landlord.

Ellsworth's activities launched a way of life that has survived to the present. Instead of the typical small independent farmer of the Hoosier frontier, wealthy individuals operated huge tracts, usually as absentee owners. Tenancy rather than owner operation became the rule.

Returns from the prairie farms were not nearly so lucrative as Ellsworth had anticipated, and by the time of the Civil War many disillusioned owners had sold to a new generation who became the cattle kings. These country barons of the corn belt amassed holdings in the thousands of acres and lived on a scale exceeding that of the southern planter aristocracy. They built huge mansions in fields where the summer heat shimmered over the rustling corn, and watched over battalions of tenants who cultivated their broad acres.

They owned land by the township instead of the section. One

farmer, with his associates, owned 65,000 acres; two others farmed 30,000 acres each. Newton County at one time contained two farms of more than 17,000 acres each, and twenty-two farms of 1,000 acres or more were scattered through Newton and Jasper counties in the days when farming elsewhere often was done on eighty-acre plots.

The cattle kings produced livestock in enormous quantities. Edward C. Sumner simultaneously fed four herds of 500 cattle each and kept twelve yoke of oxen to operate ditching machines on his 30,000 acres. Lemuel Milk owned 2,500 cattle, 10,000 sheep, 1,500 hogs, and 300 workhorses. He also owned one cornfield that covered more than three square miles. Adams Earl imported the foundation Hereford herd to America. As the cattle kings passed on and their heirs divided their holdings, farms shrank in size, but family names were planted permanently on such towns as Fowler, Earl Park, Boswell, Kentland, and Wolcott.

As the cattle kings departed, speculators moved in. Probably the most powerful was Benjamin J. Gifford of Rantoul, Illinois, who accumulated approximately 35,000 acres, mostly in marshy central Jasper County. Originally a lawyer, he promoted railroads in three states before the Kankakee country's unlimited possibilities caught his sharp eye and engaged his vivid imagination. Gifford bought land for as little as $4.50 per acre and drained it by building approximately 100 miles of ditches. His gamble paid off handsomely. In 1899 he produced 300,000 bushels of corn, 200,000 bushels of oats, 150,000 bushels of onions, and 50,000 bushels of potatoes. His farms became Chicago's pantry.

Gifford sold many tracts to his tenants, advising them to waste no time getting into the onion business. The rich soil, he told them, would produce up to 700 bushels per acre at a production cost of fifty cents a bushel. Vexed at the high rail-freight rates and requiring something better than the muddy roads, Gifford built a thirty-two-mile railroad half the length of Jasper County and made unfulfilled plans to extend it south to the Indiana coalfields and north to the steel mills along Lake Michigan. He named it the Chicago and Wabash Valley but its popular name was the "Onion Belt." Within fifteen years, Gifford shipped 15,000 cattle annually, in addition to thousands of head of other livestock and astronomical quantities of grain.

Gifford's luck ran high. When wells brought oil from the unbelievably shallow depth of 100 feet beneath his onion fields, he leased 26,000 acres and approximately 100 wells quickly began production. He then built a four-mile rail branch to a refinery constructed at a point which was named Asphaltum and bought a fleet of tank cars to add petroleum to the grain loads that rattled over his rails. The field soon gave out, however, although efforts to revive it

were made as late as 1982. For years oil oozed from scores of abandoned casings in the area and farmers used it freely to lubricate their machinery.

Gifford's domain was parceled out after his death and much of it was put into mint production. Mint stills, operated by some of America's mint kings, have long been the area's trademark. Potatoes also are an important product, along with other vegetables.

Throughout the Iroquois basin, however, the land is best known for its mammoth production of corn and soybeans. Jasper ranks seventy-first among the nation's more than 3,000 counties in corn output and stands fortieth in feeder pigs. It also is famous for another crop, which it may prefer to forget. Marijuana, the result of a U.S. government hemp-growing project during World War II, became so renowned nation-wide that location maps reportedly sold for $400 in some parts of the country.

Rensselaer, population 4,944, seat of Jasper County, is one of two cities on the Iroquois. Originally named Newton, it was located at a point known as the Falls of the Iroquois where the river tumbled in rapids over a small rock outcrop in the level prairie soil. Today its principal business is servicing the rich yield of its farmlands. It is the home of St. Joseph's College, founded by The Society of the Precious Blood, in 1889. Industries turn out transformers and cabinets.

The Iroquois winds through the center of the city and then sets out for Illinois. It serves as the setting for muddy, bankside picnics in spring when fishermen take possession of its waters, full and brown with the rich topsoil of upstream farms. Its valley is flat and scarcely noticeable as it approaches Brook and the home of its most illustrious son, George Ade.

Ade's delightful spirit has returned to Brook now that his stately English mansion, Hazelden, is restored. Throughout Ade's years, it was a place joyously alive, symbolizing good times, relaxation and pleasant memories. Ade loved people and they loved him. He built his big rambling home on 417 acres along the Iroquois in 1904, and by this time he was well on his way to becoming one of the nation's greatest writers and playwrights. He sent twelve shows to Broadway, where his *The College Widow* ran nearly a year and grossed $2 million.

When Ade built Hazelden, he spared no expense. It was pure elegance with ten acres of neatly clipped lawn and a formal garden. Ade seldom danced but his guests did, so he built a dance pavilion. He added a softball diamond, golf course, and swimming pool. From the time Ade set his house behind a grove of stately oaks until his death forty years later, Hazelden was a gay mecca for presidents, statesmen, authors, and sportsmen. When he was not busy entertain-

ing guests with such household names as Will Rogers, Gene Tunney, James Whitcomb Riley, and General Douglas MacArthur, he threw the doors open to neighborhood kids, who watched movies and circuses with spellbound attention. As a social center, Hazelden was exceeded by few places anywhere in the country.

In 1908, when William Howard Taft was in hot pursuit of the presidency, Ade invited him to fire his opening campaign gun on the Indiana prairies. Taft came and addressed 25,000 partisans and just plain curious who crowded into every corner of Hazelden, trampling the grass and threatening to smother the flowers. Taft apparently did his job well. The district of which Brook is a part sent only Republicans to Congress, with one exception, for the next sixty-six years.

At an almost legendary party for the Indiana Society of Chicago, Ade once played host to 800. His guest list read like a Who's Who—a vice president, governor, senator, mayor, and industrialists. They were a hungry bunch. Ade served 415 fried chickens, 7 hams, 2 crates of eggs, and 200 pounds of sausage—that's 1/10th of a ton—along with 50 loaves of bread and 1,500 rolls. They capped this by consuming 50 cakes for dessert and washed it all down with unlimited gallons of various liquids, for which Ade was widely known.

Hazelden fell victim to a galloping decay following Ade's death in 1944, but the George Ade Memorial Association went into action in time to save it. The beautiful home is now flanked by a hospital and a country club, both provided through Ade's generosity.

The Iroquois at one time received the contribution of Beaver Creek, which was the natural drainage from a huge swamp known as Beaver Lake. Before the state ditched an additional outlet into the Kankakee River in 1853, it covered 36,000 acres to an average depth of three and a half feet. For thirty years, however, enough water remained to make the lake a prominent resort.

As the lake was drained, it was converted into rich farmland, but by 1954 men had second thoughts and reconverted 1,500 acres into a shallow lake once again filled with ducks and geese to please the hunters. It is now part of the 9,670-acre Willow Slough State Fish and Wildlife Area.

Although the Iroquois once powered a mill at Brook, the river remains small and serene. At the Illinois line it is but fifty feet wide, its banks sandy and its valley flat. Eventually the river reaches Watseka, Illinois, the second city on its banks and a typical flat, treeless prairie county seat. The Iroquois writhes and wriggles past the city, inching by rich farmland where farmers toil endlessly in the springtime sun.

The habit of acquiring large landholdings here has continued down to the present. In the early 1960s a Watseka woman left several

*Left to right*: Potatoes are an important crop on land drained near the turn of the century. ❧St. Joseph College near Rensselaer was founded in 1889.

thousand rich acres, accumulated by her stepfather, to Iroquois County. The county sold the land to a group of Marion, Indiana, speculators and used the proceeds to build a new, ultra-modern courthouse. Purchase price: 1,085,883 hard-earned 1962 dollars. Other large landowners in the area were the children of Thomas J. Watson of International Business Machines.

The Iroquois is now more than water flowing between two banks. It is the central artery of an unbelievably rich land where farmers bring forth a bountiful cornucopia of field and sweet corn, oats, and soybeans. Iroquois County, Illinois, is the nation's third ranking county in corn acreage, fourth in soy beans, and eighteenth in sweet corn. Its total agricultural production places it forty-ninth, and it stands in the upper 3 percent in both vegetable and pullet production.

At Watseka, the Iroquois receives the offerings of its principal tributary, Sugar Creek, which shares its progress onward toward the Kankakee. The river follows a devious channel of many loops and bends, wandering about, doubling back on itself like a ribbon, moving in complete disregard of man's attempt to hurry rivers to the sea.

Suddenly the Iroquois stops playing between the winding banks and skipping among the trees and grows up. Throwing aside indecision, it makes a surprising change of direction and heads north. For sixty miles it has hesitantly paralleled the Kankakee, separated by a series of sand ridges. But now it is sure of itself. No more loops, no more windings, no more bends. The Iroquois is now broad and straight. Summer cottages line its banks. Swimmers, water skiers, and motorboaters glide over its waters. The banks ride high and the valley broadens.

Six miles above its mouth the Iroquois runs hard against a rock outcrop at Sugar Island. The shelf has held the river in check, for twenty-eight miles, slowing the current and limiting the fall to a puny five inches per mile. Now the river is unleashed and the water runs swiftly, dropping fourteen feet in the final six miles, which is half the fall of the entire seventy miles above. True, the Iroquois in fall may idle past Sugar Island with a mere nine cubic feet per second discharge, but in its newfound strength it also has been known to roar by at 27,000 second-feet.

The once-shallow stream reaches a depth of nine feet and a width of 400, which is eight times its size at the state line. It broadens into a small lake, losing its identity at last in the Kankakee, which it has been seeking for ninety-four miles.

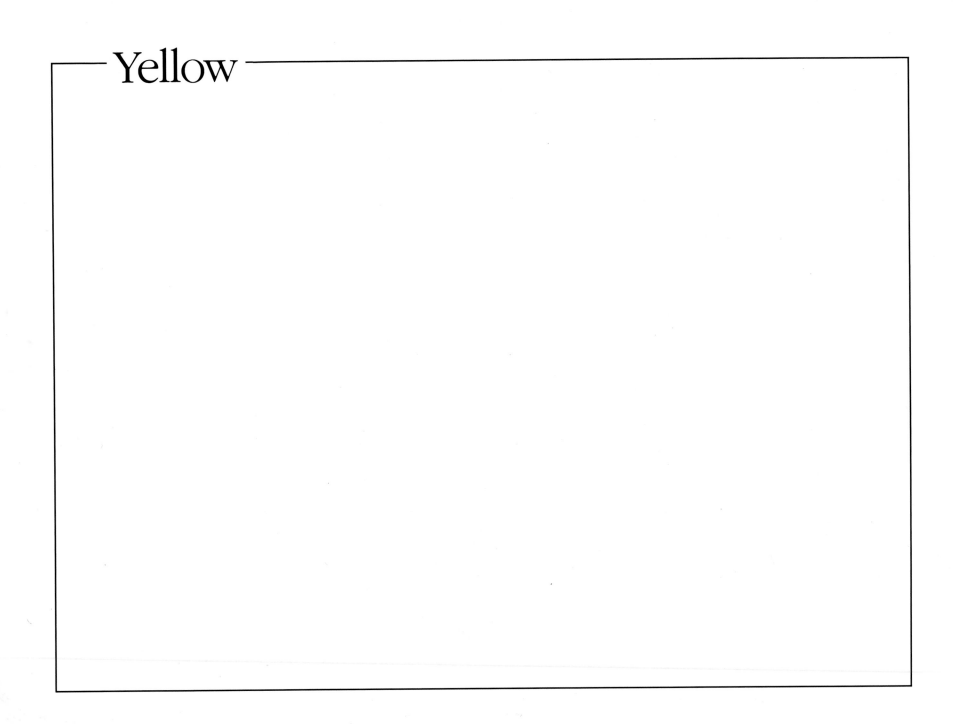

Yellow

China has its Yellow River, which is one of the world's mightiest, and the Chinese call it the Huang Ho. Indiana also has its Yellow River. The similarity ends with the name, however, for it is a tiny stream of meadow, swamp, and lake that for thirty years was considered too insignificant to be included on official state highway maps. The Potawatomi called the Hoosier river *We-thau-ka-mik*, which to them meant "yellow waters."

It is the river of three faces: There was the face of Menominee, the brave and devout Potawatomi chief, whose lands vanished from his grasp in one of the most infamous of all dealings with Indians. Then there was the face of the pioneer sportsman who came to hunt and trap in that section of the great Kankakee marsh known as English Lake. And finally the face of the modern outdoorsman who has come to fish, boat, and swim in the cool, clear lakes among which the Yellow River winds.

The story of Menominee is known as The Trail of Death. He was a chief who lived in the Twin Lakes district southwest of Plymouth, and came under the influence of French Catholic missionaries. His desire to improve the lot of his people led him to preach against the sins of murder, theft, and drunkenness, and to urge his band to abandon paganism. Imagine the surprise of the famous Indian missionary Isaac McCoy, who found that Menominee kept a long stick on which he carved a notch for every sermon he had preached, much the same as the preacher recorded his own sermons in a notebook. At Menominee's urging, a chapel was built on the lakeshore, and this is where the great drama of The Trail of Death began.

Menominee had good reason to assume that the land belonged to him permanently. With several fellow chiefs he had signed a treaty in 1832 reserving 14,000 acres at a time when other Indians were being moved west. This land, the treaty stipulated, would be theirs forever.

But neither the government nor the Indians had reckoned with the mounting pressure to permit white settlement, and four years later the reserve was sold for $14,000 at the Treaty of Yellow River, with the provision that all Indians would move west of the Mississippi within two years. Three fellow chiefs signed the treaty; Menominee would not.

In the meantime Father Benjamin Marie Petit, a brilliant young French priest, was sent to minister to the Indians. He praised the Potawatomi converts for their religious fervor and their enthusiasm in persuading other Indians to accept Christianity. In fifteen years Menominee's band had grown from a village of a few Indians housed in four huts to more than 1,000 Indians who had accepted the Christian faith.

When the time arrived for the Indians to move west, Menominee refused and his stubbornness lighted a fuse to some highly combustible tempers. In an eloquent plea to Colonel A. C. Pepper, the Indian agent, Menominee said:

> The President does not know the truth. He, like me, has been imposed upon. He does not know that you made my young chiefs drunk and got their consent and pretended to get mine. He does not know that I refused to sell my lands and still refuse. He would not by force drive me from my home, the graves of my tribe and my children who have gone to the Great Spirit, nor allow you to tell me that your braves will take me, tied like a dog, if he knew the truth. My brothers, the President is just, but he listens to the word of young chiefs who have lied. When he knows the truth, he will leave me to my own. I have not sold my lands. I will not sell them. I have not signed any treaty and will not sign any. I am not going to leave my lands and I do not want to hear anything more about it.

His resistance caused Colonel Pepper to appeal to Governor David Wallace for troops to keep the peace. The governor responded by sending General John Tipton with orders to move the Indians west of the Mississippi. The troops headed north from Indianapolis and what had been dismissed as fantastic rumor now took on the uneasy look of probability.

Action was swift and cruel. As the Indians were assembled in their chapel at prayer, the soldiers arrived, announcing their presence by a blast of gunfire. Those in the chapel immediately were taken prisoner and others were rounded up from all directions until 859 Indians, young and old, were captured and prepared for the long trek west. There was no bloodshed, but there were shouts of resistance and moans of desperation, and the forests were filled with the smoke of burning Indian villages.

Menominee resisted arrest and stood with dagger in hand, ready for any assailant. None dared approach him. Then a lasso sailed through the air, found its mark, and the proud chief was bound hand and foot, tossed into a wagon, and hauled from his home.

After sixty-one days of anguished marching in the heat of summer and the dust and drought of early fall, about 700 of the 859 Indians who had started the trip reached their new homes in Kansas. Father Petit, in poor health, accompanied his beloved converts, then returned to St. Louis, where he died at the age of twenty-seven, a martyr to his cause.

With the Indians gone, impatient settlers rushed into the Yellow River country like an engulfing tide, settling in all but the lower reaches where the river lost itself in the watery section of the Kankakee marsh known as English Lake. This was no conventional lake, but a wide soggy jungle along the Kankakee River into which the Yellow disappeared. It was seven miles long, with a maximum width of three miles, and was shut in by a bewildering mass of tall water grasses, weeds, aquatic plants, and wooded tussocks.

Before the marsh was drained, this was the heart of a great hunting area inhabited by many species of ducks, rails, sandpipers, and herons. The Yellow lay like a giant snake in the mud and marshes, hardly stirring, torpid under the sun, sleepy and satiated. It was a lost world, primitive and aloof, unfit for habitation, and surrounded, but never penetrated, by civilization. But underneath all this water the soil was unbelievably rich. The great wilderness lay there, remote and silent, awaiting the inevitable, and by the time of World War I the slimy marsh had been converted into valuable farmland.

A decade later Starke County farmers donated to the state a long narrow wedge of lake bottom for a game preserve. The state accepted the gift, and in 1933 2,300 acres of English Lake again became a marsh, now known as the Kankakee State Fish and Wildlife Area. A recent acquisition increased the acreage to 3,322. Dikes were built not to hold the water in the rivers but to keep it out, and ten miles of roads were constructed on levees so narrow that a single slip might mean a bath in the Kankakee or the Yellow.

The narrow tongue of land between the rivers is a return to the English Lake of old. It acts as a bountiful pantry for kingfisher, mallard, wood duck, and heron, and the waters teem with bass, bluegill, and catfish. Tremendous gloomy trees sit knee-deep in marshes, and eerie, glassy stretches of water mirror the silent, forbidding forest.

For fifty days in late fall reverberations of nearly 5,500 hunters' guns shatter the unearthly quiet. Before daybreak they come, drawing lots at 4:30 A.M. for the nearly forty blinds that line the swamps and rivers; three men to a blind. A campground accommodates the more rugged types. At noon the shooting stops and hunters head for home, each hopefully carrying the bag limit of his favorite waterfowl.

The wildlife area is Yellow River's last exciting chapter before flowing into the Kankakee at the village of English Lake. It is an invitation to adventure in its final miles, a lonely highway between dark walls of green trees. The banks are low, edged with river birch, silver maple, and cottonwoods and the trunks of fallen trees that lie prone in the shallows. Sandbars speckle the muddy, brown water. As though it were loathe to lose its identity, the Yellow for nearly five miles keeps a slender finger of land between itself and the larger river whose tributary it is, one of four closely parallel streams that come together like the fingers of a giant hand.

The original predrainage Yellow River writhed and twisted its way across the full width of Starke County, carving oxbow cutoffs and bayous in the swampy land. But artificial drainage has changed all that. The Yellow now flows on a beeline from Knox to the wildlife area, bisecting luxuriant soybean fields that are protected from flooding by banks thrown up by ponderous dredging machines.

*Preceding page*: River carves its way through the Maxinkuckee Moraine.
෴*Left to right*: Chicago Kiwanis clubs built a handicapped children's camp near Twin Lakes in 1911.
෴Statue of Menominee, the Potawatomi chief, near Plymouth.

Above Knox, the river, now in its natural bed, carves its way through the massive Maxinkuckee Moraine, a high belt of land thrown up by the retreating glaciers 15,000 years ago. Turning beautiful before your eyes, it winds through a ruggedly picturesque valley that slopes between the crouching hills and passes a long, green trough which contains a chain of refreshing lakes. Lying in a nameless fold in the hills, these cool, green, clear lakes are busy in summer with fishermen, boaters, and water skiers and in winter attract skaters and ice fishermen.

Among the lakes a Kiwanis-operated camp for physically handicapped children slopes down to the water. Founded in 1911, it spreads over fifteen acres of woodland and beach, serving campers from the Chicago area and northern Indiana. Thirty staff members supervise 120 campers each summer who come, forty at a time, to study nature, swim, learn crafts, and to enjoy the outdoors. The camp offers games, nutritious food, entertainment, and lots of love. What more could a wheelchair-bound city child ask?

One-quarter mile south of the camp, a heroic-sized statue of Chief Menominee in full Indian regalia gazes from a lofty stone pedestal across the land that once was his. Made possible in 1909 by a $2,500 legislative grant, it is the first monument, it is said, that any state erected to an Indian.

Lakes are the special glacial legacy of Marshall County, and south of Donaldson, in as tranquil a scene as can be found anywhere, they provide a beautiful setting for the massive towering buildings of Ancilla Domini College. Seven miles east lies Plymouth, largest city in the valley, whose residents keep busy producing automotive parts, plastics, paper products, and heat transfer equipment. A vast bounty of cucumbers and pickles, which ranks Marshall among the top 3 percent of the nation's counties, finds its way into the local food processing industry.

As one moves backward to its source, the Yellow changes in appearance as it becomes a quiet highway moving between comfortable rows of trees. Contours of the land grow gentle as rich farmland falls away from either bank, interrupted only briefly by the outlet of beautiful, 416-acre Lake of the Woods.

In the area near Bremen, where the main river finally gathers its upper branches and becomes one, the Yellow officially has its source. Two deep ditches, willow-choked and songbird-enhanced, join within fifty yards of a lonely farmhouse. From this insignificant beginning flows the Yellow—through the fertile fields, past the beautiful lakes, and into the land that Menominee believed was his "forever."

# The Muscles of Industry

# Grand Calumet

Flowing scarcely twenty miles and confined in its Indiana portion to a single county, the Grand Calumet River is the liquid backbone of one of America's greatest industrial complexes. Despite its distinguished name, it is only one-third as long and both shallower and narrower than its companion stream which is designated modestly: "Little Calumet."

The Grand Calumet is a river of amazing contradictions; it is a stream that doesn't know which way to go. Although it now flows due west, originally it flowed east. Now narrow, now wide, now deep, now shallow—every mile brings a changing look to this stream that slithers a foot deep on the spot where lake boats once steamed. Many a man is made by a river, but the Grand Calumet is a river made by man.

Its bed contaminated by the foul discharge of the state's heaviest concentration of commerce, industry, and population, this dirty, slimy workhorse needs a bar of Lava soap and a thorough scrubbing, not only on Saturday but on every night of the week. It is burdened, abused, contaminated; its surface is oily and scummy. It is polluted, offensive, and unable to support fish life. No swimmers dare use its waters. It is an ecologist's nightmare.

Army engineers, in a rare instance when they preferred to leave nature strictly alone, reluctantly dredged the channel many years ago to permit commercial navigation. But waste flowed in faster than the engineers could dredge it out, and so they abandoned hope and handed the river back to nature. Thus silted over, it reverted to a minor drainage ditch, which periodically becomes a candidate for navigational improvements. The Grand Calumet is a prime example of what ought not to be.

In the kaleidoscopic social and economic history of a region that is simultaneously a bottleneck, a gateway, and a transfer point, the Grand Calumet is at once a river of sand dunes and steel mills, swamps and oil refineries, national melting pot and homegrown American ingenuity, political intrigue and cities born in full bloom. It is sluggish, inaccessible, and refuse-laden; an eyesore in an ugly land. As a water highway, it is a failure.

The river was not always thus. Go back more than 300 years, and Father Jacques Marquette, exploring 4,000 miles from his native France, pitched camp on a desolate Lake Michigan beach and gazed up a river flowing toward him from the west. Father Marquette—now cast in a heroic-sized statue—still stands there looking west, but the stream which flowed eastward into the lake has disappeared and in its place a series of picturesque lagoons give birth to a river flowing in the opposite direction. It is uniquely a man-made stream and it has survived great change as man has relocated its course, dredged its channel, put huge boats on its surface, and erected colossal monuments to commercial enterprise and business daring.

The Calumet the Indians knew was a marshy stream, more a bayou than a river, and shaped like a huge letter U lying on its side. It rose in a hilly lake region south of what is now Michigan City and flowed west to a short distance beyond the Illinois state line, where it abruptly reversed itself and paralleled its course, sometimes as close as three miles. Then it entered Lake Michigan in what is now the Miller section of Gary. This is the river that Father Marquette found.

But a century and a quarter later sandbars choked the river's mouth, so the Indians, pushing their canoes continuously through the flat, reedy marshes, opened a new outlet near the Illinois state line. Thereafter, the lower river reversed itself and flowed westward; this section became known as the Grand Calumet. The upper parallel section was designated the Little Calumet, and the new channel into Lake Michigan simply the Calumet.

For decades the lonely wilderness of the Calumet waited, remote and silent, for man's settlement, and it came nearly a half-century after pioneering had gone out of style in most of Indiana. The river was the winding thread stitching together the area's variegated cities. It gave the region its name, which is derived from the French word for "reeds," which grew in profusion along the banks and were used by the Indians for ceremonial pipes. The name also is translated from Indian dialects as "still, deep water." The river's story begins at the mouth as far as man is concerned. This is the direction from which settlement came as Chicago spilled over its boundaries and men set out to search for new land.

The Calumet region was uninhabited for a very simple reason: It was too harsh an environment for any but the hardiest souls. The entire area was a succession of sand ridges separated by swampy sloughs through which no man could penetrate. The river, barely flowing, was so choked by vegetation that even light canoes, in some places, could not navigate, and to approach it through the thick growth of marsh grasses and wild rice was impossible.

The great Kankakee swamps effectively cut off immigration from the south and migration from the east stopped elsewhere long before it reached the Calumet region. There were no suitable harbors along Lake Michigan. The sloughs and ridges, remnants of beach lines left by Glacial Lake Chicago, paralleled the lake, and often the only way to move from ridge to adjacent ridge was to travel miles to the end of the swamp, cross over, and work back.

But men of vision see opportunity in such hopeless scenes and the first of a long procession of these was George H. Hammond. He was instrumental in developing the railroad refrigerator car, so that for the first time dressed meat as well as live animals could be transported safely. This new transport flexibility allowed packers to locate their plants wherever supplies were favorable.

Consequently, Hammond in 1869 established his huge State Line Slaughter House along the Grand Calumet's banks in what is now the city of Hammond. It was an ideal location. Ice from nearby lakes and streams cooled the refrigerator cars and the river was a handy place to dispose of waste. The packing plant, in fact, used the river as a private sewer to such an extent that it helped end navigation and set a precedent for unparalleled pollution, which is only now being combated.

Hammond's city, which bears his name, was the first in the Calumet region. Others followed in orderly geographic succession, like a man walking across the desert and leaving his footprints, each neatly spaced. After Hammond came Whiting and East Chicago and finally the biggest of them all—Gary. Each was created to serve some gigantic new industry, so that each bypassed the usual development stage and sprang full-blown from the swampy soil.

In the process, the cities swallowed the scattered tiny settlements that previously had sprung up in the area and then, in turn, attempted to swallow each other, so that within a short period a resident might find himself a citizen of two or three cities without ever having moved. In this manner, settlements like Roby, Robertsdale, Tolleston, Miller, and Aetna merged into Hammond or Gary, leaving only their names to designate some particular section of the larger city. Grandiose dreams led Hammond to annex and then disannex

Whiting, East Chicago to annex both, and Gary to annex all three. Officials eventually came to their senses and the old boundaries were restored. The region developed a fierce independent spirit very early, picking up a few bad habits that had been developed across the line in Illinois and relying on the long distance from the Indiana statehouse to escape attention. Some habits apparently haven't been kicked yet.

Back at Hammond, before the other Calumet cities appeared, George Hammond was operating what came to be called "the greatest single dressed beef plant in the world" and relying on the railroad to keep in business. Others, however, saw potential value in all that water lying around unused and urged the federal government to improve the Grand Calumet for navigation.

The year after Hammond opened his packing plant, work began on a harbor at the mouth of the Calumet River, which is just across the Illinois state line. Despite an unfavorable report by U.S. Army engineers, Congress yielded to local pressure and extended improvements to the Grand Calumet after a sixteen-year battle. A ten-foot channel was dredged three times within seven years, but man threw too much refuse in and the sluggish current took too little out. After 1903, navigation was a subject only for antiquarians.

Although the principal source of pollution was removed in 1901

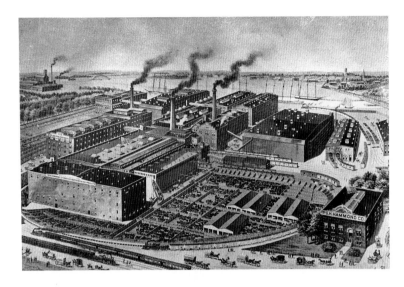

*Preceding page*: Teeming steel into ingots at a basic oxygen steelmaking shop.
~~Left to right~~: George H. Hammond's packinghouse, around 1900.
~~Cargo ship *Cap Delgado* loading grain at the Garvey Grain Elevator.

when the packing plant burned, other industries continued the problem. Steel mills and refineries began to line the river and at times the marsh-bordered stream seemed to be one-third sand from the swampy dunes, one-third sludge and one-third pickle liquor from the vast steel mills that transformed the region into one of astonishing productivity. As late as 1965 the U.S. Public Health Service said that streams in the Calumet area were characterized by "unsightly appearance in the form of floating debris, oil, discoloration and turbidity." It called the Grand Calumet the worst of all.

The future, however, looks better for the weary old river. United States Steel, meeting standards set by the Indiana Stream Pollution Control Board, switched to deep wells or filtration to dispose of its acid wastes and the river no longer runs red with iron oxide. Other industries have joined the battle to cleanse the river, but antiquated and overburdened waste water disposal plants continue to be troublesome.

Cities along the Grand Calumet have grown by explosive leaps. Hammond, the region's first, had a population of fewer than 700 during its infant years, but a decade later, 5,400 inhabitants had swelled the wilderness village to city size. As late as 1910 every third resident was a native or first-generation German or Austrian, and as late as World War I scores raised their melodious voices in activities of the

nine German cultural or singing societies. By the '30s, however, eastern Europeans had largely supplanted this element.

In 1893 Hammond, needing Lake Michigan frontage to assure an adequate water supply, reached for the communities of Roby and Robertsdale, which blocked it from the lake. This annexation gave Hammond more than a lakefront. Into the bargain went Roby's gambling casino, three horse-racing tracks which were used successively to circumvent a state law, and a 12,000-seat arena where the faithful lined up to shout their way through boxing matches.

Since Illinois prohibited prizefighting, a gambling syndicate had moved in from Cicero, Illinois, and relied on the wilderness separating Roby from Hammond proper to discourage any official interference with the sport, which was equally illegal in Indiana. The theory may have been good, but the attending commotion grew so loud that the governor dispatched two National Guard companies, which effectively put an end to the boxing business in Indiana. A law followed which prohibited betting on horse races, so the promoters packed what equipment they could and quietly returned to Illinois.

As industrialization marched eastward, the Standard Oil Company began to construct a gigantic refinery at a sandy, swampy, and mosquito-ridden location known as Whiting's Crossing. The year was 1889. The population immediately exploded in true Calumet fashion,

and within six years the refinery had attracted 3,000 persons. Standard Oil then set the pattern for succeeding Calumet cities by building homes for its supervisors. Hammond, in a brief delusion of grandeur, annexed most of Whiting in 1894, but handed it back two years later.

Whiting gave America one of its greatest industrial triumphs and without it we might have become a "have not" oil nation. As the burgeoning automobile industry sharply increased the demand for gasoline, it became obvious that something better than the existing 11 percent recovery from crude oil would have to be devised.

A young chemist, Dr. Robert E. Humphreys, attacked the problem under the direction of Standard's general manager, Dr. William M. Burton. Working with a personally designed still and oblivious to the dangers of heat, pressure, and explosion, Dr. Humphreys invented the cracking process which became universally used. It doubled the quantity of gasoline obtained by former methods, averted a future gasoline famine, and assured the future of the automobile age.

About the time that Standard Oil established Whiting, the town of East Chicago was incorporated in the impenetrable swamps to the east. Speculators had considered the area since 1881 when the East Chicago Improvement Company bought 8,000 acres of worthless sand, swamps, and sloughs. But once the company owned the land, it

apparently didn't know what to do with it. First it attempted to build a ship canal which would connect the recently dredged Grand Calumet with Lake Michigan. Although it was soon abandoned, the work was later revived and after twenty years of fits and starts was partly completed. The federal government accepted the final section for maintenance in 1925.

In the meantime, twenty years and six owners later, Inland Steel erected a huge plant in 1902 employing 1,200 men at what became known as Indiana Harbor. Other industries, including a second steel mill and four refineries, followed. In reality, the area was in East Chicago and often was called the "Twin Cities," since the canal diagonally bisects the area. It was a roaring place. One hundred ten saloons were going full blast by 1910. Bursting with expansive hopes, East Chicago swallowed up Hammond and Whiting, but before it could digest its gains it was in turn swallowed by Gary. City officials subsequently annulled these municipal marriages.

Gary, like its sister cities, leapfrogged its infancy and was born an adolescent. In 1906, U.S. Steel acquired 9,000 acres of lakefront, sand ridges, and swamps and immediately set out to build not only a huge steel mill but a city to house its workers. It moved the Grand Calumet and re-channeled it.

The river cut the millsite in two and at flood times spread out

until it was a thousand feet wide. The steel company simply picked it up bodily, giving it new and contrasting characteristics, and set it down in a newly excavated mansonry and slag-lined channel one-fifth mile south of its former course. Imprisoned between its walls, the river carried away waste, flowing straight as a Dutch canal.

There were problems from the beginning of Gary. Surveyors found it impossible to cross the swampy sloughs, so they tied their stakes to dogs and urged them to swim to crews stationed on the opposite side. Working like ants, they slowly and laboriously laid out the city.

As the mills roared into production, Europeans migrated like an engulfing torrent. In two years the population exploded from 334 to 10,246. The steel company sold business and homesites as rapidly as the deeds could be processed and retained control only of the four liquor stores it established.

As Gary quickly outgrew itself, an area called "The Patch" sprang up to the south. This was a roaring boomtown, wide open with its "Bucket of Blood" and "First and Last Chance" saloons and as full of life and color as a Roman candle lighted at both ends and going full blast.

Politics in Gary was rough and tumble from the first and setting off political fireworks became an ingrained habit. Fantastic charges and countercharges, politically inspired, ushered in the first election, and the night before the polls opened the entire police force was arrested. Mayor Tom Knotts was arrested fourteen times during his first two years in office on charges ranging from election fraud to perjury and embezzlement, although none was ever proved. Saloons, which numbered one for every seventy-seven residents, kept their doors open through unique protection arrangements despite sporadic attempts at civic purification.

Four years after Gary's founding, nearly three of every four residents were of foreign birth or of first-generation descent. This ratio changed abruptly during World War I when Negroes and Mexicans filled production vacancies in the steel mills. With more than 70 percent of the present population black, Gary became the nation's first major city to elect a black mayor.

A trip down the Grand Calumet today is an amazing journey in contradictions. The river rises in Marquette Park, a 250-acre sand-circled oasis that U.S. Steel purchased at a tax sale and resold to the city of Gary. What was the river's mouth in Marquette's day is now a green valley filled with tennis courts and bordered with trees. Nearby the river flows westward from the Calumet River lagoons, which are bordered by oaks and cottonwoods, connected by artistic little Japanese bridges. A marker explains that Octave Chanute, the

aviation pioneer, experimented with gliders here and that the Wright brothers studied his findings.

Against this green, tranquil setting stand the steel mills in the distance. Vast, vast steel mills. Slag piles. Dusty buildings. Hard hats. Security guards. Gates. Movement, always movement. Endless railroad cars shuttling noisily back and forth. Trucks thundering along dusty roads. But motion, always motion, which never ends. Through the steel mill grounds, the Grand Calumet flows straight as an arrow in her artificial channel, a stream of clumsy bridges and discoloring pollutants, bordered by hideous buildings.

Passing beneath the Indiana East-West Toll Road, the river spreads itself out into a soggy pond, bordered by rushes and cattails and covered with lily pads. It wriggles through the area like a snake until finally the surface lies motionless between encroaching fields of fill dirt. A slight greenish scum appears on the water. There is no perceptible current. The Grand Calumet has become the river that does not move.

Now the channel narrows and it is again a river. The backdrop changes slightly as the stream eases into East Chicago and Hammond, but the theme is familiar: Railroad trains, heavily laden. Power lines to feed the factories. Air heavy with the black smoke of factory chimneys. Abandoned buildings—empty, windows gone, ghostly.

Then the Grand Calumet shrinks into a small stream with an almost indefinable channel. It glides under a bascule bridge, apparently a relic of the navigation days but looking a little silly because of the minuscule flow of water beneath it. A quarter-mile away a pipe culvert carries the entire river under Sohl Avenue in Hammond. The channel is narrow and reed-bordered. A railroad crosses on a rotating bridge but the tracks end in an open field and go nowhere. Another quarter-mile away a triple culvert carries the tiny stream under a busy street. A channel gauge records the depth as one foot where busy steamers once churned the water. The water is oily. It moves at a crawl.

Now the Grand Calumet flows past the site of the State Line Slaughter House and into Illinois. The green of Burnham Woods Forest Preserve and its adjoining golf course suddenly transforms the land into a thing of beauty, and the ugliness, for a brief moment, vanishes like Cinderella's coach at midnight.

Shortly the Grand Calumet meets the Little Calumet and the end of its journey in the Calumet River. In a characteristic scene, a sunken barge, rusty and grimy, lies grounded at its mouth. Man has much to do to erase from the Grand Calumet its stigma of being "the worst of them all in the Calumet area."

Little Calumet

Six miles south of Michigan City, on the steep, rolling flank of the massive Valparaiso Moraine, a narrow valley bordered by beautiful lake basins forms the pathway for a tiny stream. To locate the stream's origin, you push your way through the weeds and briars, isolated from today except for the whine of traffic on the nearby Indiana East-West Toll Road. The streambed you find is perhaps a yard wide and half that deep and contains a few inches of water. What you see is hard to believe because scarcely sixty miles away this same stream will float a 1,000-foot hull stuffed with 68,000 tons of cargo and start it on a journey that may end 6,000 miles away.

This is the Little Calumet, Indiana's river of contradictions. It is short, small, obstreperous, and reversible. It is nearly as old as the glaciers, as modern as today, as unpredictable as tomorrow.

Wandering and charming in its upper course, it glides among Lake Michigan's famous sand dunes, sharing their mysterious, silent isolation and the grandeur of an unspoiled nature tucked away in another world. It has watched over the puzzling habits of that famous hermit, "Diana of the Dunes," and guarded the secrets of Indiana's last frontier.

But in its lower reaches it is busy and burly, carrying hulking ships bound for distant ports and fouled with the wastes of home and industry. It crosses a land so flat that it may flow upstream, downstream, or not at all, depending on the whims of the weather. By turns it may be a stagnant bayou or a roaring flood. Here it is crowded, unkempt, and cantankerous, defiled by trash dumps and reclamation fills until it bears little resemblance to the adolescent river a few miles upstream.

Before man began his incessant meddling, the Little Calumet was the upper part of a longer river that flowed westward across the present Porter and Lake counties into Illinois, where it abruptly turned and retraced its course, approaching as close as three miles, until it flowed into Lake Michigan. But man, beginning with the Indians, changed all that and now only the upper portion of the hairpin-shaped stream is known as the Little Calumet. The remainder, although shorter and less significant, had somehow attained the impressive name of "Grand Calumet" and flows opposite to its original direction. Where the two meet, a channel begun by the Indians and completed by the federal government connects with Lake Michigan. This is known simply as the Calumet River.

The original Little Calumet was a lazy river, moving slowly between sandy ridges, idling among tall reeds, groping through waterlogged swamps and marshes. Three marshes were so singular and

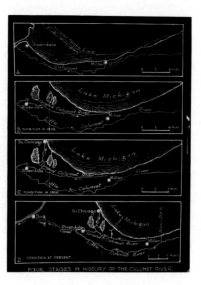

*Left to right*: Four stages in the history of the Grand Calumet and the Little Calumet rivers. ◆§ Twenty-ton capacity rope trolley unloaders, Bethlehem Steel, Burns Harbor.

vast as to earn individual names—Cady Marsh on the west, Cowles Bog near the center section, and Pinhook Bog near the river's source, the latter two registered National Natural Landmarks. Pinhook occupies a deep ice-block depression and is a type rare in Indiana, although common in the northern lake states and Canada. Orchids blossom in summer, and rare sundew and pitcher plants keep busy trapping the insects on which they thrive. Blueberry bushes provide an annual harvest. Sphagnum mosses cover the ground. Between the marshes, Little Calumet varies between a swamp wasteland which holds back a surging urbanization and a narrow ditch given over to scores of pleasure craft. It was a silent partner in the battle for the dunes and an interested sidewalk superintendent during construction of Indiana's deepwater port.

In the fifty-six-mile journey from hill to lake, it goes through countless changes in size, width, depth, mood, pace, surface, and surroundings. It is by turns a winding meadow brook, a stagnant bayou, and a broad, deep bearer of commercial burdens. Finding its way westward among the hills that surround its source, Little Calumet first makes its way through two lakes, then emerges into an embayment of Lake Michigan's prehistoric ancestor. Here it is wholly rural, a brook so small that only the sharpest eye will detect the stream of

water flowing among the lush, green meadow grasses. This is the springtime of the river's life.

As the land changes slowly from hilly to flat, the stream enters a broad plain over which it wanders aimlessly. Vast acreages of corn, soybeans, wheat, and hay line its course before it plunges into cool, green woods. Soon it slips through a rustically beautiful valley past the twin communities of Chesterton and Porter. This was the valley that attracted Joseph Bailly, the French fur trader, who became the Calumet area's first settler in 1822. Located on the trails connecting Fort Dearborn (Chicago) with Fort Wayne and Detroit, Bailly's home and trading post became a meeting place for whites and Indians, an oasis for travelers, and a religious and cultural center. It's still there, a registered National Historic Landmark and an object of study by the Historic American Buildings Survey.

Suddenly, however, Little Calumet abandons its rustic environment and runs headlong into the workings of Randall W. Burns, the man who drained its uppermost swamps, provided a shortcut into Lake Michigan, and gave it the dilemma of both coming and going. The Calumet region, since its discovery, has strangely attracted men of practical vision who believed that rich resources could be wrung from its sandy, swampy wastes. Burns was among the last of these. He

owned 1,200 acres of marshland which produced great fishing and hunting and not much else. But he could see this land reclaimed and converted into rich farms, busy commercial tracts, and vast housing developments.

Burns fought through the courts for fifteen years before he won his battle. When the Burns Ditch was completed in 1926, it emptied the upper river into Lake Michigan through a one-and-one-eighth mile channel that knifed through the dunes left by the lake's prehistoric ancestor. This shortcut reversed the river from near the point where it received the contribution of Deep River and provided six-and-a-half miles of flowing waterway. Twenty thousand soggy acres had been effectively drained. Burns's project also helped provide the state with a site for Burns Waterway Harbor at Portage, which gives Indiana access to the Great Lakes and the St. Lawrence Seaway.

Burns Ditch, however, was more than a waterway. It was a social and economic force that created thirty square miles of new land and brought the Glen Park section of Gary, which once had been isolated by a mile-wide swamp, into closer association with the remainder of the city.

Burns Ditch wrought great changes, but the Little Calumet survived them. Beyond the end of Burns Ditch, it was the same old Little Calumet, still demanding that men spend money and energy dealing with its eccentricities. Melting snows or heavy showers send the river on rampages that inundate homes, cover roads, and interrupt the trade of anyone who has the temerity to settle in the shallow valley. Some stretches are swampy bayous studded with the trunks of long-drowned trees. From either side march truck farms, green with cabbage and onions when the waters are behaving. In Gary's Gleason Park, the river is a stagnant lily-choked pond and west of the park its banks are a veritable jungle. In this area, which is so flat that the river may flow either direction if it flows at all, anyone with authority is busy with a plan.

The U.S. Army Corps of Engineers is casting an eager eye on the water and proposes, after a three-and-a-half-year study authorized in 1976, to protect the area against floods. If approved, construction may start by the late '80s. The state-appointed Little Calumet River Basin Development Commission likewise seeks a solution to the river's ills. Indiana governors and congressional representatives also have shown concern. The Indiana Department of Natural Resources has investigated potential recreational benefits. Approximately 70 percent of a proposed 4,300-acre linear corridor has been acquired between Burns Ditch and the Illinois Waterway for future improvement of the unruly river.

East and west of this troubled area men have busied themselves

*Left to right*: Local, state, and federal agencies are attempting to tame the flooding of the Little Calumet. ⋖ᴣBurns Waterway Harbor, Portage, port of Indiana, opened in 1959 near the Burns Ditch.

for years improving the stream, or at least pushing the problems from place to place. More than sixty years ago, the Chicago Sanitary District completed the Calumet-Sag Channel, which captured Little Calumet and diverted its western waters into the Illinois river system so that barges could travel from the Great Lakes to the Mississippi. Congress then authorized further improvements with the result that draglines and dredges were busy for another twenty years.

An early channel improvement was at the Dutch town of Munster, where a major tributary, Hart Ditch, enters. Waters entering Little Calumet here normally flow west to the Mississippi through the Calumet-Sag Channel, while water above this point may flow east through the Burns Waterway to Lake Michigan. As a result, a "continental divide" sometimes appears in the streambed.

Numerous highway bridges and narrow railway culverts near the east edge of Gary sometimes block eastbound waters. Then, as the western portion of the stream empties, they may glide back past their point of beginning and enter the Illinois Waterway.

Little Calumet continues westward to Blue Island, Illinois, where it makes a surprising change of direction and heads back toward Indiana. But soon the tiny, winding, willow-bordered stream is swallowed up by the Calumet-Sag Channel and its identity is lost completely. Once again, its flow is artificially reversed. Beyond this point,

there is no similarity to the original river. It is nearly a city block wide, nine feet deep, and carries 7,000,000 tons of shipping annually.

Upstream—which formerly was downstream—Little Calumet heads toward Indiana but shortly before reaching the state line it meets the Grand Calumet and abruptly turns northward to Lake Michigan. The combined river, closely controlled by the O'Brien Locks and Dam, is termed simply the Calumet.

Now the Calumet is overwhelmingly a river of man. It is a busy artery of commerce—a wide, deep, majestic bearer of nearly 18,000,000 tons of shipping annually to and from the Port of Chicago. Bridges divide and rise to the hoot of whistles as cargoes begin their journeys to every part of the world.

Steel mills, metal fabricators, grain elevators, and dry docks on a vast scale line the Calumet's final miles. Huge buildings topped by monitor-roofed ventilators and filled with furnaces holding floods of molten steel border the river. It is a smoky land of chimneys, retorts, steam, and furnaces all bound together by the clattering steel hoops of busy railroads. Serbian, Hungarian, and Croatian churches and lodge halls that look down upon the bustling streets tell the story of a melting pot of men who have come together from a score of nations to provide the brawn of a great industrial region.

The scene now shifts back to the Little Calumet's rustic headwaters and the wild dunes alongside. Indiana long ago recognized the value of preserving this unusual region and established 2,200-acre Indiana Dunes State Park near Porter in 1925. This was the wildest of the modern dune country—sand, swamps, blowouts, blue lake frontage, white sand beaches, birds, game, and the meeting place of vegetation from the Arctic and the tropics.

The region was isolated, inaccessible, mysterious. Conservationists wanted to keep it that way. Although two towns sprang up, Ogden Dunes and Dune Acres, they are unlike other towns. Homes sit perched on the steep, shifting sands and the roads that thread through them are so steep that automobile hoods cut off forward vision. Both are wrapped in the silent, enigmatic isolation of the dunes. Ogden Dunes has its Diana Road, which brings to mind the strange story of "Diana of the Dunes," who spent a decade living as a recluse among the sands. An intellectual who fled the restraints of civilization, she first lived alone. Then she married but remained among her beloved dunes until she died in 1925. Among the dunes are wetlands like Cowles Bog near Dune Acres. A registered National Natural Landmark, the bog is named for Professor Henry C. Cowles, whose studies made the dunes famous as the birthplace of North American plant ecology.

The unique combination of nature brought the National Park Service out from Washington intent on preserving thousands of acres of dunelands and neighboring areas. But industry had now overflowed from the Calumet River and was marching eastward along the lake intent on acquiring land wherever needed. The inevitable battle developed.

Congress authorized the Indiana Dunes National Lakeshore in 1966 but it was not formally established until 1972. Meanwhile, a long, emotional conflict raged which finally brought its compromises. Two steel mills rose near the mouth of Burns Waterway. Indiana built its long-sought deepwater port between them amid predictions that it would revolutionize northwestern Indiana. Park plans were revised in both directions, ultimately coming to rest with approximately 13,000 acres in several scattered tracts that encompass a great variety of the region's natural assets. In addition to thirteen miles of Lake Michigan's white sand beaches for the swimmers, there are dunes, wetlands, and woods for the naturalists, a historic district for students of the past, ski trails for winter sportsmen, and hiking trails for just about everyone. In 1982, nearly 1,500,000 visitors swarmed into the park, intent not only on enjoying the spectacular beaches but viewing the Little Calumet in the only area that resembles the stream the Indians knew.

# Select Bibliography

## Books

Baker, Ronald L., and Marvin Carmony. *Indiana Place Names*. Bloomington: Indiana University Press, 1975.

Banta, R. E., comp. *Indiana Authors and Their Books, 1816–1916*. Crawfordsville: Wabash College, 1949.

Barce, Elmore. *The Land of the Miamis*. Fowler, Ind.: The Benton Review Shop, 1922.

Barnhart, John D., and Donald F. Carmony. *Indiana from Frontier to Industrial Commonwealth*. New York: Lewis Historical Publishing Co., 1954.

Barnhart, John D., and Dorothy L. Riker. *Indiana to 1816: The Colonial Period*. Vol. 1 of *The History of Indiana*. Indianapolis: Indiana Historical Society and Indiana Historical Bureau, 1971.

Bartlett, Charles H. *Tales of Kankakee Land*. New York: C. Scribner's Sons, 1904.

Bassett, John S. *A Short History of the United States*. New York: The Macmillan Company, 1939.

Benton, E. J. *Wabash Trade Route in the Development of the Old Northwest*. Baltimore, Md.: Johns Hopkins University, 1903.

Bestor, Arthur E., Jr. *Backwoods Utopias*. Philadelphia: University of Pennsylvania Press, 1950.

Dunn, Jacob Piatt. *Indiana*. Boston and New York: Houghton Mifflin Co., 1888.

——. *Indiana and Indianans*. Chicago and New York: The American Historical Society, 1919.

——. *True Indian Stories*. Indianapolis: Sentinel Printing Co., 1908.

Esarey, Logan. *A History of Indiana*. Fort Wayne: The Hoosier Press Studies, 1924.

Fatout, Paul. *Indiana Canals*. West Lafayette: Purdue University Studies, 1972.

Fowke, Gerard. *The Evolution of the Ohio River*. Indianapolis: The Hollenbeck Press, 1933.

Galloway, Joseph A., and James J. Buckley. *The St. Joseph Valley Railway*. Chicago: Electric Railway Historical Society, 1955.

German, Harry O. *Whitewater Canal*. Indianapolis: Society of Indiana Pioneers, 1944.

Gould, George E. *Indiana Covered Bridges Thru the Years*. Indianapolis: Indiana Covered Bridge Society, 1977.

Griswold, B. J. *The Pictorial History of Fort Wayne, Ind.* Chicago: Robert O. Law Co., 1917.

Hampton, Taylor. *The Nickel Plate Road*. Cleveland and New York: World Publishing Company, 1947.

Hargrave, Frank F. *A Pioneer Indiana Railroad*. Indianapolis: William B. Burford Printing Co., 1932.

Harlow, Alvin F. *Old Towpaths*. Port Washington, N.Y.: Kennikat Press, 1926.

Hilton, George W. *Monon Route*. Berkeley, Calif.: Howell-North Books, 1978.

Hilton, George W., and John F. Due. *The Electric Interurban Railways in America*. Stanford, Calif.: Stanford University Press, 1960.

Holliday, Murray. *The Battle of the Mississinewa*. Marion: Grant County Historical Society, 1964.

——. *Indiana: A Guide to the Hoosier State*. Works Progress Administration. New York: Oxford University Press, 1941.

Isaacs, Marion C. *The Kankakee: River of History*. N.p., 1964.

——. *The Old Kankakee*. N.p.: Izaak Walton League, n.d.

Kelly, Fred C. *One Thing Leads to Another*. Boston and New York: Houghton Mifflin Co., 1936.

Ketcham, Bryan E. *Covered Bridges on the Byways of Indiana*. Oxford, Ohio: n.p., 1949.

Kleber, Albert. *History of St. Meinrad Archabbey*. St. Meinrad, Ind.: Grail Publications, 1954.

Klein, Benjamin and Eleanor, eds. *The Ohio River Handbook*. Cincinnati: Young and Klein, Inc., 1954.

Klinger, Ed. *How a City Founded to Make Money Made It*. Evansville: University of Evansville, n.d.

Knollenberg, Bernhard. *Pioneer Sketches of the Upper Whitewater Valley*. Indianapolis: Indiana Historical Society, 1949.

Lilly, Eli. *Prehistoric Antiquities of Indiana*. Indianapolis: Indiana Historical Society, 1937.

Lindsey, Alton A., Damian V. Schmel, and Stanley A. Nichols. *Natural Areas in Indiana and Their Preservation*. Lafayette: Purdue University, 1969.

Lindsey, Alton A., ed. *Natural Features of Indiana*. Indianapolis: Indiana Academy of Science, 1966.

Lockridge, Ross F., Sr. *The Old Fauntleroy Home*. New Harmony: New Harmony Memorial Commission, 1939.

——. *The Story of Indiana*. Oklahoma City: Harlow Publishing Corporation, 1961.

Lockwood, George B. *The New Harmony Movement*. New York: D. Appleton and Company, 1905.

Logan, W. N., and others. *Handbook of Indiana Geology*. Indianapolis: The Department of Conservation, 1922.

Madison, James H. *Indiana through Tradition and Change: A History of the Hoosier State and Its People, 1920–1945*. Vol. 5 of *The History of Indiana*. Indianapolis: Indiana Historical Society, 1982.

Marlette, Jerry. *Electric Railroads of Indiana*. Indianapolis: Hoosier Heritage Press, 1980.

——. *Michigan: A Guide to the Wolverine State*. Works Progress Administration. New York: Oxford University Press, 1949.

Miller, John W. *Indiana Newspaper Bibliography*. Indianapolis: Indiana Historical Society, 1982.

Misek, Frank J., ed. *Electric Railways of Indiana*. 2 vols. Chicago: Central Electric Railfans Association, 1957, 1958.

Moore, Powell A. *The Calumet Region*. Indianapolis: Indiana Historical Bureau, 1959.

Nichols, Fay Folsom. *The Kankakee: Chronicle of an Indiana River and Its Fabled Marshes*. Brooklyn, N.Y.: T. Gaus Sons, 1965.

Peat, Wilbur. *Indiana Houses of the Nineteenth Century*. Indianapolis: Indiana Historical Society, 1962.

Peckham, Howard H. *Indiana*. New York and Nashville: W. W. Norton & Company, Inc., and American Association for State and Local History, 1978.

Pence, George, and Nellie C. Armstrong. *Indiana Boundaries*. Indianapolis: Indiana Historical Bureau, 1933.

Phillips, Clifton J. *Indiana in Transition: The Emergence of an Industrial Commonwealth, 1880–1920*. Vol. 4 of *The History of Indiana*. Indianapolis: Indiana Historical Bureau and Indiana Historical Society, 1968.

Reed, E. A. *Tales of a Vanishing River*. New York: John Lane Co., 1920.

Rehor, John A. *The Nickel Plate Story*. Milwaukee: Kalmbach Publishing Co., 1965.

Schwartz, Lois Fields. *The Jews of Ligonier—An American Experience*. Fort Wayne: Indiana Jewish Historical Society, 1978.

Shumaker, Arthur W. *A History of Indiana Literature*. Indianapolis: Indiana Historical Society, 1962.

Slocum, Charles E. *History of the Maumee River Basin*. Defiance, Ohio: n.p., 1905.

Sulzer, Elmer G. *Ghost Railroads of Indiana*. Indianapolis: Vane A. Jones Co., 1970.

Thompson, Donald E., comp. *Indiana Authors and Their Books, 1917–1966*. Crawfordsville: Wabash College, 1974.

——. comp. *Indiana Authors and Their Books, 1967–1980*. Crawfordsville: Wabash College, 1981.

Thornbrough, Emma Lou. *Indiana in the Civil War Era, 1850–1880*. Vol. 3 of *The History of Indiana*. Indianapolis: Indiana Historical Bureau and Indiana Historical Society, 1965.

Van Natter, Francis. *Lincoln's Boyhood*. Washington, D.C.: Public Affairs Press, 1963.

Warren, Louis A. *Lincoln's Youth*. Indianapolis: Indiana Historical Society, 1959.

Werich, J. Lorenzo. *Pioneer Hunters of the Kankakee*. Logansport: Chronicle Printing Co., 1920.

Wilson, George R., and Gayle Thornbrough. *The Buffalo Trace*. Indiana Historical Society Publications, vol. 15, no. 2. Indianapolis: Indiana Historical Society, 1946.

Wilson, William E. *The Wabash*. Rivers of America Series. New York: Farrar & Rinehart, 1940.

Winger, Otho. *A Brief Centennial History of Wabash County*. North Manchester: n.p., 1935.

——. *The Frances Slocum Trail*. North Manchester: n.p., 1933.

——. *The Last of the Miamis*. North Manchester: n.p., 1933.

——. *Little Turtle*. North Manchester: The News-Journal, 1942.

——. *The Lost Sister among the Miamis*. Elgin, Ill.: The Elgin Press, 1936.

——. *The Potawatomi Indians*. Elgin, Ill.: The Elgin Press, 1939.

Woehrmann, Paul. *At the Headwaters of the Maumee*. Indiana Historical Society Publications, vol. 24. Indianapolis: Indiana Historical Society, 1971.

Zink, Maximilian A., and George Krambles, publication directors. *Electric Railways of Indiana*. Chicago: Central Electric Railfans Association, 1960.

### Books, Miscellaneous

County histories. Entire Indiana State Library collection that pertains to the 85 counties through which Indiana's rivers flow.

*Illustrated Historical Atlas of the State of Indiana.* Chicago: Baskin, Forster & Co., 1876.

Indiana Industrial Directories. Indiana State Chamber of Commerce and Harris Publishing Co., Twinsburg, Ohio. Various issues.

Official Guide of the Railways. New York: National Railway Publication Company. Various monthly issues.

Various publications and reprints in the Allen County Public Library.

World Almanac.


## Newspapers and Periodicals

*Chicago Tribune.*
*The Denver Post.*
*Detroit Free Press.*
*Evansville Courier.*
*Fort Wayne News-Sentinel.*
*Indiana Magazine of History.* Bloomington: Indiana University and Indiana Historical Society.
*The Indianapolis News.*
*The Indianapolis Star.*
*The Indianapolis Star Sunday Magazine.*
*Jasper Herald.*
*Logansport Journal.*
*Logansport Pharos.*
Louisville *Courier-Journal.*
*Marion Chronicle.*
*Marion Leader-Tribune.*
*The Newton County Enterprise.*
*Outdoor Indiana.* Indianapolis: Indiana Department of Natural Resources.
*Railway Progress.* Washington, D.C.: Federation for Railway Progress, February 1955.
*Trains.* Milwaukee: Kalmbach Publishing Co., various issues.


## Reports and Proceedings

Indiana Academy of Science, various proceedings.
Indiana Junior Historical Society, various publications.
"The Kankakee 'Marsh' of Northern Indiana and Illinois" by Alfred H. Meyer. Michigan Academy of Science, Arts and Letters, 1936.
Kankakee Valley Draining Co., Prospectus of, 1869.
"Lost River." National Audubon Society.
"Lost River." National Speleological Society.
"Ohio River Basin Study." Washington, D.C.: League of Women Voters, 1964.
*The Ohio River: Pathway to Settlement* by Donald T. Zimmer. Indianapolis: Indiana Historical Society, 1982.

*A Pioneer Experiment in Teaching Agriculture* by Otho Winger. Indianapolis: Society of Indiana Pioneers, 1939.


## Government Reports and Documents

Illinois
Basin Studies of Iroquois, Kankakee, and Vermilion rivers.
Indiana
Durbin, Governor Winfield T., Messages, 1902–1904.
Fisheries and Game, Report of the Commissioner for 1901–1902.
Indiana Board on Geographic Names, Findings, 1963 and 1965.
Indiana Canal Commissioners, various official reports.
*Indiana Canoeing Guide.* Department of Natural Resources, 1983.
Indiana Crop and Livestock Reporting Service, Lafayette.
Indiana Geological Survey, various publications.
Indiana State Geologist, annual reports, 1869–1916.
Kankakee River Commission, Reports to the Governor, 1890, 1891, 1895.
Lost River Watershed Work Plan, Soil Conservation Service.
Master Plan for Conservation and Recreation, Indiana Department of Conservation.
Wabash River Basin Study, Water Resources Planning.
*Whitewater Valley, Study of Water Conservation and Recreation Resources in the,* by Dennis O'Harrow and Lester Engel. Indianapolis: State Planning Board, 1937.
United States
St. Joseph-Kalamazoo River Basin Planning Report. Federal Power Commission, 1965.
U.S. Army Corps of Engineers. Various publications relating to Grand Calumet, Little Calumet, and Ohio rivers and Brookville, Mississinewa, Patoka, Salamonie, and Huntington reservoirs and Cataract Lake.
United States Census Bureau, various population reports.
United States Department of Agriculture: ranking agricultural counties.


## Maps

Canoe navigation maps. Indiana Department of Conservation.
Official highway maps. Indiana Department of Highways, various editions.
Ford, Grundy, Iroquois, Kankakee, Livingston, Vermilion, and Will counties, Illinois. Portage Township (St. Joseph County), Indiana. Hillsdale and St. Joseph counties, Michigan. Auglaize, Darke, and Mercer counties, Ohio.

Indian Place Names by E. Y. Guernsey. Indiana Department of Conservation, 1932.

Indiana Electric System Network and Generating Stations. Indiana Electric Association, 1983.

United States Geological Survey topographic maps, various quadrangles.

## Pamphlets and Brochures

Allen County-Fort Wayne Historical Society.
Burns Waterway Harbor.
Danville, Illinois, Chamber of Commerce.
Department of Natural Resources, Indiana.
Forest Glen Preserve, Danville, Illinois.
Fort Wayne Chamber of Commerce.
Historic Fort Wayne, Inc.
Historic Madison, Inc.
Howe Military School.
Indiana Dunes National Lakeshore.
Madison Chamber of Commerce.
Muscatatuck Wildlife Refuge.
National Register of Historic Places in Indiana.
St. Meinrad Archabbey.
Toledo, Ohio, Chamber of Commerce.

## Personal Correspondence

Abbott's Magic Manufacturing Co., Colon, Michigan.
Callahan, T. M., Rensselaer.
Cassell, Frank A., University of Wisconsin-Milwaukee.
Central Soya Co., Inc., Fort Wayne.
Commonwealth Edison Company, Chicago.
First Mennonite Church, Berne.
Indiana & Michigan Electric Co., Fort Wayne.
Indiana Canal Association, Fort Wayne.
Jasper Desk Company, Jasper.
Lost River-Springs Valley Conservancy District, Paoli.
May Stone and Sand, Inc., Fort Wayne.
Michigan Department of Natural Resources, Lansing.
Northern Indiana Public Service Company, Hammond.
Northwood Institute, West Baden.
Penn Central Transportation Co., Philadelphia.
University of Illinois, Champaign-Urbana.
Officials of Hillsdale and Calhoun counties and Centreville, Hillsdale, Jonesville, Marshall, and Sturgis, Michigan.

# Acknowledgments and Credits

**Front Matter.** iii: Pigeon River Below Mongo—Indiana Department of Commerce. xi: Indiana Rivers map—Guy Fleming.

**Wabash.** 3: George Rogers Clark National Memorial, Vincennes—Indiana Department of Commerce. 4: (a) George Winter painting—Nineteenth Century Paintings Department, Atelier Dore, Inc., San Francisco; (b) Richard S. Simons. 5: D.A.R., Vincennes. 6: Richard S. Simons. 7: Richard S. Simons. 8: Standard Oil of New Jersey Collection, University of Louisville Photographic Archives. 9: (a) Indiana State Library; (b) Indiana Historical Society Library.

**Eel (north).** 13: Bridge at Roann—Ed Breen. 15: Simons Collection. 16: Richard S. Simons. 17: Richard S. Simons.

**Mississinewa.** 19: Cliffs below Marion—Simons Collection. 21: Simons Collection. 22: Richard S. Simons. 23: Richard S. Simons. 24: Simons Collection.

**Salamonie.** 27: Salamonie Reservoir—Neal Case. 28: Richard S. Simons. 29: Simons Collection. 31: Richard S. Simons.

**Tippecanoe.** 33: Near Warsaw—Darryl Jones. 34: Tippecanoe County Historical Association. 35: Winona Lake Christian Assembly. 36: Richard S. Simons. 37: Simons Collection.

**Vermillion.** 39: Bridge near Danville, Ill.—Ed Breen. 41: (a,b) Richard S. Simons. 42: Simons Collection.

**Maumee.** 45: Early Fort Wayne—Allen County Public Library. 47: Indiana Historical Society Library. 48: *Outdoor Indiana*. 49: Richard S. Simons. 50: (a,b) Richard S. Simons.

**Little.** 53: Above Aboite—Ed Breen. 55: Richard S. Simons. 56: (a,b) Richard S. Simons. 57: Richard S. Simons.

**St. Joseph (of the Maumee).** 58: Fort Wayne—Indiana Department of Natural Resources. 59: Three Rivers Festival race, Fort Wayne—Darryl Jones. 60: (a) Richard S. Simons; (b) Indiana Department of Commerce. 61: Richard S. Simons.

**St. Marys.** 65: Swinney Park, Fort Wayne—Ed Breen. 66: Richard S. Simons. 67: Richard S. Simons. 68: (a,b) Historic Fort Wayne. 69: Allen County Public Library.

**St. Joseph (of Lake Michigan).** 71: Mishawaka—Ed Breen. 72: Simons Collection. 73: Indiana State Library. 74: Indiana State Library. 75: (a) University of Notre Dame; (b) Richard S. Simons.

**Ohio.** 78: Sherman Minton Bridge, New Albany—Darryl Jones. 79: Near Aurora—Darryl Jones. 83: (a) George Tilford; (b) Glenn A. Black Laboratory of Archaeology. 85: (a) Simons Collection; (b) Richard S. Simons. 86: (a) Richard S. Simons; (b) New Albany-Floyd County Public Library. 88: (a) Metropolitan Evansville Chamber of Commerce; (b) Indiana Port Commission. 89: Indiana Department of Commerce.

**Whitewater, East and West Forks.** 91: South of Cedar Grove—*Outdoor Indiana*. 92: Richard S. Simons. 94. Richard S. Simons. 95: Richard S. Simons.

**Patoka.** 99: Above Jasper—Ed Breen. 103: (a,b) Simons Collection. 104: Richard S. Simons. 105: Richard S. Simons.

**Anderson.** 107: Near Huffman—Ed Breen. 109: (a) Lincoln Boyhood National Memorial; (b) Richard S. Simons. 110: (a) St. Meinrad Seminary; (b) Richard S. Simons.

**White, East and West Forks.** 112: Hindostan Falls, below Shoals—Indiana Department of Commerce. 113: Near Butler University, Indianapolis—Darryl Jones. 115: Conner Prairie Pioneer Settlement. 116: (a) Woolpert Consultants, Dayton, Ohio; (b) Indiana Historical Society Library. 117: Indiana State Library. 118: (a) Indiana State Library; (b) Richard S. Simons. 119: Simons Collection.

**Big Blue.** 121: Dam at Edinburgh—Indiana Department of Commerce. 122: Richard S. Simons. 123: Buck Kern Collection. 124: Simons Collection. 125: (a) Simons Collection; (b) Richard S. Simons.

**Flat Rock.** 127: Near Geneva—Ed Breen. 129: (a,b) Richard S. Simons. 130: (a) Balthazar Korab; (b,c) Richard S. Simons.

**Lost.** 133: South of Orangeville—Ed Breen. 135: Richard S. Simons. 136: Richard S. Simons. 137: (a,b) Richard S. Simons. 138: Indiana State Library.

**Muscatatuck.** 141: Below Vernon—*Outdoor Indiana*. 144: (a,b) Richard S. Simons. 145: (a) Richard S. Simons; (b) U.S. Fish & Wildlife Service.

**Blue:** 147: Below Milltown—Indiana Department of Commerce. 148: Simons Collection. 149: *Frank Leslie's Illustrated Newspaper*, August 8, 1863. 150: (a,b) Richard S. Simons. 152. Indiana Department of Commerce.

**Eel (west).** 155. Cataract Falls—*Outdoor Indiana*. 158: Richard S. Simons. 159: (a,b) Richard S. Simons. 160: Richard S. Simons. 161: Richard S. Simons.

**Elkhart.** 162: Bonneyville Mill, near Bristol—Ed Breen. 163: Southeast of Ligonier—*Outdoor Indiana*. 166: (a,b) Richard S. Simons. 167: Richard S. Simons.

**Fawn.** 169: Near Howe—Ed Breen. 171: Richard S. Simons.

**Pigeon.** 173: Below Mongo—*Outdoor Indiana*. 174: Richard S. Simons. 175: Richard S. Simons. 177: Simons Collection.

**Kankakee.** 181: State Fish and Wildlife Area—Ed Breen. 185: Indiana Department of Natural Resources. 186: Richard S. Simons. 187: (a) Richard S. Simons; (b) Simons Collection. 188: Richard S. Simons. 189: (a) Simons Collection; (b) Richard S. Simons.

**Iroquois.** 191: Above Brook—Ed Breen. 192: Richard S. Simons. 195: (a,b) Simons Collection. 196: Richard S. Simons. 197: Richard S. Simons.

**Yellow:** 199: Below Plymouth—Ed Breen. 201: Richard S. Simons. 202: (a) Syl. Szymczak; (b) Richard S. Simons.

**Grand Calumet.** 205: Gary—Ed Breen. 207: Simons Collection. 208: Indiana State Library. 209: U.S. Army Corps of Engineers. 210: Richard S. Simons. 211: (a) Indiana State Library; (b) James B. Lane.

**Little Calumet.** 213: North of Chesterton—Nature Conservancy/George Svihla, photographer. 215: (a) Simons Collection; (b) Bethlehem Steel. 216: Little Calumet River Basin Commission. 217: Indiana Port Commission.

RICHARD S. SIMONS is a frequent contributor to *The Indianapolis Star Magazine*, vice president of the Indiana Historical Society, and a member of the New Harmony Commission. He received a Distinguished Alumni Award in 1984 from Indiana University, where he has also taught journalism.

THE RIVERS OF INDIANA
Richard S. Simons


*editor*: Jane Rodman
*book designer*: Sharon Sklar
*jacket designer*: Sharon Sklar
*typeface*: Garamond Light
*typesetter*: G&S Typesetters, Inc.
*printer*: Dai Nippon Printing Company, Ltd.
*paper*: Topkote
*binder*: Dai Nippon Printing Company, Ltd.
*cover material*: T-Saifu